America
1803 - 1853

AMERICA
1803 - 1853

The Lewis and Clark Expedition
and the Dawn of a New Power

Denis Vaugeois

Translated from the French

by Jane Brierley

Véhicule Press

MONTRÉAL

Published with the generous assistance of The Canada Council for the Arts, the Book Publishing Industry Development Program of the Department of Canadian Heritage and the Société de développement des entreprises culturelles du Québec (SODEC).

The author expresses his thanks to the librarians and archivists who assisted him in his research, as well as Michel Chaloult, Gaston Deschênes, and Ferdinand Grenier for their judicious comments. He also greatly appreciated the collaboration of museum curators and staff. Every effort has been made to gain permission for material reproduced, although in some cases this proved impossible. Finally, the author thanks Catherine Broué, Raymond Wood, and Bob Moore for the data that they provided.

Cover and interior design by J.W. Stewart
Cover painting is a detail from "View of the Bear Paw Mountains from Fort McKenzie" by Karl Bodmer, Joslyn Art Museum, Omaha, Nebraska.
Printed by AGMV-Marquis Inc.

Originally published as America: *L'éxpédition de Lewis & Clark et la naissance d'une nouvelle puissance* by Septentrion, 2002.
The author has taken the opportunity of this translation to revise parts of the original text.

Library and Archives Canada Cataloguing in Publication

Vaugeois, Denis, 1935-
    America : the Lewis & Clark expedition and the dawn of a new
power / by Denis Vaugeois ; translated from the French by Jane Brierley.

Translation of: America, 1803-1853.
Includes bibliographical references and index.
ISBN 1-55065-172-2

    1. Lewis and Clark Expedition (1804-1806). 2. West (U.S.)—Discovery and exploration. 3. West (U.S.)–History–To 1848. 4. Canadians–West (U.S.)–History–19th century. I. Brierley, Jane, 1935- II. Title. III. Title: The Lewis & Clark expedition and the dawn of a new power.

F592.7.V3813 2003   917.804'2   C2003-903218-3

Véhicule Press
www.vehiculepress.com

Canadian Distribution: LitDistCo, 100 Armstrong Avenue, Georgetown, Ontario, L7G 5S4 / 800-591-6250 / orders@litdistco.ca

U.S. Distribution: Independent Publishers Group, 814 North Franklin Street, Chicago, Illinois 60610 / 800-888-4741 / frontdesk@ipgbook.com / www.ipgbook.com

Printed in Canada

Preface

"We the People of the United States," asserted the Constitution of 1787. Within a century, the new country's citizens would say, in heart and spirit, "We are America."

From being a somewhat chilly seaboard country, the United States suddenly became part of a continent. Before long it would regard itself as stretching "from sea to shining sea." This did not come about solely because of Lewis and Clark or even Jefferson, but it all began with them.

The United States took shape between 1803 and 1853, and it is this fifty-year period that interests us. Lewis and Clark's journey is the lens through which we have chosen to focus on the period from a number of different angles, first that of Jefferson himself, then of the early *Canadiens* and the later "French Canadians" who have been rather overlooked in the expedition's history, and finally of Native Americans. It was these last who made it possible for whites to settle and adapt to what was, for them, a new land. And it was these same Native Americans who were swept away and annihilated before they could take advantage of the whites' technology and knowledge. After all, both parties had something to offer, but the giving was all one way.

In this book you will find not only the now famous leaders, but the humble, the disenfranchised, the unsung heroes of the great adventure without whom the success of the Lewis and Clark Expedition would not have been possible.

Table of Contents

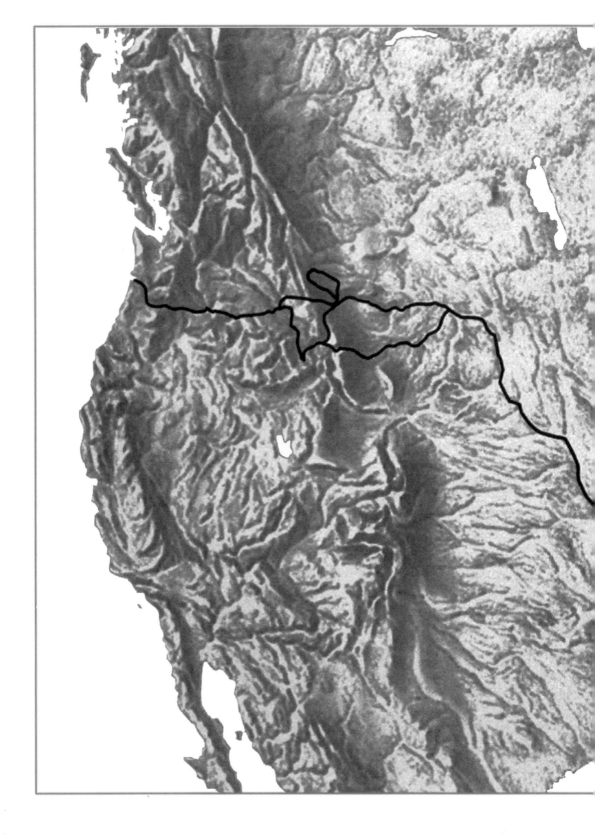

INTRODUCTION

"La Verendrye Discovers the Rocky Mountains"
Painting by Charles M. Russell

In their search for the Western Sea, La Vérendrye and his sons reached the Missouri in 1738. In the years that followed, they pushed toward the Rockies. *See pages 59-63.*

– I –

Prelude to Power

For many Americans, Lewis and Clark are a single entity. One might just as well write "LewisandClark" for all the difference it would make. For over two years, from May 1804 to September 1806, these men were inseparable — united by a common goal and a profound and loyal friendship.

Lewis and Clark met in the army, and it was there that they came to appreciate each other's qualities. William Clark was four years older than Meriwether Lewis and highly respected, his reputation strengthened by the military exploits of his brother, George Rogers Clark, during the American War of Independence. Each had his dreams and plans. Lewis, in particular, dreamed with all his heart of exploring the West. Thomas Jefferson, before becoming president in 1801, had encouraged several proposed expeditions. His objective was clear: "Find the shortest & most convenient route of communication between the U.S. & the Pacific ocean" (Jackson 1993: 76).

The United States of Jefferson's day consisted of sixteen states, three-quarters of which lay along the eastern seaboard. The inland states were Pennsylvania, straddling the Alleghenies, and Kentucky and Tennessee, both clearly in the West (*see maps on pages 15+17*). One American in ten, some five hundred thousand people, lived west of the mountains in Kentucky, Tennessee, and the bordering territories. It may seem astonishing to modern readers, but a good many of these people had such a different outlook from the coastal population that they had come to consider the possibility of eventually seceding from the United States. Jefferson was aware of this and ready to accept such a separation, but only if necessary.

Events moved faster than anyone had foreseen. The settlers in the West had every intention of using the river system leading to the sea via the Ohio and Mississippi rivers. However, while the Ohio ran entirely through American territory, the Mississippi did not. The river's western shore was controlled by Spain, as was the city of New Orleans, even though it was on the eastern bank *(see page 73-74 for discussion.)* The Americans of Kentucky and Tennessee, several hundred miles from the Gulf of Mexico, were at the mercy of the power ruling New Orleans.

Jefferson fully recognized the threat of secession, and he was determined to remove any basis for it. He was equally determined that Americans should be able to navigate the Mississippi unhindered.

When Jefferson became president, King Carlos IV of Spain had already given in to pressure from Napoleon, who demanded the return of Louisiana to France. Readers may remember that France had quietly ceded Louisiana to the Spanish shortly before signing the Treaty of Paris in 1763. France and Spain had a long-standing family compact with a tradition of secret deals—a tradition to which Napoleon subscribed. At San Ildefonso in Spain on October 1, 1800, the two countries signed a secret accord filled with all sorts of conditions, the main feature being the return of Louisiana to France.

The two powers wanted to hide this fact as long as possible, fearing that the Americans might react violently. Jefferson, who had a hunch that he might have to settle the New Orleans question with France rather than Spain, discovered this duplicity in the spring of 1801, barely days after being sworn in as president.

It was a serious affair. The appearance of French troops in Louisiana would present a *casus belli* to the fledgling president. In a letter of April 18, 1802, to Robert R. Livingston, U.S. minister to France, Jefferson wrote, "There is on the globe one single spot, the possessor of which is our natural and habitual enemy. It is New Orleans, through which the produce of three-eighths of our territory must pass to market." Could so warlike a tone be adopted toward France—the heroic nation that had given the Thirteen Colonies such crucial aid, the civilized, *douce* France of Louis XVI where the Francophile Jefferson had been welcomed as minister plenipotentiary in 1785? Normally the new president would have hesitated, but dealing with Napoleon, the ambitious upstart, was another matter entirely.

Jefferson was a practical man, and before arming the United States against France he reasoned, as had his friend Benjamin Franklin earlier when speaking of Canada, that it might be better to buy the territory than conquer it, and cheaper in the bargain.

Robert Livingston and James Monroe were sent to France with a mandate to negotiate the purchase of New Orleans. They returned with the territory of Louisiana in their pockets—in other words, the entire drainage basin west of the Mississippi. Why not get hold of the western section of Florida and, while they were at it, a vast territory to the east of the Rio Grande that was the future state of Texas? The Americans had developed a keen appetite. They wanted land, although at the time there was no pressing need for it. But they had absolutely no idea of what lay west of the Mississippi.

Livingston and Monroe acquired the Louisiana Purchase for about three cents an acre. There were souls miserly enough to take offence at the cost. What use were these huge stretches of land, no doubt crawling with prehistoric animals straying through endless deserts, perhaps like the fabled Lost Tribe of Israel that might possibly be found there as well?

One might ask how things would have turned out had the United States not bought Louisiana in 1803, but such questions are not for historians. The territory was purchased, and we know what happened.

The French: Walking, Exploring, and Mapping a Continent

In 1492 the Americas had loomed as an obstacle on the route to the East Indies. In the northern hemisphere, Europeans were stubbornly looking for a passage of some kind. They soon identified four ways of penetrating the interior of North America: Hudson Strait in the north, the St. Lawrence and Hudson rivers on the east coast, and the Mississippi River in the south.

The Dutch settled along the Hudson River early in the seventeenth century, but were ousted by the British some fifty years later. The French challenged Great Britain for possession of Hudson Bay for some time before giving way in 1713, when they also ceded Acadia and Newfoundland to the British. Meanwhile they were resolutely colonizing the St. Lawrence. Settlement along the Mississippi would be for the future.

Throughout the seventeenth century the French learned how to drive deep into North America. They were looking, more or less, for a navigable route to the Pacific. The fur trade enabled them to finance these exploratory journeys.

By 1615 Samuel de Champlain had already reached Lake Huron via the Ottawa River and Lake Nipissing, following an Indian trail that became the route of the *Canadiens*. Others pushed on from this base to the end of Lake Superior, Lake of the Woods, Lake Manitoba and the immense Lake Winnipeg at the southern end of the Hudson Bay drainage basin. The river system gradually unlocked its secrets,

The European Powers Invade North America

This map of North America shows the approximate positions and movements of Russia, Spain, Holland, Great Britain, and France between 1650 and 1713. It is based on Carl Waldman's Atlas of the North American Indian.

What is most surprising is the small amount of territory occupied by the British, in contrast to the remarkable movement of French expansion, which stretched from the St. Lawrence Valley to the Gulf of Mexico.

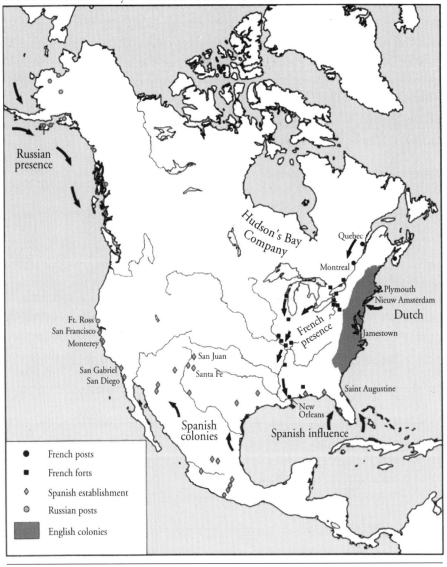

and chains of forts stretched from Montreal to Sault Sainte Marie at the juncture of lakes Huron, Michigan, and Superior.

Other explorers chose to go south rather than west and journeyed down Lake Michigan. Among them was Louis Jolliet, an intrepid and astute businessman, accompanied by the Jesuit Jacques Marquette. Their Indian guides led them to the Mississippi via Green Bay, and the Fox and Wisconsin rivers. They stopped some 700 miles (1,100 kilometres) from the Gulf of Mexico, realizing they were approaching Spanish settlements. On their journey down the Mississippi they had identified three important watercourses: the Missouri coming from the west, and the Ohio and Illinois rivers coming from the east. On the return trip they followed the Illinois River, which led them to the Chicago portage and the southern end of Lake Michigan.

The ambitious Cavalier de La Salle, accompanied by his indefatigable lieutenant Henri de Tonty, set out in the footsteps of Jolliet and Marquette, preceded by the Recollet Louis Hennepin, whose travel accounts were widely read.

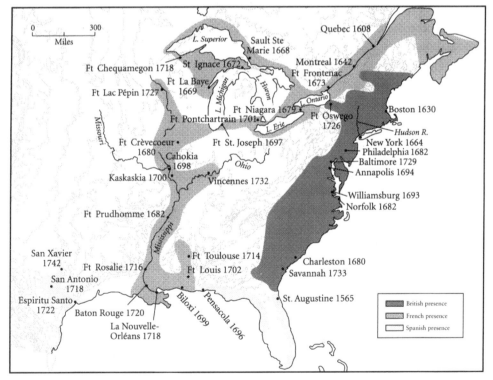

European powers establish a foothold in North America

In April 1682, after many misadventures, the French reached the mouth of the Mississippi. A new chain of French settlements sprang up: Fort Prudhomme in 1682, Cahokia in 1698, Kaskaskia in 1700, Fort Rosalie in 1716, New Orleans in 1718, and Baton Rouge in 1720.

The Ottawa River shortcut had not prevented other *Canadiens* from using the St. Lawrence as a water route to the interior. Very soon forts were built at strategic points—Fort Frontenac in 1673 at the eastern end of Lake Ontario, Fort Niagara in 1679 between Lake Ontario and Lake Erie, and Fort Pontchartrain du Détroit in 1701 between Lake Erie and Lake Huron.

Coureurs des bois (fur traders), missionaries, explorers, and soldiers were criss-crossing North America. In Paris, cartographers did their part, compiling reports and travel accounts to create increasingly accurate maps of the continent. Champlain had already revolutionized mapmaking. Men like Sanson and Delisle, working in a studio, completed the task of on-site explorers like Raffeix, Jolliet, and Franquelin.

The French advance seemed unstoppable. The lure of furs, ever more beautiful and less costly for those who were willing to go farther afield, continued to be a powerful stimulus. The added attractions of wide-open spaces, adventure, and freedom made exploration almost irresistible to the *Canadiens*, although these temptations caused the authorities and missionaries of New France considerable misgiving.

Nothing could be done about the wandering propensities of the *Canadiens*, however. The white man needed the Indian woman for his comfort and survival, as well as to establish a climate of confidence and build a network of alliances. Indians generally were given to adopting outsiders, and the *Canadiens* became part of their communities, "going native" as the expression was and initiating a deep-rooted intermingling. New France maintained its position not through the size of its population but by means of an extraordinary network of French and Indian alliances and a genuine convergence of interests.

Another Model: the British Colonies

Meanwhile the British colonies were developing along quite different lines. Immigration was considerable, stimulated by political and religious crises at home. The British colonist arrived with his family. He had come to stay and he wanted land.

The French practised cohabitation, whereas the British clustered along the coast where the Indian was not useful—indeed, even *de trop*. Initial contact

Source: Encyclopedia of American History, Jeffrey B. Morris and Richard B. Morris

North America following the Royal Proclamation of 1763

Royal Proclamation of 1763

In 1762, France ceded the western drainage basin of the Mississippi, (that is, part of the old Louisiana), to Spain. A few months later, in February 1763, it ceded to Great Britain what remained of its empire in North America. The British were forced to act quickly to improvise the framework of a new administration. On October 7, 1763, George III signed a royal proclamation determining the frontiers of "Four distinct and separate Governments" to be established in North America — that is, the Province of Quebec along the St. Lawrence River, East Florida and West Florida on the Gulf of Mexico, and the Grenada archipelago in the Caribbean. Especially important was the provisional reservation of land for the exclusive use of the Indian population. In the second paragraph of the excerpts from Article 4 of the Proclamation given below, note the words, "for the present." These words didn't appear on the draft for the proclamation, but were added *in extremis*.

Excerpts from Article 4:

And whereas it is just and reasonable, and essential to our Interest, and the Security of our Colonies, that the several Nations or Tribes of Indians with whom We are connected, and who live under our Protection, should not be molested or disturbed in the Possession of such Parts of Our Dominions and Territories as, not having been ceded to or purchased by Us, are reserved to them, or any of them, as their Hunting Grounds, We do therefore, with the Advice of our Privy Council, declare it to be our Royal Will and Pleasure, that no Governor or Commander in Chief in any of our Colonies of Quebec, East Florida, or West Florida, do presume, upon any Pretence whatever, to grant Warrants of Survey, or pass any Patents for Lands beyond the Bounds of their respective Governments, as described in their Commissions.

… And We do further declare it to be Our Royal Will and Pleasure, for the present as aforesaid, to reserve under our Sovereignty, Protection, and Dominion, for the use of the said Indians, all the Lands and Territories not included within the Limits of Our said Three new Governments [i.e., Quebec and the two Floridas], or within the Limits of the Territory granted to the Hudson's Bay Company, as also all the Lands and Territories lying to the Westward of the Sources of the Rivers which fall into the Sea from the West and North West as aforesaid.

And We do hereby strictly forbid, on Pain of our Displeasure, all our loving Subjects from making any Purchases or Settlements whatever, or taking Possession of any of the Lands above reserved, without our especial leave and Licence for that Purpose first obtained.

… We do, with the Advice of our Privy Council strictly enjoin and require, that no private Person do presume to make any purchase from the said Indians of any Lands reserved to the said Indians, within those parts of our Colonies where, We have thought proper to allow Settlement: but that, if at any Time any of the Said Indians should be inclined to dispose of the said Lands, the same shall be Purchased only for Us, in our Name, at some public Meeting or Assembly of the said Indians, to be held for that Purpose by the Governor or Commander in Chief of our Colony respectively within which they shall lie.

between the British and Indians had been positive. It should be remembered that the Massasoits and early Pilgrims celebrated Thanksgiving together in 1621. The charm of the encounter was soon shattered, however, and persistent conflict set in. The French were not loath to fuel the fire. Although the British population was thirty times greater, its colonies lived in fear of the combined forces of the French and Indians. These conflicts, known as the French and Indian Wars, ended on September 8, 1760, with the capitulation of Montreal, although the flame of the French-Indian alliance flared up for a time with Pontiac's Rebellion and a few isolated cases of resistance.

In February 1763 France admitted defeat, and North America became largely British territory with the Treaty of Paris. In reality, British North America was made up of a number of parts. First and foremost were the Thirteen Colonies, established for over a century along the Atlantic seaboard. A fourteenth colony, the "Province of Nova Scotia," was rising on the ruins of the former Acadia, and a fifteenth colony, "the Province of Quebec," was created along the St. Lawrence for the descendants of the French. Far to the north an immense territory was ceded to the Hudson's Bay Company. Between this and the frontiers of the Province of Quebec, lay a huge stretch of land running further south between the Mississippi and the Thirteen Colonies. It was reserved "for the present" for Indians placed under the protection of the British Crown.

The British had not ousted the French in order to give the Indians back their hunting grounds. The "Indian reserve" created in 1763 would prove unable to resist the pressure of colonists and colonial administrators.

American colonists had wanted to eliminate New France to give themselves elbow-room. They felt distinct from the European British in much the same way as the *Canadiens* felt distinct from the European French. These Anglo-Americans dreamed of expanding their territory and their power. They wanted access to the south shore of the St. Lawrence. British cartographers such as John Senex and Henry Popple were aware of this and made a point of extending the sphere of influence of the Thirteen Colonies on their maps.

In the event, the second Treaty of Paris (1783), while recognizing American independence, did not give the young republic the south shore of the St. Lawrence except between Lake Ontario and near present-day Massena in northern New York State, where it touches the forty-fifth parallel. What the Americans *did* gain was the vast, long-coveted region between the Great Lakes and the confluence of the Ohio and Mississippi rivers. The territory further south, east of the Mississippi, fell to them almost by default—at least as far as the Floridas, which were returned to Spain by Great Britain in the same year. In other words, in 1783 the United States extended from the St. Lawrence River (or within a few miles of it) and the Great Lakes to the Floridas, and from the Atlantic seaboard to the Mississippi.

Exactly twenty years later, Louisiana was handed to the Americans on a platter. For them it was uncharted ground. For French Canadians (as they were to be known) who had survived the demise of New France and the disappearance of what they had known as Canada, it had become a land of refuge. Rather than being British subjects, many had chosen to serve Spain after 1763.

In St. Louis on March 9, 1804 (and in New Orleans a few weeks earlier), various dignitaries officially handed over power from Spain to France. The tricolour was flown until the following day, it is told. Then on March 10, as the guns of American troops fired the salute, the Stars and Stripes rose in its place. The French Canadians watched, some with tears in their eyes, others stoic, as the Americans took possession of the upper part of Louisiana. Soon afterward, the transfer of the entire territory had been completed. In the space of a few months, power over this huge stretch of country had passed from the Spanish to the French, then to the Americans. First had come the rumours, then the confirmation.

Meriwether Lewis and William Clark, who had spent the winter at Camp Dubois on the eastern shore of the Mississippi, were present at the ceremony in St. Louis. Captain Amos Stoddard, representative of the United States and future governor of Upper Louisiana, personally invited his friend Lewis to act as an official witness. Three years later, Jefferson offered Lewis the post of governor of Upper Louisiana.

– II –

The Expedition

At President Jefferson's request, Meriwether Lewis and William Clark prepared to form an expeditionary corps that would eventually number some forty people. Technically speaking, it was an infantry company of the U.S. Army. Its mandate was to reach the Pacific Ocean, starting from St. Louis, a small town at the mouth of the Missouri River.

This expedition, popularly known as the "Corps of Discovery," has become famous for a variety of reasons. To begin with, it was successful. In 1793 Alexander Mackenzie, the Scottish-born Canadian fur trader and explorer, had been the first European to reach the Pacific by an overland route and return to his starting point. It was a remarkable exploit, and the publication of his travel journal created a sensation. Mackenzie was actually one of the factors that triggered the mission entrusted to Lewis.

Unlike Mackenzie, who travelled light and moved quickly, as though his one aim was to do the round trip while gathering a minimum of information, Lewis and Clark took over two years to complete a mission that that was both political and scientific in nature, as well as having commercial dimensions.

The expedition's primary objective was to find a navigable route, as direct as possible, to the Pacific and ultimately to China. According to Jefferson's theory, the Missouri River led to the foot of a western mountain range at about the same latitude as the source of the Columbia River. As such a route would be used for trade, it was essential to make sure that friendly relations were established with the Indians living in the regions through which the Missouri passed. If necessary, peace should be established among the various tribes, and those living between the Mississippi and the western mountains would be told that this vast territory had a new master—the president of the United States. It was a serious undertaking. With this in mind, Lewis had prepared a supply of medals, flags, certificates, and gifts such as handkerchiefs, mirrors, beads, and hats.

Jefferson was a man of great knowledge and culture. Everything interested him, particularly precise observations on topography, fauna and flora, and the Indians—their numbers, languages, mores, characteristics, beliefs, and so on.

The Fascinating Journals

Lewis and Clark had no choice but to take copious notes, a task they performed with exemplary diligence. Each was required to keep his journal, even if it meant transcribing or basing himself on his colleague's notes. Above all, Jefferson had insisted they do so as a precaution against loss.

It soon became clear that Lewis had a greater gift for narration than Clark, and no doubt found it more to his taste. Clark was often satisfied with simply copying his partner's notes. His strength lay in recording scientific data, drawing small pictures, and making marvellous maps.

The quality of the Lewis and Clark journals certainly helped establish their reputation. Writing in a lively style, both narrators keep their readers in continual suspense. Even if we know in advance that the expedition will succeed, we don't know exactly how. Each day brings its share of fresh challenges. With evening comes anxiety for the morrow. At what time of day did Lewis or Clark write in their journals? To tell the truth, it often seems as though they did it in the heat of action. If a grizzly chases Lewis, we know he'll escape because he's telling the story, but he does it so skilfully that we almost fear for his life. The Teton Sioux bend their bows, the soldiers point their guns, we are there, and anything is possible.

Lewis was especially skilful in bringing each day's events to life for us. He was more sensitive than Clark, a little poetic in style, sometimes nostalgic or even troubled. We sense that he liked to write—and to surprise his readers.

On August 18, 1805, he launched into a curiously introspective exercise. It was his thirty-first birthday—a midlife milestone—and he fully realized that he "had done but little, very little indeed" for the happiness of humanity "or to advance the information of the succeeding generations." He thought of all the time wasted, of all the knowledge he could have accumulated that would have been so useful to him at the present juncture. He resolved to turn over a new leaf. From now on, wrote Lewis, he would "live for *mankind*, as I have heretofore lived *for myself*" (Thwaites, 2: 368).

Clark never had such moods. And yet he was not a cold, impassive man: quite the contrary. He was attentive to the needs of others, generous, and humane. He was less expressive, more concise, and probably aware of his spelling difficulties—although these make delightful reading today. He compensated by using his scientific instruments to maximum advantage. This was no small accomplishment.

A Terrific Team

Lewis and Clark were excellent leaders of men, soldiers by trade and in spirit. They were methodical and disciplined, and would tolerate no misconduct. These qualities were the key to their success.

They recruited the members of the expedition with care, making a point of hiring people with complementary skills and training: hunters and cooks, of course, but also a blacksmith, carpenter, tailor, gunsmith, and so on. Were they aware of recruiting a peerless second-in-command in the person of John Ordway? Probably not. Did they think that Georges Drouillard would be far more than an interpreter or Pierre Cruzatte other than an excellent guide? They certainly couldn't have realized that they had assembled a cast worthy of a blockbuster film, able to capture the imagination and become quasi-legendary: a young Indian woman with her baby, a black slave, and a loyal Newfoundland dog, as well as numerous bit players in the form of the Indians, always unpredictable but generally helpful and friendly, with their eloquent, shrewd, and energetic chiefs.

The story of Lewis and Clark is so complex that there is something in it for everyone. With time it has acquired new meaning, sustaining and then justifying the American dream of "manifest destiny." It opened the trail to the West, the path of inexorable territorial expansion. It is a story that has become a founding myth.

The Expedition Sets Off: From St. Charles to the Mandan Villages

On May 21, 1804, a flotilla of three boats—a fifty-five-foot long keelboat and two pirogues manned by six to eight paddlers—left the tiny village of St. Charles, some twenty miles west of St. Louis. A little further upstream, they hailed the last white settlement, the village of La Charette.

The Missouri was an unknown quantity for Americans, but not for French Canadians or Creoles. It was a difficult river to navigate, dotted with snags, floating driftwood, and sandbars, among other obstacles. The expedition had barely got under way when it met convoy after convoy of canoes coming mainly from Omaha or Pawnee villages. Invariably, they were steered by what Lewis and Clark called "Frenchmen." One of the first was Régis Loisel, an important member of the Missouri Fur Company of St. Louis. Loisel took the time to tell the Americans what to expect, advising them to stop at Cedar Island, about a thousand miles upriver. There they would find his associates, Pierre-Antoine Tabeau and Joseph Garreau.

On June 12 the Americans met Pierre Dorion coming down the Missouri with two rafts. He said he had been living among the Yankton Sioux for some twenty years and agreed to accompany the expedition upstream as far as his people.

By the time two months had passed since leaving St. Charles, the expedition had covered nearly 600 miles (1,000 kilometres) and encountered dozens of so-called Frenchmen, but not a single Native American.

It wasn't until August 3 that Lewis and Clark could hold their first meeting with Indians—the Otos, with whom the Missouris lived, sad survivors of recent epidemics. Not far away lived the Omahas, whose population had also been decimated by smallpox in 1800-1801. Despite their wretchedness they were at war with the Otos, fighting over mere trifles. Peace was possible, nevertheless. Lewis and Clark were more than willing to help, but the Omahas were nowhere to be found. They were off hunting.

Encounters with the Otos were amicable, but nothing more. The Indians were interested in trading with any and all whites.

By the end of August, discussions with the Yankton Sioux were proceeding on a friendly basis to the point where they had agreed to go to Washington in the spring with Pierre Dorion. For the moment, however, they wished the expedition good luck, alluding to the hostile welcome by the Teton Sioux that would certainly await the Americans. The Tetons' reputation was well known. The explorer Jean-Baptiste Trudeau had escaped from them by the skin of his teeth in 1794, and he issued serious warnings in his journal. Everyone had repeated these to Lewis and Clark. They were forewarned. When the expedition finally met the Tetons, the result was three days of ruses, altercations, warnings, and threats. Like many other tribes, the Tetons intended to profit from their geographical position. Did they have any choice? If traders from St. Louis could reach the Arikaras, Mandans, or Hidatsas without paying, what advantage was left to the Tetons? At least, they reasoned to themselves, they could make people passing through pay dearly. It gave them a chance to get a few goods and allowed the chiefs to reassert their authority.

One of the Tetons, a man called the Partisan, was especially provoking to the Americans, who came within a hair's breadth of exchanging blows with the Indians. The Tetons began to threaten the Americans. "I felt My self Compeled to Draw my Sword," wrote Clark, upon which Lewis ordered the men to prepare for action. Clark, in his fury, "Spoke in verry positive terms" to the warriors (Thwaites,

1: 165). But the captains opted for negotiation and gradually pushed their way past the Tetons with the consent of Chief Black Buffalo, a more conciliatory man than the Partisan. They proceeded on, thankful to leave the Tetons behind. They would meet them on the way back—but that was a bridge to be crossed another day.

For the moment the Americans continued on their way. On October 1 they met another French-Canadian trader, Jean Vallée, who told them about the region. A week later they met Joseph Gravelines, Pierre-Antoine Tabeau, and several other Frenchmen among the Arikaras, a tribe devastated by epidemics. The Americans quickly realized that the Arikaras were trading with the North West Company's French-Canadian agents. What sort of welcome awaited Lewis and Clark? The Arikaras' reputation wasn't as fearsome as that of the Tetons, but they too stood guard over the passage to the Mandans, sometimes levying payment or blocking the way for traders from St. Louis.

This time Lewis and Clark had good interpreters—something they'd lacked in dealing with the Tetons because Dorion had stayed behind with the Yanktons. The presence of interpreters made all the difference. It took time for them to come to terms. There were issues on which both sides disagreed resulting in numerous parleys. The length of the discussions allowed the men of the expedition to get used to the very warm hospitality offered by the Arikara women—something of a prelude to what awaited them when they wintered over with the Mandans.

The Corps of Discovery reached the Mandans on October 24 and went no further before the spring. It was five months since the expedition had left St. Charles. With great difficulty it had covered the 1,600 miles (2,580 kilometres) to the Mandan village. Now it was time to stop; winter wasn't far off.

Near the two Mandan villages were three Hidatsa villages on the Knife River— 4,000 Indians in all, of which 1,300 were warriors. The atmosphere remained friendly, but the expedition took no chances. Lewis and Clark had the men build a fort.

Winter at Fort Mandan passed pleasantly—more than pleasantly in some cases. The Americans got to know a few French Canadians who lived with the Indians, among them Toussaint Charbonneau. The brush with the Tetons had made the Americans realize the importance of having interpreters. They hired Charbonneau in this capacity. His young Shoshone wife, Sacagawea, would accompany him. The Shoshones lived near the Rocky Mountain foothills and were known for their horses. The presence of the young Indian woman might be invaluable when it came time to negotiate for mounts. Sacagawea gave birth to a son, Jean-Baptiste, on February 11, 1805, and as a matter of course he joined the expedition along with his mother.

From Mandan Country to the Pacific

On April 7, 1805, the Corps of Discovery set off once more. The keelboat was sent back to St. Louis laden with specimens and reports for President Jefferson. It took the expedition a little over two months to cover the 1,000 miles (1,600 kilometres) separating the Mandan country from the "great falls" mentioned by the Hidatsas. (Unlike the Mandans, the Hidatsas had no qualms about going as far as the Rockies.) The report regarding great falls gave Lewis and Clark some idea of what to expect. Baptiste Lepage, whom they recruited among the Mandans, had already reached the River "Rochejhone" (later known as the Yellowstone River), but beyond that point Lewis and Clark believed they would be the first whites to travel so far west—a highly unlikely supposition that, in any case, didn't take into account the epic voyages of men like the La Vérendryes.

To their amazement, the men of the expedition would encounter not one but five great falls on the Missouri, requiring an interminable portage. After this ordeal they continued for some distance in dugout canoes, but the Missouri became increasingly difficult to navigate. The captains realized that they would soon have to leave their boats behind.

Mountains were rising on the horizon. In order to reach the source of the Columbia River, Lewis and Clark must first cross them. They would need horses, but where were the Shoshones, those famous breeders? Since leaving Fort Mandan, the expedition had not met a single Indian. Where were the Crows, Flatheads, and Nez Percés mentioned by the Hidatsas?

Sacagawea reassured the leaders. She recognized the spot where her people had been attacked by Hidatsas and where she had been kidnapped. The Shoshones couldn't be far off. At last, in mid-August, the much desired encounter took place — and in the nick of time: the Shoshones were getting ready to leave for the buffalo hunt. Would they be willing to part with a few horses and supply guides to take the expedition over the mountains?

Sacagawea was called on to act as interpreter. Lewis spoke in English to Labiche or Drouillard, who translated his words into French for Charbonneau, who in turn passed the message on to his wife in Hidatsa. Sacagawea was to be the expedition's spokesperson with the Shoshone chief. Suddenly Lewis, who had occasionally remarked on Sacagawea's impassive manner, discovered a totally different woman. When she recognized Cameahwait, the Shoshone chief, as her brother, she "ran and embraced him" (Jackson, 1978, 2: 519) and was equally overjoyed to see a Shoshone woman, captured at the same time as herself, who had escaped from her kidnappers.

Although much moved by the reunion, Cameahwait kept a cool head. His people were at the mercy of the Blackfeet, who were given guns and ammunition by the French Canadians of the North West Company, whereas the Shoshones' Spanish allies had always refused to trade firearms to them. Lewis promised to do this, and in return obtained horses and at least one guide to take the Americans up into the mountains.

On the road — but "road" is a euphemism here — the men of the expedition, dog-tired, starving, and despondent, happened on a band of Salish (Flathead) Indians who proved to be extremely co-operative, thanks to Old Toby, the Shoshone guide. They shared what little food they had with the expedition and agreed to exchange a few of their best horses for the expedition's skinny hacks. In his journal, Joseph Whitehouse expressed his colleagues' feelings when he wrote, "They are the likelyest and honestst Savages we have ever yet Seen" (Thwaites, 7: 150).

He could have said the same of the Nez Percés who came upon the expedition on September 20, 1805. Lewis and Clark's people were in a state of extreme exhaustion. The temptation must have been very strong. The Indians had at hand as many firearms as they could possibly want, just for the taking. However, a woman of the tribe urged them to do no harm to the strangers. She had been captured by the Blackfeet and sold to a white trapper who had treated her kindly. Later, she had found her way back to her people (Thwaites, 3: 83, n. 1).

The Nez Percés treated the expedition generously, both going and returning. They provided food and showed the men how to build canoes. They even acted as pilots on the tumultuous waters of the Clearwater River where, on October 7, 1805, the expedition could travel downstream for the first time since their departure.

Since passing the Missouri's Great Falls, the expedition had covered about 350 miles (565 kilometres), including 140 miles (225 kilometres) of terrifying mountain trails. After the Clearwater, there remained 600 miles (967 kilometres) to cover before reaching the ocean. The corps would have to travel down the Snake River, then the Columbia, reaching its mouth in mid-November. There was no time to lose: the expedition set off, paddling with great daring though a succession of rapids.

On the way, they met the Wanapams and Yakimas encamped at the juncture of the Snake and Columbia rivers. These people gave the Corps of Discovery a warm welcome. The Umatillas, in contrast, were distinctly unwelcoming, but nothing serious took place. As the expedition got closer to the coast, the Indians were more accustomed to seeing whites. They were also more demanding and struck harder bargains. They insisted on getting the maximum for the dried fish and dogs that the corps had to eat for lack of game. The Americans' nerves were frayed and they were worried about their dwindling store of trade goods. They almost began to dislike the Indians, whose penchant for petty thievery provoked anger and exasperation.

At last the expedition came to the Pacific. The men were proud of their achievement, but they were in a state of collapse. The weather was dismal, the region inhospitable, and food hard to come by. They built a fort near the Clatsop Indians. Everything seemed ugly. The Clatsops especially seemed dirty, squat folk according to the journals, scantily dressed and given to wearing outlandish garments and decorations (Thwaites 4: 183-191). All in all it was a gloomy winter that couldn't even be enlivened by an old Chinook woman—none other than the chief's wife!—offering to sell the favours of her six daughters and nieces (Thwaites, 3: 241).

The men of the Corps of Discovery had reached the end of their outward journey and the end of their tether.

The Return Journey

Even before spring came, the men were ready to leave. Did they lack a canoe? Lewis decided to steal one. The price asked was considered too high, and in any case weren't the Americans justified in taking it as compensation for six elk stolen by the Clatsops? A real theft, that, although the Clatsops had actually offered a few dogs in payment.

The fact was that Lewis was itching to get going. On March 23, the expedition left Fort Clatsop without regret. The Indians warned them that they would reach the Rockies too soon. Trails would be completely snowed in, almost impassable, and—most important of all—there would be no grazing for the horses.

Lewis and Clark decided to kill some time among the Nez Percés and kept busy looking after the sick. But they were restless and set off once more—far too quickly, and even worse, without their guides. They resigned themselves to waiting for the guides to catch up. At last all was well, and by June 30, 1806, the terrible Bitterroot Mountains were finally behind them. Lewis and Clark could breathe easy. Their confidence returned: they would reach St. Louis before the winter. In that case, why not profit from the opportunity to split up and explore as much as they could? Lewis would go east, keeping to a virtually straight line, to reach the Missouri as near as possible to the Marias River, hoping to verify the latter's source. This was a question of some importance. The territory acquired by the United States in 1803 corresponded to the western drainage basin of the Mississippi. What was its northern boundary? It could well be the source of the Marias.

Clark would head for the Yellowstone River and follow it to where it emptied into the Missouri. The two captains would rendezvous there. To reach this point, Clark would cover a distance of some 1,000 miles (1,600 kilometres) and Lewis a little less—about 800 miles (1,300 kilometres). As the crow flies, the juncture of the Missouri and Yellowstone rivers was 500 miles (800 kilometres) from where the two parties separated. They set off on July 3 and met again, a little to the east of the appointed place, on August 12, 1806. All were safe and sound. Six weeks later they reached St. Louis. Nothing had been heard of them for so long that they were presumed dead, but in fact everyone had survived except Sergeant Charles Floyd, who had died of an appendicitis attack at the beginning of the expedition.

Taking Stock

To reach the mouth of the splendid Columbia River, Lewis and Clark had covered 3,555 miles (about 5,700 kilometres) in roughly the following segments: 2,575 miles (about 4,100 kilometres) on the Missouri from its mouth to the Great Falls; about 340 miles (600 kilometres) more to reach a navigable route west of the Rockies, and finally 640 miles (about 1,000 kilometres) descending three successive waterways: the Clearwater (Kooskooske or Tête Plate), the Snake (Lewis), and the Columbia.

During their long adventure, Lewis and Clark met over twenty Indian nations and became relatively familiar with the Yankton and Teton Sioux, the Arikaras, Mandans, Hidatsas (Minitaris or Gros Ventres), Shoshones, Flatheads, Nez Percés (Chopunnish), Chinooks, and Clatsops. They parleyed with the Otos, Missouris, Yakimas, Wanapams, Walla Wallas, Umatillas, Wishrams, Wascos, Sahaptians, Skilloots, Multnomahs, Kathlamets, and Wahkiakums. Lastly, they acquired information about dozens of other tribes such as the Osages, Kansas, Pawnees, Foxes, Cheyennes, Kristinas, Blackfeet, Assiniboins, and others.

Their reports included estimates of native populations; what is striking is the small number of Indians scattered in numerous tribes and bands. Also noteworthy is the absence of native peoples in some of the great open spaces. The expedition encountered no Indians from St. Charles to the mouth of the Platte and from Mandan country to the Great Falls. When they finally met some, they were few in number. The abandoned villages bore witness to the ravages of recent epidemics that probably coincided with the arrival of whites. The Arikaras, for example, had only three sparsely populated villages left, whereas they previously had eighteen, and the Mandans had only two out of five left.

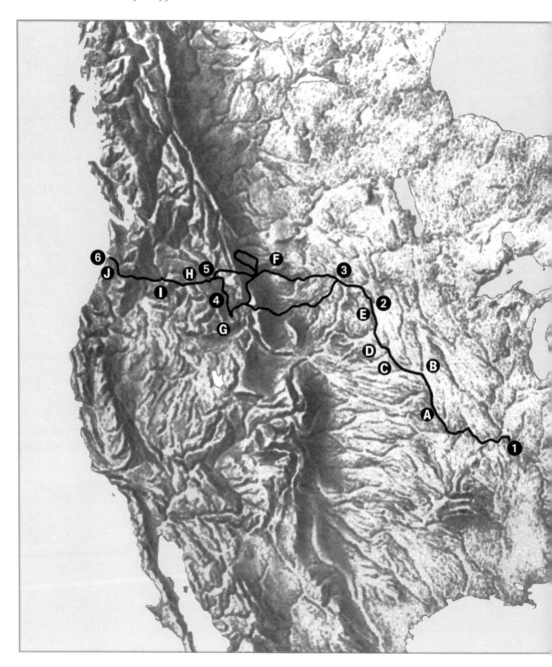

A few geographical points

1. St. Louis at the mouth of the Missouri.
2. Fort Mandan, where the Corps of Discovery first wintered over. The region had been frequented by the French Canadians and British for years.
3. Mouth of the Yellowstone River, named the "Rochejhone" by the French Canadians.
4. The Bitterroot Mountains.
5. Travellers' Rest where the expedition stopped on the way west (September 9, 1805) and on the return journey (July 4, 1806.)
6. Fort Clatsop, south of the mouth of the Columbia River, where the expedition spent the second winter.

Some of the tribes encountered

A. The Otos, among whom lived the remnants of the Missouris.
B. The Yankton Sioux, with whom Pierre Dorion lived.
C. The warlike Teton Sioux.
D. The Arikaras, with whom Joseph Gravelines and Pierre-Antoine Tabeau were staying.
E. The Mandans and their neighbours, the Hidatsas (also called Gros Ventres or Minitaris/Minitarees).
F. The Blackfeet, who confronted Lewis near the Marias River
G. The Shoshones (Snakes).
H. The Nez Percés (Chopunnish).
I. The Walla Wallas and Yakimas.
J. The Chinooks and Clatsops.

How many Indians remained along the Missouri between 1804 and 1805? A few thousand, and these would be wiped out by another smallpox epidemic in 1837.

Initially, Clark estimated an Indian population of 69,040 people in the region traversed by the expedition. He revised his estimate, suggesting 80,000. These small numbers are astonishing. In all, the Chinook family had less than 1,000 members, divided among a dozen or so tribes. The Chinooks north of the Columbia numbered 400, and the Clatsops, settled across the river, about half that. The Nez Percés had some 2,000 people.

Jefferson had stated his precise expectations regarding the Indians. The two captains did their work admirably. They gathered an amazing amount of information covering every imaginable aspect of their subject.

Nor was geography neglected—far from it. The captains noted everything: the longitudes and latitudes of various places, characteristics of the landscape, distances, and obstacles. Indian or French place names were noted, but new names appeared, chosen by the captains. They used the names of expedition members: Floyd, Shields, Gibson, Bratton, Goodrich, Thompson, Shannon, and so on, not to mention their illustrious sponsors back in Washington—Jefferson, Gallatin, Madison, and Dearborn.

Even Sacagawea's son, young Jean-Baptiste Charbonneau (nicknamed Pomp), left his name on a rock in the Yellowstone River: Pompey's Tower, later Pompey's Pillar. Almost everyone except the black slave York had the honour of having some geographical feature named after him.

It might well be said that Lewis and Clark named everything. Animals and plants received special attention. On occasion, Clark slipped little drawings into his journal. Among the most popular were the eulachon (a fish) and the "cock of the plains" or sage grouse. Above all, Clark devoted himself patiently to drawing maps of amazing quality.

In a word, the journals of Lewis and Clark are a treasury of inexhaustible information. Perhaps no exploratory mission has brought back so much scientific data—information that helped guarantee Lewis and Clark's entry into the pantheon of great explorers.

The keelboat and the two pirogues leaving St. Charles in May 1804.
Painting by L. Edward Fisher.

– III –

Dream or Destiny?

Lewis and Clark had reached the Pacific. They had followed the planned itinerary, only to establish that it was not a practical route. The 140-mile (225 kilometre) trek through snowbound mountains posed too many problems, and for this reason they had questioned the Indians about other possible routes.

The "Rochejhone" (Yellowstone) River offered a way of avoiding the Missouri's Great Falls and reaching the Three Forks area. But what route should be followed from there? The Indians said they knew of several and used certain of these with their families. For the moment, however, the Rockies remained a powerful challenge and a terrifying obstacle.

For 150 years, nature and circumstance had prompted British Americans to settle along the Atlantic seaboard. Behind them to the west rose the Appalachian Mountains—and the Indians. There were also the French, who occupied a wide corridor running the length of the Mississippi. They had rapidly established a chain of forts that led as far as the Gulf of Mexico. Furthermore, they had formed alliances with the Indians, and in 1701 had invited various Indian nations to Montreal in order to conclude the Great Peace. Most of these nations came from central North America.

Eliminating New France

Great Britain had brought France to its knees in 1763. North America became British. The Thirteen Colonies—New Hampshire, Massachusetts, New York, Rhode Island, Connecticut, Pennsylvania, New Jersey, Delaware, Maryland, Virginia, the two Carolinas, and Georgia—found their family enlarged by Britain's acquisition of the former French colony, a small part of which became the "Province of Quebec," in addition to the Province of Nova Scotia, which had already been acquired under the Treaty of Utrecht in 1713. Now there were fifteen British colonies.

Nevertheless the Thirteen remained the Thirteen. At the signing of the Treaty of Paris the Duc de Choiseul, the French minister, had felt that this might be the case and murmured to his entourage, "Nous les tenons!" — an enigmatic comment meaning "They've lost them!" that veiled a premonition. William Pitt the Elder, the British prime minister and great victor of the Seven Years' War, shared this view. The fall of New France might remove the Thirteen Colonies' reason for being attached to England. Once the French rival was driven from North America, how would the Thirteen react? Would they try to distance themselves from Great Britain? Pitt feared they would. He was ready to return Canada to France in exchange for Guadeloupe and Martinique.

The powerful sugar lobby in London felt threatened by this possible competition. Opposition to Pitt's views caused him to resign, and he took no further part in negotiations for the Treaty of Paris. New France was taken off the map and a new British colony appeared along the St. Lawrence. At the same time Britain became aware of the fact that the drainage basin west of the Mississippi no longer belonged to France. The French had transferred it to Spain by secret treaty on November 3, 1762, several months earlier.

In any case the British ministers had their hands full. How should they rearrange their new possessions? They improvised a vast Indian reserve that lay to the west of the Thirteen Colonies and bordered on the Province of Quebec to the north. It was a provisional measure, but the Colonial Office hadn't time to find a better solution. In 1774, realizing that the Thirteen Colonies were trying to move west with the consent, voluntary or not, of the Indians, London decided to extend the boundaries of the Province of Quebec to the confluence of the Ohio and Mississippi rivers, basically taking in the whole Great Lakes region. It wasn't so much a concession to the French Canadians as a means of trying to keep control over these vast regions from Quebec City, the British capital in North America.

The Thirteen Colonies Rebel

The Thirteen Colonies were enraged by the Quebec Act of 1774. The spectre of New France had not disappeared, and fear of the French and Indians was still very much alive. That was all it took to light the fuse, and in 1775, as the revolution moved into high gear, the Americans decided to invade the Province of Quebec and submit it to their will. However, the former French colonists weren't taken in by the official American position proposing that French Canadians profit from the chance to take revenge on the conquering British. The invasion failed, and as a result the Province of Quebec became a garrison colony from which Great Britain tried to dominate the British-American rebels.

Although the French Canadians had no taste for a paltry revenge, the same was not true of the continental French. They would aid the Americans, who had nothing to fear from such assistance since there was no question of France profiting from the occasion to recover pieces of its old North American empire.

American Independence

In 1783, Britain resigned itself to recognizing the independence of the United States in the Second Treaty of Paris. Twenty years had been enough to prove that Choiseul and Pitt were right. Apart from nature's obstacles, there was nothing to stop the United States from expanding to the Mississippi. Two new states, Kentucky and Tennessee, were created west of the Appalachians, and colonists on the Atlantic seaboard learned to go around or across the mountains.

Nevertheless, in 1801 the United States was still a coastal country, all the more ambivalent about western expansion because a small secessionist movement had emerged among the settlements between the Appalachians and the Mississippi.

Some leaders of the seaboard states had trouble seeing beyond the Appalachians, but there were others, including the newly-elected president, Thomas Jefferson, who could see as far as the Mississippi and were preoccupied with ensuring that Americans would have free access to it.

Expectations ended there. No one in the United States in those days was interested in the land west of this majestic river. However, the few French Canadians in the Ohio Valley, Illinois country, Kaskaskia, Cahokia, and other small settlements on the eastern shore were already gravitating toward the Mississippi's western bank.

It was at this point that, against all odds, the United States gathered up what was left of the immense French Louisiana of the eighteenth century—the territory west of the Mississippi, extending to the sources of its tributaries. It was so far away that even Jefferson, the visionary, couldn't imagine what to do with it except create an immense Indian reserve; he planned to encourage the rare (as he thought) whites on the west bank to return to the east. As for the Indians east of the Mississippi, either they would voluntarily become farmers and cede their vast forests to the federal government, or they would exchange them, willingly or not, for equivalent territories west of the Mississippi.

The Conquest of the West

American entrepreneurs such as John Jacob Astor lost no time in heading west, although not in the footsteps of Lewis and Clark. The Platte River wasn't navigable, but after the spring floods its hard sand shores were suitable for horses and wagons. Beyond that people were sure someone would discover a reasonably practical passage over the Continental Divide and the barrier of the Rockies.

Settlers rushed toward Oregon, and American authorities did the rest, negotiating a frontier with the British to the north. Mississippi tributaries extended to the forty-ninth parallel, and this would be the frontier between Canada and the United States. Roughly speaking, Canada occupied the northern slope or watershed of the continent, much of which consists of the Precambrian Shield left by the receding Wisconsin Glacier, while the United States occupied the southern slope. The reality is more complicated, especially if we follow the forty-ninth parallel westward. Readers need only think of the Columbia River with its main source in the immensely long Columbia Lake, well to the north of the parallel. Initially the river flows north for more than 200 miles (300 kilometres) before turning due south, then west.

Despite such anomalies, the limits of the Louisiana Purchase provided a basis for negotiating a frontier with the British, masters of Canada. From the Americans' standpoint, it was in their interest to settle the question of the northern frontier. They had enough on their hands with their southern border. Moreover, both British and Americans could rely on a shared cultural background that would incline them to resolve the matter without further bloodshed.

War in the South

After the Louisiana Purchase—in a move that was part bravado, part pure arrogance toward the Mexicans—the Americans had claimed that the new territory extended as far as the Rio Grande, although this river isn't a tributary of the Mississippi. The future of what would become Texas was in question.

Jefferson's rather surprising position contrasted sharply with Spain's view of the boundaries. The Spanish minister of state, Manuel Godoy, didn't hesitate to exclude the Illinois country and the Upper Missouri from the Louisiana Purchase. He fixed its western frontier at Fort Natchitoches on the Red River, in present-day Louisiana. Clearly, Godoy's Louisiana had nothing in common with that of the Americans who, as a curious sidelight, were claiming territories they knew nothing about.

In all logic, the Spanish felt they must put a stop to American exploration.

The United States between 1783 and 1853

The United States mainland acquired its present form in stages, beginning with the core Thirteen Colonies lying between the Appalachian Mountains and the Atlantic. Britain had received a huge section of the continent in 1763. In 1783, with the official recognition of American independence, Britain ceded the territory south of the Great Lakes as far west as the Mississippi to the new republic.

In 1803, Napoleon pressured Spain into giving back Louisiana (the western drainage basin of the Mississippi) to France. He then offered it to the United States. The Louisiana Purchase spurred the expansion of the United States and stimulated the American appetite for territory. The U.S. government redefined "Louisiana" to include enlarged borders. The country's northern border was quietly delineated at different moments: in the Northwest along the forty-ninth parallel (1818 and 1846) and in the Northeast (Maine, 1842). To the south, the U.S. acquired the Floridas from Spain in 1819, claimed and then annexed Texas in 1845, went to war with Mexico and obtained, by the Treaty of Guadalupe Hidalgo (1848), an immense territory (1,191,061 square miles or 3,084,851 square kilometres) that included Texas. In this treaty Mexico gave up all claim to land beyond the Rio Grande and ceded territory in the West that corresponded to the present states of Arizona, Nevada, California, Utah, and parts of New Mexico, Colorado, and Wyoming. The treaty was ratified by Congress despite fairly strong opposition from the Senate, which demanded the annexation of Mexico as a whole. By 1853 the process was completed with the acquisition of a new piece of land in the south. This was the Gadsden Purchase (29,649 square miles or 79,791 square kilometres), named after the American negotiator, James Gadsden. The goal was to have territory through which to put a railroad to the Pacific.

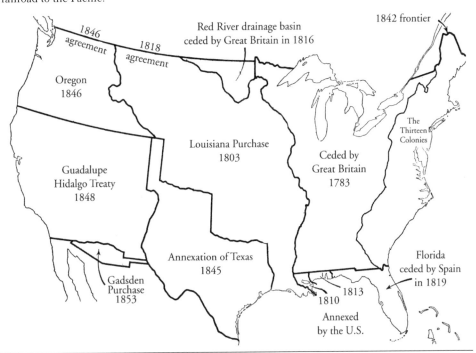

They therefore tried to block Lewis and Clark, but couldn't find them, although they would have more luck with Zebulon Pike and several other explorers.

At the same time, the Spanish certainly intended to make good their rights "of discovery." The noted Mexican scholar, Father José Antonio Pichardo, launched into a huge survey of the frontiers of Texas and Louisiana (thirty-one volumes with a total of 5,127 pages). The question was and is a complex one.

While some sharpened their quills, others polished their muskets. Spanish and Americans were on the verge of taking up arms when two fairly questionable commanders decided to define a demilitarized zone between Natchitoches and the Sabine River (the present border between the states of Texas and Louisiana). Before long, this neutral zone was swarming with fugitive slaves, outlaws, and criminals of all sorts, waiting to head into Texas.

Manifest Destiny

What explained this mad rush toward the West? The Americans have a surprising expression that dispenses them from all logical explanation: "manifest destiny," irresistible and implacable. *New York Morning News* editor John L. O'Sullivan coined the magic formula, asserting in the *United States Magazine and Democratic Review* (July-August 1845) that, "Our manifest destiny is to overspread the continent allotted by providence for the free development of our yearly multiplying millions."

This "overspreading" would lead to Indian massacres and cruel wars waged against the Mexicans. No explanation would be needed. It was manifest destiny.

The West was a dream. In history, one comes to recognize the power of fashion and taste. A taste for spices provoked the most daring enterprises. A totally frivolous fashion for beaver hats gave birth to the French empire in America, enabling a handful of Frenchmen to control nearly a whole continent for over a hundred years.

Dreams are of the same order as fashion. They can become mirages, chimeras, utopias. Dreams can also give birth to a mysterious force, invincible, conquering, even annihilating.

The conquest of the West belonged to this realm of dreams that fired great enterprises. Obstacles were overcome one after another: the Appalachians, the French-Indian barrier, the Mississippi River, the Great Plains, the Rockies. Nothing could stop this westward drive — coldly implacable, often inhuman, moving with the power of a steamroller. Its principal victims were the Indians who had survived the epidemics. Weakened, impoverished, and duped, they were finally crushed.

The irony is that their ancestors could have wiped out the members of Lewis and Clark's expedition many times over. The Teton Sioux could have massacred them; so could the Arikaras, Mandans, and Hidatsas. The Nez Percés had them at their mercy. The Chinooks could have leagued with their people against the Americans.

All in all, it must be admitted that the Indians proved themselves hospitable. They were traders and lived by commerce. Each of these nations believed they would gain some advantage from the arrival of new trading partners.

1803-1853: The United States Takes Shape

A new power was born in 1783 with the official recognition of American independence in the Second Treaty of Paris. This power assumed impressive dimensions in 1803. Fifty years more sufficed for it to acquire its present form, then another hundred years for it to establish order within its own frontiers before taking on the internationally predominant role it has chosen to play.

THE EXPEDITION:
PERSPECTIVES AND PERSONAE

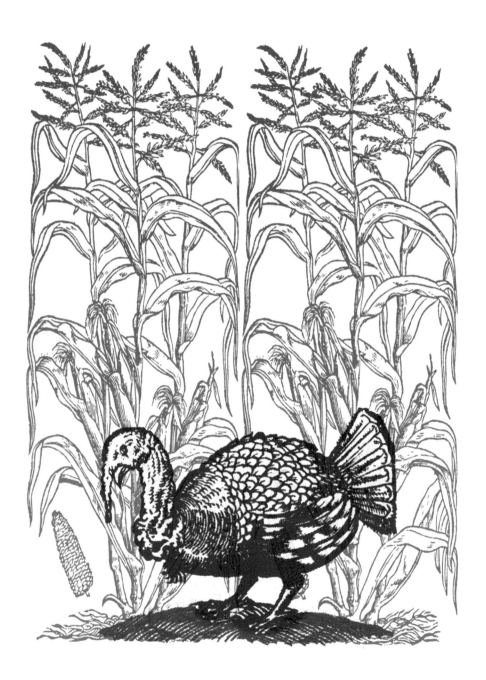

Chapter 1

The Western Sea

In 1492 Christopher Columbus thought he had reached the East Indies. Instead, he had run up against a wall blocking his route. This continent, which French mapmakers would call America, was to provide abundant resources that would change the world, but for all that, the Orient and its mysteries were not forgotten.

For three centuries explorers would search the Atlantic coast carefully, hoping to find a waterway that would lead them to the Western Sea.

The French succeeded in reaching the heart of North America, and then went down the Mississippi, a journey of some 3,100 miles (5,000 kilometres). Explorers like Cavelier de La Salle and the La Vérendrye family are well remembered. Forgotten are men like the Mallet brothers or Viénard de Bourgmont, the sometime lover of the amazing Madame Montour, a Métis woman from Trois-Rivières who has yet to find her place in the history books.

This first chapter provides the background to exploration of the Missouri. By the end of the eighteenth century there was a fair amount of fur-trading traffic on the river, but it went not much farther than the Mandan country on the Upper Missouri—the hub of a vast trade network that brought firearms from the north and horses from the south. And epidemics from all sides.

Little by little the Missouri came to dominate the public imagination as the most likely way west. The Pacific coast had been explored by ships going round the tip of South America. A giant river, the Columbia, had been discovered. It fascinated explorers.

Exactly three hundred years after Columbus's first voyage, almost to the day, an American captain, Robert Gray, finally calculated the longitude of the Columbia's mouth. This enabled Thomas Jefferson to determine the width of the North American continent. Now all that remained was to find the most practical navigable route for the east-west journey, a voyage equal in distance to the earlier north-south Mississippi explorations.

But which route? The question haunted Jefferson. As soon as he became president of the United States he made it a personal goal to find the answer. Jefferson organized the greatest expedition ever sent into the continent's interior. It would change the course of history.

In 200 B.C. the Greek geographer Eratosthenes calculated Earth's circumference with amazing accuracy. American historian Daniel J. Boorstin, in his outstanding work, *The Discoverers* (1983), noted that Eratosthenes had the genius to figure out a way of doing this. Ptolemy set out to correct his learned predecessor, estimating Earth's circumference to be 17,475 miles (28,000 kilometres), just 7,489 miles (12,000 kilometres) short of the actual figure. Ptolemy extended Asia's coastline further east than it really is, thus reducing the distance between Europe and Asia. Columbus relied on Ptolemy and his disciple, French prelate and scholar Pierre d'Ailly, whose Imago Mundi (1483) suggested reaching the Indies by sailing west. Columbus found land where he expected Asia to be and was able to return to it three times. He had charted a new Atlantic route that led to the Americas. (Côté et al., 1992: 13)

Christopher Columbus believed that Earth's circumference was about 28,000 kilometres (17,360 miles). Leaving Palos in Spain on August 3, 1492, how far west would he have travelled by October 12, after two months at sea? According to his calculations, he was certainly somewhere in the Orient. The islands he visited quite naturally became the West Indies, and their inhabitants Indians. The name stuck. Later the almost miraculous maize plant, the result of five thousand years of genetic manipulation, would be known as Indian corn, and the guinea pig (originating in South America) would be referred to in French as a *cochon d'Inde*, just as the celebrated Thanksgiving turkey would be called a *poule d'Inde*—hence a *dinde* or *dindon*.

Numerous explorers set sail across the Atlantic in the wake of Columbus. Among them was the Italian, Amerigo Vespucci, who journeyed in the southern hemisphere for sixteen months, remarking in his travel accounts that the Great Bear constellation was invisible.

The geographers of Saint-Dié in Lorraine called Vespucci *l'homme sagace*, the astute man who had discovered a fourth part of the Earth—the others being Europe, Africa, and Asia. Early in 1507 the

Amerigo-America

America was given its name by geographers in Saint-Dié, France, inspired by the name Amerigo/Americo Vespucci, but given an ending that corresponded to the Latin names of the continents Europa, Asia, and Africa. The accounts of Vespucci's four voyages were very popular and reached the Saint-Dié geographers before Columbus's reports. When they finally did see the latter, it was too late. "America" had been adopted by a number of other mapmakers, including Mercator, who inscribed it on his great world map published in 1538. The writer Stefan Zweig took an interest in this monumental historical error. When he died he left a manuscript on the subject, translated and published in English as *Amerigo Vespucci: Comedy of Errors in History* (New York: Viking, 1942).

At left: Diagram of Martin Waldseemüller's map, above. See also margin notes on p. 50.

✳ In 1520 the Portuguese explorer Ferdinand Magellan succeeded in rounding Cape Horn at the southern tip of South America — a long and perilous route to the Pacific.

❷ The Americas were called the New World, but this was an error. It may have been new for Europeans, but certainly not for its inhabitants. A truly new world would be born as a result of the growing contact and exchange that began with crossing the Atlantic, but very soon extended to every part of the globe. Africa also received its share of the new foods brought from the Americas, and as a result experienced major population growth. By a strange fate, it was as slaves that Africans were taken to the Americas, source of the food that had increased their numbers and of the medicines that had made raiding slave traders more daring.

♛ Although Europeans had gained a foothold in North America, they soon learned that its riches paled in comparison to those of Central or even South America. This made them more eager than ever to find a route to the Orient.

Saint-Dié mapmakers, working in Latin, prepared the *Cosmographiae Introductio* and gave the name America (as in *Europa* and *Asia*) to the "land" described by Vespucci in the accounts of his "four navigations." An immense map, over three square metres or yards in size, accompanied this publication. Mapmaker Martin Waldseemüller inscribed the name "America" on what appeared as two narrow strips of land, one above the other, running the length of the Atlantic from south to north. They presented an unexpected obstacle on the route to Asia. Could one sail around it or cross it in some way? ✳

For centuries to come the challenge would be to find a passage to the Western Sea. Not that the Americas themselves were without interest. These continents were home to ancient civilizations that had developed over thousands of years, with a total population comparable to that of Europe. Mexico City probably had the largest population of any agglomeration and was consequently one of the best organized of the age. This "old world" of America was to alter the destiny of that other old world of Europe and Asia. From this encounter a truly new world would emerge. ❷

Onward to China

Whatever the riches of the Americas, those of the Orient were not forgotten. Cathay (China), Cipangu (Japan), and the East Indies lured explorers onward, and the search for a passage to Asia became an obsession, especially for Holland, England, and France. ♛ Backed by these countries, which sent out increasing numbers of expeditions, Europeans established a foothold on North America's Atlantic seaboard. Giovanni Verrazzano, working for France, sailed along the coast looking for a promising break in the shoreline, but without success. Like Samuel de Champlain at a later stage, Jacques Cartier was full of hope as he penetrated the continent by sailing up the St. Lawrence River (Allen,

1991: XXI). Henry Hudson, in the service of England, searched for a passage toward the far north and left his name on a famous strait and bay. Halfway down the North American coast he reconnoitred what became the Hudson River as far as the site of Fort Orange (now Albany). Later the Dutch settled along the Hudson River Valley, moving out from Nieuw Amsterdam (New York), their base on Manhattan Island. The English settled along the seaboard from Plymouth to Jamestown, biding their time before ousting the Dutch and later the French. Thirteen British colonies came into being one after another, representing successive migrations. More than a century and a half passed before the settlers in these colonies began a massive move into the hinterland.

After an ill-fated attempt to establish a colony at St. Augustine in Florida, ✳ the French settled hesitantly along the St. Lawrence and in Acadia on the east coast (the region that is now Canada's Maritime Provinces and part of southeast Quebec). The fishing off Newfoundland was miraculous. Basques and Bretons were familiar with the Grand Banks, teeming with cod, and gradually discovered the possibilities of fur trading. It was Champlain who drew the French into the interior.

As Canadian historian Lionel Groulx remarked, things then proceeded by giant steps. The French formed numerous alliances with native peoples, journeyed round the Great Lakes, and reached the Mississippi. Louis Jolliet and Father Jacques Marquette travelled down the great river by canoe as far as the Arkansas River, noting as they went the immense Missouri coming in from the west. Could this be the water route to the Western Sea? Another French explorer, René-Robert Cavelier de La Salle, pinned his hopes on the Mississippi itself.◉

The French surveyed, explored, and mapped North America. As they advanced, they encircled the British colonies. Both France and Britain wanted the

✳The Spanish massacred the French in St. Augustine. Jacques LeMoyne de Morgue was among the very few to escape. His drawings and those of John White inspired the Protestant Theodor de Bry and his family of engravers to publish a large collection of maps entitled *America*, with an accompanying text that castigated the Roman Catholic Spanish colonizers for their cruelty toward the Indians.

◉ Robert Cavelier de La Salle hoped the Mississippi would lead to the Western Sea—so much so that, intentionally or not, he placed its mouth much farther west than it actually was. He influenced many mapmakers of his day. China was his goal. His seigneurie near Montreal was named La Chine as something of a joke, but the name stuck.

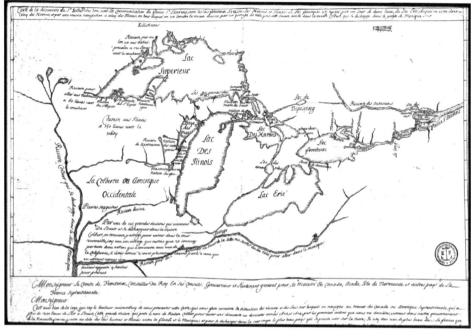

Jolliet's map

*Map of the Discovery of Sieur Jolliet, showing the connection of the Saint Lawrence River with
Lake Frontenac [Ontario], Lake Erie, Lake Huron, and Lake Illinois [Michigan]. Lake Frontenac
is separated from Lake Erie by a drop of half a league, after which one passes into Lake Huron, and
thence into Lake Illinois, at the end of which one enters the Divine [Illinois] River by a portage of a
thousand rods, and this river empties into the Colbert [Mississippi] River,
which empties into the Gulf of Mexico.*

Although undated, the map is accompanied by a long dedication to Governor Frontenac.
Jolliet noted that a great river "runs through the finest land in the world" and he was
anxious to settle in Illinois country. Colbert, the French minister, refused to consider it
(although the explorer had done him the honour to name the future Mississippi River after
him), and Jolliet turned his attention to the Mingan Islands in the St. Lawrence. Jolliet
shows various routes to the Mississippi: through Lake Erie and the Ohio River, as La Salle
had done; out the bottom of Lake Michigan and into the Illinois River; or through the Baie
des Puants (Green Bay) and the Fox and Wisconsin rivers. Jolliet prepared this map from
memory (there are several versions), having lost all his documents when his canoe capsized
as he reached Montreal.

same resources. They challenged each other over fishing, and very soon thereafter over furs and fur trading routes.

Up the Missouri

The Treaty of Utrecht in 1713 left New France shorn of Hudson Bay, Newfoundland, and Acadia, despite the fact that the French and their *Canadien* colonists hadn't lost a significant battle in North America during the War of the Spanish Succession. The British also took it upon themselves to establish a sort of protectorate over the Iroquois.✳ The objective was clearly to create a zone where British Americans could move about freely in Iroquois country, particularly south of the Great Lakes. This gave them access to the Ohio Valley and cut New France in two, isolating Louisiana from Canada.

✳ "[T]he French subjects and other inhabitants of Canada shall disturb or molest in no wise the Five Nations or Indian cantons, which are under the dominion of Great Britain" (Treaty of Utrecht, Article 15).

The Louisiana of those days comprised the entire Mississippi basin, east and west. Canada was basically the St. Lawrence Valley and, according to some, the *Pays d'en Haut*—the territory upriver that we would now describe as the Great Lakes region.

☙ So apt was this description that many people considered the Missouri to be the "real" Mississippi.

From Montreal the *Canadiens* soon worked their way to the far end of the Great Lakes—that is, Lake Superior and Lake Michigan. They then established several routes to the Mississippi. They could go through the far end of the Baie des Puants (today Green Bay) into the Fox and Wisconsin rivers. They could also leave Lake Michigan at its lower end and follow the Illinois River. Then there was the Ohio—*la Belle Rivière* as they called it.

The Mississippi, it transpired, did not lead to the Western Sea. Explorers considered various tributaries as alternative routes. The Missouri seemed the most likely. The Chevalier de Rémonville, a friend of La Salle's "interested in the Compagnie du Mississippi," remarked, "The Mississippi isn't really the Mississippi after the Missouri [joins it]. When the waters of this river mingle with those of the Mississippi, heretofore fine and clear, they become murky and silt-laden" (Margry, 1888: XIII and 179).☙

The Missouri, described as "a considerable river," caught the attention of all explorers and was mentioned in reports to the French court by various administrators of New France. Nicolas de La Salle, apparently no relation to Cavelier de La Salle although he accompanied the latter in 1682, was curious about the Missouri's source. In a letter dated October 16, 1708, he proposed taking an expedition of a hundred men to explore this river that traversed "the finest country in the world." Several others followed suit. Among them was the Jesuit father, Pierre-François-Xavier de Charlevoix, whom the Duc d'Orléans (at that time regent of France), sent in 1719-1720 to "investigate the numerous rumours about the existence and location of a western sea between the New World and the Orient" (Hayne, *DCB*, 3: 104). Father Charlevoix left Paris in June, 1720, and reached the mouth of the Missouri on October 10, 1721. He stayed at Kaskaskia, Cahokia, and Natchez. Regarding the Western Sea, he explained to the French minister, Comte de Morville, in a letter sent from Paris on April 1, 1723, that "he could see only two courses of action to find the western sea," one of which was to go up the Missouri River, "whose source is certainly not far from the sea," as "all the Savages have unanimously assured [us]" (Hayne, *DCB* 3, 106; Margry, 1888: 534).

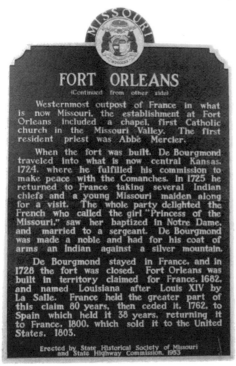

Historical plaque at Fort Orleans erected by the State Historical Society of Missouri and the State Highway Commission in 1953. Described as the "Westernmost outpost of France in what is now Missouri," the exact location of Fort Orleans is uncertain, but many agree that it was probably near Brunswick in Carroll Country, central Missouri. Note the alternate spelling of "de Bourgmond." The spelling "Bourgmont," used in the present work, is current in many references, including Frank Norall's interesting biography of the explorer.

A Famous Precursor

Of all the Frenchmen who travelled the Missouri early in the eighteenth century, the most significant was certainly Étienne Véniard de Bourgmont.

Following a pitiful performance at Fort Détroit in 1706, when he became acting commander of the fort in the absence of Antoine de Lamothe Cadillac and Alphonse de Tonty, de Bourgmont preferred to make himself scarce. He deserted his post with two soldiers (Jolicoeur and Pichon, *dit* Larose). He also took his interpreter,

Isabelle Couc, whose husband of the moment, Pierre Tichenet, had just been killed in battle (Vincens: 199). Did de Bourgmont and Isabelle stay together long? Not surprisingly, we have no written trace of the lovers' flight, but we soon find Isabelle at the side of her brother, Louis Couc Montour, who was doing a brisk business with Albany traders—a covert but frequent practice. Governor Vaudreuil was frustrated by this contraband trading, and Montour became a marked man. The governor's protégé, Chabert de Joncaire, took it upon himself to dispose of Montour. Isabelle Couc became known as Isabelle Montour. And where was de Bourgmont? According to Villiers du Terrage (1925), he had left for less dangerous parts.

✳ Two documents from this expedition have survived. One, regarding navigation, is highly technical; the other is more descriptive and refers to tribes, including the "Aricaras," settled north of the Platte River. Did de Bourgmont actually get this far? Or is this second-hand information? Historians differ on this point.

De Bourgmont surfaced around 1712 at Fort Détroit when it was under attack by the Foxes. The French, helped by local Indians, emerged victorious. De Bourgmont continued on his way, apparently accompanying the Missouris to their territory. In 1713, he travelled through Louisiana and the following year began exploring the Missouri, going upriver at least as far as the Platte, a distance of some 1,000 kilometres (620 miles).✳

In the fall of 1723 de Bourgmont returned to the Missouri under orders to get the Padoucas (Comanches) to make peace. He had Fort d'Orléans built on the Missouri north shore, 74 miles (120 kilometres) from where the river flows into

Illinois country, based on Norall (1988).

the Mississippi. On June 25, 1724, he set out for Comanche country at the head of a small corps consisting of two detachments. De Bourgmont took the land route with one hundred and sixty-four Indians and six whites, while Robert Groston de Saint-Ange, an officer in the colonial regular troops, followed on water with some twenty men. On July 8, the Kansas welcomed him with a gift of two horses. The Kansa chief told him, "We have seen you for years past, you have never wronged us, you have crossed the Great Lake, you promised us you would return and you have kept your word. Thus we love you … and will follow you wherever you wish to go." That very evening de Bourgmont learned that fever had appeared in de Saint-Ange's group. In the days that followed, the expected pirogues failed to materialize. The Indians became anxious, as several of them "had fallen ill with the hot fever." De Bourgmont prepared "medicines" while his men made wine with grapes brought by the Indians. The mood became ominous on July 17. The Kansas refused the merchandise offered in exchange for each horse. It wasn't enough, they said, pointing out that the French had given double the amount the previous year. De Bourgmont was offended and drew back. The Indians were uneasy and tried to mollify him. All ended well, however. The Kansas, "always of good will," with great ceremony presented de Bourgmont with the grand chief's daughter, who was thirteen or fourteen years old, "so that he might marry her." De Bourgmont explained that Frenchmen weren't permitted to have two wives. Would his son take his place, then, the Indians asked? The boy was

---

De Bourgmont Accompanied by Many *Canadiens*

Pierre Margry, the nineteenth-century historian who edited a work of several volumes on the discoveries and settlements of the French in North America between 1614 and 1754, included several documents dealing with de Bourgmont, among them his 1724 account of his travels. While he and a fairly large body of men journeyed on horseback, Monsieur de Saint-Ange following by boat. In de Bourgmont's group were Messrs. Renaudière, Bellerive, D'Estienne Roulot, and one Derbet (probably the drummer), a *Canadien* named Hamelin, an engagé named Gaillard, and de Bourgmont's servant, Simon. (It must be remembered that in those days all permanent residents of New France were called *Canadiens*.)

Monsieur de Saint-Ange was accompanied by Sergeant Dubois, two corporals, eleven privates, five *Canadiens*, and two engagés. They include such names as La Jeunesse, Bonneau, Poupard, Mercier, Quesnel, and Rivet—names that would take root in French colonial Louisiana. Anyone interested in de Bourgmont should read Frank Norall's *Bourgmont, Explorer of the Missouri, 1698-1725* (1988).

Isabelle Montour is the subject of a marvellous work entitled *Madame Montour et son temps* (1979) by Simone Vincens. William A. Hunter also gives an excellent biography of this extraordinary woman under her other name, Elizabeth Couc, in *DCB* 3, 147-148. On the topic of her numerous descendents, see my article in *Le Devoir* of June 5, 1993.

---

only ten years old,✳ but de Bourgmont assured the Indians that he would be very pleased if his son desired the marriage later on, when the boy was older. The chief replied that he was content and would keep the girl for several years so that the boy's decision could be known (Margry, 1888: 398-449).

Good relations were maintained, but unfortunately good health was not. The fever was spreading. By July 31 de Bourgmont himself could no longer stay on his

✳ In 1719, while he was exploring the Lower Missouri, de Bourgmont is reputed to have had a son by a Missouri Indian woman.

Missouri Remembers

Véniard de Bourgmont's childhood remains a mystery for historians, but his last days are now better known. On his return to France he spent two months in Paris, parading a delegation of nine Indian chiefs and an Indian princess around the royal court and the city. The princess received the solemn sacrament of baptism in Notre Dame Cathedral before being married to one of the men of the expedition, Sergeant Dubois. De Bourgmont was subsequently ennobled and then retired to Clerisy Belle-Étoile in Normandy with his French wife, Jacqueline Bouvet des Bordeaux. He died in December 1734 without known descendants. His three European children had died young. It is probable that a child was born of his brief union with Isabelle Couc, but she raised her numerous brood without caring much about the fathers. Then there is a Missouri Indian woman's child, who was most likely entrusted to the Indians at the end of his 1724 expedition (Norall, 1988). The mural by artist Ernest L. Blumenschein, *shown below*, is in the Missouri State Capitol. It represents the return of the Indian princess and her French husband. Missouri remembers.

horse. He decided to return to Fort d'Orléans and sent emissaries to inform the Comanches of the delay. On September 20 he set out once more, and a month later was parleying with the Comanches. He returned to Fort d'Orléans on November 5, 1724, his mission accomplished.

De Bourgmont's two expeditions enabled cartographers to produce more accurate maps of the Mississippi Basin. Around 1716, the groundbreaking cartographer Guillaume Delisle had already prepared a map of the Missouri from its mouth up to the Panis (Platte) River. Two years later the Delisles, father and son, produced their famous map of Louisiana, which owed much to Jolliet, Hennepin, La Salle, Tonty, and de Bourgmont.

The Mallet Brothers

De Bourgmont's exploits had been remarkable. Equally amazing was the expedition led by Pierre and Paul Mallet. They left Fort de Chartres on the Mississippi and travelled up the Missouri, passing through Missouri, Kansa, and

This map by Guillaume Delisle (1718) was the accepted authority for half a century. Among other features, it showed the correct configuration of the Mississippi delta. The "Mission de los Teijas" (Texas), founded in 1716, appears on the map, as well as information gathered by Juchereau de Saint-Denis. Note that the French ascribe to themselves all the land between the Appalachians and the Rockies—a way of consoling themselves for the losses sustained under the terms of the Treaty of Utrecht.

Otoctata country to reach the mouth of the Panimahas River. From there they headed for Ricara (Arikara) country, thinking the Missouri River would carry them toward the southwest. However, the Indians pointed out that this wouldn't take them to the land of the Spanish, "that large nation of small men with very big eyes, an inch to each side of the nose, dressed like Europeans, always booted, with spurs and gold spangles on their boots" (Margry, 1888: 385).

The Mallet brothers and their small group allowed themselves to be persuaded and returned by land, retracing their footsteps almost parallel to the Missouri. On June 2, they came upon a river from the west that they called *la rivière Plate* — "the flat river." ✳

The brothers continued travelling south overland. They passed several rivers and "tongues of land," and at last on June 30 "found marks of the Spanish . . . on some stones." On July 6, they met a Ricara slave among the Laïtaines. He knew the way to the Spaniards, who had baptized him, and agreed to guide the expedition. On July 14 the Mallets came within sight of a Spanish post, a mission called "Piquouris" (Picuries in New Mexico). They continued to the missions of Santa Cruz and Cagnada, then stopped in "a town called Saint-Marie" (Santa Maria). On July 22, 1739, they reached Santa Fe, having covered "265 leagues" from the "river of the Panimahas" (Margry, 1888: 455-462). After various adventures they returned to New Orleans by the Arkansas River, leaving behind them two companions who had married Spanish women and three others who wanted to go north to Illinois country. ☙

✳ According to Margry (1888: V), the Mallet expedition gave the Platte ("flat") River this name because of its width — often "six thousand feet" (1.8 kilometres) — while the river was no more than five or six feet (about two metres) deep. Father de Smet, the Catholic missionary who ministered to the Indians west of the Missouri in the mid-nineteenth century, made a point of mentioning that although the Platte might not be navigable at certain times of year, it was always possible to ride along its hard sandy banks. It was the Platte that accounted for the Oregon Trail.

☙ To get a good idea of the extraordinary scope of the Mallet brothers' expedition, see *The Atlas of North American Exploration: From the Norse Voyages to the Race to the Pole*, by William H. Goetzmann and Glyndwr Williams (1992: 98-99). The Mallet brothers actually started at New Orleans, went up the Mississippi to the Missouri, then up the Missouri to the Pawnee country. The Pawnees suggested that they should cut overland toward the south. The Mallets were accompanied by seven trappers from the Illinois country, including one Moreau, who was later married in Mexico (Margry, 1888: 460). According to other sources, two French Canadians were married in Mexico.

The La Vérendryes in Mandan Country
The Mallet brothers' objective was Spanish territory, the land of silver and wealth. For Pierre Gaultier de la Varennes et de La Vérendrye (1685-1749) and his sons, riches lay in beaver pelts, but they couldn't escape the dream of the Western Ocean. Ever since Columbus, European explorers had kept on searching for a

passage to the Orient. Throughout the seventeenth century, the French travelled North America in every direction, describing their journeys. In Paris, mapmakers took up the torch. Nicolas Sanson d'Abbeville (1600-1667) and his sons, then Claude Delisle (1644-1720), also with his sons, amalgamated this acquired knowledge in graphic form. ✷

✷ Trained as a historian, Nicolas Sanson (1600-1667), rather than copying his contemporaries, undertook a close study of the writings and accounts of the period. His sons, Nicolas, Guillaume, and Adrien, continued in this tradition, as did his grandson, Pierre.

Claude Delisle's son Guillaume (1675-1726) became what was probably the greatest mapmaker of his day. With his three brothers, Simon Claude, Joseph Nicolas, and Louis, he enabled France to triumph over Dutch dominance in cartography. Aware of the importance of the network of rivers leading to the sea, Guillaume carried on the work of his father (1644-1720), focusing on the St. Lawrence, the Great Lakes, and especially the Mississippi drainage basin.

La Vérendrye left Montreal on June 18, 1738, intending to reach Mandan country. By September 22, he had got as far as the Assiniboine Fork, where the Red and Assiniboine rivers meet. He continued on until the Assiniboine Portage and Lac des Prairies (Lake Manitoba), where he built Fort La Reine. On October 18 he left this fort and reached the "Mandanes" on December 3. He returned to Fort La Reine on February 15, 1739, leaving two Frenchmen with the Mandans to learn the language.

The North American continent gradually took shape in people's minds: to the southeast lay the Gulf of Mexico, to the southwest the Gulf of California (*la mer Vermeille* or "the Golden Sea"), to the north Hudson Bay (*la mer Glaciale*). And to the west? Why wouldn't there be a large inlet, some immense bay, some vast gulf opening onto the Pacific? There it was, the Western Sea—the dream of European scholars and politicians, among them Philippe, Duc d'Orléans. The duke had encouraged de Bourgmont to venture forth to explore the Missouri and pacify the Comanches. He also kept the French court interested in finding that famous and elusive Western Sea. The Comte de Maurepas, minister for naval and colonial affairs, followed the regent's lead in this respect. This gave rise to a coolness between French authorities and the La Vérendryes, who, in the opinion of Maurepas, paid more attention to commerce than to exploration. Historians are still divided on this question. Controversy aside, however, we have an extremely impressive list of the innumerable voyages of Pierre de La Vérendrye and his four sons: Jean-Baptiste, Pierre, François, and Louis-Joseph (Chevalier).

In the spring of 1737 Maurepas clearly indicated his impatience in a letter to Governor Beauharnois, stating that La Vérendrye took more interest in the beaver trade than in discovering the Western Sea. What, he wondered, was La Vérendrye waiting for to reach this "Western Sea or Bay" that the Delisles had shown on their manuscript maps since 1696? Wasn't it big enough to be easily spotted and within reach of the western forts or posts established by the La Vérendryes themselves? Beauharnois urged his minister to be patient, especially as he felt that the commercial side of the venture was not insignificant. He made his protégé La Vérendrye agree to reach Mandan country—that land of mystery and promise—by 1738 (Zoltvany, *DCB*, 3: 252). On December 3, 1738, after an exhausting journey, Pierre de La Vérendrye entered the first Mandan village ♛ at the head of a large group that included hundreds of Assiniboins, two of his sons—Chevalier (Louis-Joseph) and François—and some twenty Frenchmen (Margry, 1888: 590). The return journey was to prove even more difficult. According to his own account, he came back very ill and

♛ The Mandans (or Mandanes) were Indians of the Upper Missouri belonging to the Sioux family (as did the Crows, Hidatsas, Omahas, Osages, Kansas, Winnebagos, Poncas, and others). Victims of smallpox, as well as being attacked by Assiniboins and Dakotas, the Mandans began losing a large part of their population after 1750. By the time of the Lewis and Clark Expedition there were about 1,250 Mandans, but their numbers would be virtually wiped out by a new epidemic in 1837, leaving about one hundred survivors.

The Sea or Bay of the West is shown on this map prepared by Philippe Buache, based on the memoirs of Monsieur de l'Isle (circa 1752). Its title translates as *Map of New Discoveries in the North of the Southern Sea, both to the East of Siberia and Kamtchatka and to the West of New France*. (From *Trésors des Archives nationales du Canada*, 1992: 32-33).

On his return voyage, Chevalier de la Vérendrye buried a lead plaque as a reminder that, in the name of the king of France, he had taken possession of this territory on March 30, 1743. He wrote that he had placed a lead plaque on a rise near the fort, on which appeared "the arms in inscriptions of the King" (Margry, 1888: 609). The date is on the reverse side shown here. The plaque was found in 1913 and is today carefully preserved in the Cultural Center of Pierre, the capital of South Dakota.

✳ Louis-Joseph de La Vérendrye remarked that it was among the Horse People that he asked if anyone knew about the nation that lived by the sea. They replied that no one from their nation had ever been there, as the way was barred by the Snake People; also that La Vérendrye and his companions would be able to see some nations that traded with the white people from the sea. He was also told that all the nations of that country had horses, donkeys, and mules (Margry, 1888: 601, 602). Note that the La Vérendryes saw the Rockies south of the forty-ninth parallel. These weren't the Canadian Rockies!

worn out to Fort La Reine. To add injury to insult, he was burdened with debt.

One of his sons, Pierre, made another journey, but it produced nothing because he lacked a guide. In April 1742, La Vérendrye decided to send Chevalier and François to the Mandans once more. They were looking for, and eventually found, "the Horse People" who talked about white men and quoted some remembered words of their language, which Chevalier recognized as Spanish (Margry, 1888: 613). These people guided the Frenchmen to the Bow Indians, who invited them to join a huge expedition of allied tribes planning to fight the dreaded Snake Indians (Champagne, *DCB*, 3, 242).

In early January, 1743, the La Vérendrye brothers, travelling with some 2,000 Indians, came within sight of the mountains. As it turned out, even this large contingent couldn't dispel fear of the Snakes, and the Indians would go no further. The Bow chief guiding the two explorers had to give up. "It's too bad," he told Chevalier, "that I have led you this far and can go no further."

"I was much mortified at not being able to go up the mountains," noted Louis-Joseph in his journal. They had been riding for twelve days toward these mountains "which are for the most part well-wooded, and seem very high."✳ Faced with terrified Indians, the brothers decided to turn back. In fact, a band of about fifteen hostile Indians did attack them shortly afterward. Louis-Joseph decided to "fire off a few gunshots, . . . this weapon being highly respected among all those nations that are unfamiliar with it" (Margry 1888, 605-606).

The journey home was done in stages. By May 18 they were among the "Mantanas." Finally, on July 2, they reached Fort La Reine where they found their father anxiously awaiting them. The La Vérendryes had reached the Missouri by the north from Fort La Reine on the Assiniboine River—a route not to be forgotten. It was probably the trail followed by François-Antoine Larocque, the North West Company agent whom Lewis and Clark met among the Mandans on November 27, 1804.☉

Larocque Meets Lewis and Clark

Since leaving St. Louis, Lewis and Clark had met a considerable number of French Canadians. Most were independent traders like René Jussaume and Toussaint Charbonneau, usually living with Indians. Others worked for a St. Louis company. The meeting with Larocque, accompanied by Charles Mackenzie, Jean-Baptiste Lafrance, and four other voyageurs, probably surprised the Americans somewhat, although they were mostly annoyed by it.

☉ François Larocque noted in his journal for 1805 that, when he arrived at the Mandan village in the fall of 1804, he found a party of forty Americans commanded by two captains, Lewis and Clark, sent by their government to explore the Upper Missouri and the regions of the North West as far as the Pacific. They spent the winter with the Mandans, he added, and left on March 28, 1805, to continue their explorations (Larocque: 87). In fact, the American expedition left on April 7, 1805. Larocque was accompanied by "Charles McKenzie, Baptiste Lafrance, and four voyageurs" (Thwaites, 1: 283; 227, n. 1).

"Seven Traders arrived from the fort on the Ossinoboin from the NW. Company one of which Lafrance took upon himself to speak unfavourably of our intentions," noted Clark tersely on the day of the meeting, clearly irritated (Thwaites, 1: 227). The next day he was concerned about the medals and flags that the "British trader M. Le rock" might distribute among the Indians. He told the "Grand Chief of the Mandans" that "those simbiles were not to be receved by any from them, without they wished [to] incur the displeasure of their Great American Father" (Thwaites, 1: 228). The Americans had nothing to fear, explained Larocque in his own account of the matter. "I had neither flags nor medals" (Thwaites, 1: 229, n. 1).

In the late winter each party moved off in a different direction. "Mr. Larocke leave[s] us to day," Clark noted on February 2, 1805, adding in parentheses, "this man is a Clerk to the NW. Company & verry anxious to accompany us"

✳ Larocque wrote that he suggested accompanying Lewis and Clark, but that for reasons connected with the U.S. government they did not accept his proposal. The Americans embarked in seven pirogues, since the boats in which they had been transported previously had been sent back with a collections of minerals, roots, plants, carcasses and pelts, all things that they felt would interest the educated world (Larocque: 87).

◑ His father, François-Antoine Larocque, was a businessman. In 1792 he was elected to the Legislature of Lower Canada "without having solicited this honour" and died on October 31. He was unable to take his seat in the legislature, as it opened on December 17, 1792 (Vaugeois, 1992: 124). The young orphan studied at the Collège de Montréal and did a term of training in the United States to learn English. He then joined the XY Company before it became part of the North West Company. There he prepared reports in English, and this was to be the language of his interesting travel journal. Larocque was an educated man and a keen observer. He described people and places in detail, and recounted the incidents of his expedition, continually explaining and commenting on all that he saw or experienced.

(Thwaites, 1: 252).✳

While Lewis and Clark continued their journey toward the Pacific, Larocque prepared to explore the Rocky Mountains. On June 2, 1805, he remarked in his journal that his expedition's departure affected everyone, as it seemed likely that he and his men would not return. He left Fort de la Bosse near the Souris River with a heavy heart (Larocque: 12). Just twenty years old at this time, Larocque had been born in Assomption near Montreal on August 19, 1784. ◑

On September 10, after a three-month march, he reached the Yellowstone River, noting its size, its strong current, and the fact that the Indians said it had no falls (Larocque: 47). He explored the surrounding country, and after visiting Crow territory to see if it had any beaver, hired Crows to hunt in accordance with instructions received from "Monsieur Chaboillez" and prepared for the return journey. By October 22, 1805, Larocque was back at the mouth of the Souris River.

Meanwhile Lewis and Clark had almost reached the Columbia River and were fraternizing with the Wallawallas, handing out small gifts and medals. On November 7, 1805, in one of his rare moments of emotion, Clark wrote, "Great joy in camp we are in *view* of the Ocian" (Thwaites, 3: 210). He had just glimpsed the splendid estuary of the Columbia. In 1792 Captain Gray had given Jefferson its position: longitude 124° west, latitude 46° north *(see note next page)* 🌿. At that latitude, North America was about 3,000 miles (5,000 kilometres) wide. The challenge was to find a water route to cover this distance. Had Lewis and Clark at last fulfilled the dream that had captured the imaginations of Europeans for three centuries and inspired Thomas Jefferson?

※ On May 11, 1792, Captain Robert Gray entered the estuary of the Columbia River (named after his ship) and was able to calculate the latitude and longitude of his position (or possibly learned it from George Vancouver). In any case, both men exchanged the information that confirmed James Cook's calculations made on his voyage of 1780.

Longitude (Meridian) and Latitude (Parallel)

Strange to say, the ideas of longitude and latitude are poorly understood in our day. In the early era of North American exploration, from the time of Champlain to William Clark, all the great explorers knew how to use highly complex instruments that allowed them to establish their position.

Latitude is calculated in degrees moving north or south from the equator. Thus "49° latitude north" means 49° from the equator, which, by convention, is set at zero. The north (or south) pole is at 90°.

To calculate longitude, it was first necessary to choose an agreed point zero. Many were suggested. Greenwich in England was finally chosen. Thus "124° west" means that Astoria, for example, was 124° west of Greenwich.

Until the invention of a variety of chronometer by John Harrison, it had been extremely difficult to calculate longitude. To do it fairly easily (all is relative), you needed to know what time it was in Greenwich at the moment when you took the reading of your position. Harrison, originally a simple carpenter, developed an instrument that could keep exact Greenwich time despite the ship's movement, and would not be affected by cold, heat, or humidity. In 1772-1773 King George III ordered the use of the Harrison chronometer to be officially adopted (Sobel: 146-150).

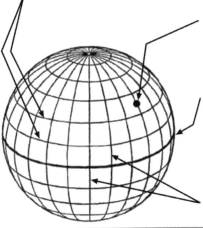

Latitude is a line parallel to the equator. The distance between two parallels equals the degree of distance from the equator.

Greenwich, England, site of the Royal Naval College, has been the point of reference for calculating longitude since 1884.

The equator is the point of reference for calculating latitude.

These vertical lines encircling the globe are called meridians. Each meridian coincides with a longitude.

Thomas Jefferson

Chapter 2

A Jeffersonian Obsession

There is no question that Thomas Jefferson was a visionary. Being a visionary, however, doesn't necessarily mean seeing things clearly. Jefferson had dreamed of independence for his country, but this independence was not so much an objective as a means, a set of tools.

Independence would serve to initiate a move westward. Indians lay along this route. They would either have to integrate with white society or agree to be relocated. If Indians posed a problem in Jefferson's view, what can we say about blacks? This brings up the most astonishing paradox of all in this man who regarded blacks with contempt but loved a mulatto.

A man of contradictions, a man with an obsession, Jefferson intended to act before others could realize his dream.

Nothing was run of the mill with Thomas Jefferson. The best example of this is probably his election to the United States presidency in February 1801.

Jefferson had been narrowly defeated in the preceding election by John Adams, whose vice-president he became in accordance with the Constitution as then framed. On February 11, 1801, Jefferson had an eight-vote lead over the president, but was running neck-and-neck with another Republican, Aaron Burr. The electoral college had reached an impasse. The House of Representatives, where the opposing Federalists were in the majority, had to decide the question. Exactly thirty-six successive ballots were needed to give Jefferson the minimum majority of votes needed to become president.

Jefferson was man of paradoxes. His ambiguous and contradictory nature was

✳ In a letter to Thomas Jefferson dated January 8, 1802, Dr. Caspar Wistar, a member of the American Philosophical Society, reported that the explorer Alexander Mackenzie was "at New York, on his way to the North West Country, & that he has provided himself with the vaccine virus for the benefit of the unfortunate natives" (Jackson, 1993: 121). Inoculation against smallpox had existed for years, and had taken an important step forward with the work of Edward Jenner.

Jefferson was a fascinating person. To get a comprehensive view of his ideas about the settlement and expansion of the United States, one of the best works to read is probably Donald Jackson's *Thomas Jefferson & the Stony Mountains: Exploring the West from Monticello* (1993). Jackson, in my opinion, gets to the heart of the matter on all the important questions. His aim is to get at the truth, based on solid documentation, rather than take an adulatory stance toward his subject. On the approaching fate of the Indians, see Anthony F.C. Wallace, *Jefferson and the Indians: the Tragic Fate of the First Americans* (1999).

The United States in 1801

Thomas Jefferson was sworn in as third president of the United States on March 4, 1801. At the time the country had a population of 5,308,483, of which twenty percent were black slaves. Officially the U.S. extended from the Atlantic coast to the Mississippi, and from the Great Lakes to the Gulf of Mexico—a territory of about 1,000 miles east to west, and 1,000 miles north to south. Only a small part of this area was inhabited by whites, with two-thirds of the population living at least fifty miles from the Atlantic. There were only four passable routes over the Appalachians, one from Philadelphia to Pittsburgh, another from the Potomac to the Monongahela, a third crossing the southern part of Virginia to Knoxville in Tennessee, and the fourth leading to Kentucky via the Cumberland Gap.

reflected not only in his words, but in his life. He had opinions on almost everything under the sun and took a genuine interest in many matters, from prehistoric animals to the fate of the American Indians. He believed they were the equals of other men, yet wanted them to vanish from the scene—in other words, to be assimilated. He was especially conscious of the dangers of smallpox epidemics and a strong advocate for making vaccination available to the native population (Jackson, 1993: 124). ✳ He firmly believed in the virtues of farming as a means of forming upright citizens (Ronda, 2000: 29). He also understood that by accepting this new way of life the Indians would no longer need their immense territories and that these could therefore be put to use by whites.

Jefferson also felt that the proximity of Indians and whites would produce a Métis population that would gradually lead to assimilation and eventually bring an end to fighting and confrontation between whites and Indians. If it didn't, the Indians would have to be displaced to distant areas. Jefferson's dream was to see them resettled west of the Mississippi.

Jefferson's ideas about Indians in no way applied to the black population. He himself owned slaves, in flagrant contradiction to the official policies of the young republic (Lewis and Onuf, 1999: 20-21). His paternalistic behaviour toward his own slaves didn't constitute an excuse for this anomaly. Jefferson's theories on the subject of blacks were clear—or at least clearly expressed. In his writings he repeatedly mentioned his aversion to "negroes" and stated in no uncertain terms his views on the low intellectual capacities of Africans and African-Americans (Gordon-Reed, 1997: 134-140). He even went so far as to wish they could simply go back to Africa.

Although Jefferson believed that mixing white and Indian blood was a good thing, he strongly disapproved of similar mixing with blacks (Lewis and Onuf, 1999: 22). And yet Jefferson had a black woman as his intimate companion for thirty-eight years, from about 1788 until his death in 1826. They seem to have had seven children, the first conceived in Paris around 1788 and the last at Monticello when Jefferson was sixty-five.

♕ American novelist Barbara Chase-Riboud wrote her version of Sally Hemings' story in the award-winning *Sally Hemings*, the hypotheses of which were hotly debated at the time. However, conclusive DNA tests have since proved that Jefferson and Sally Hemings have both black and white descendants. *Time* magazine featured an article by Tamala M. Edwards on the subject, "Family Reunion" (November 23, 1998).

The question is not a trivial one; it touches on the most profound aspects of American history. Many specialists have taken an interest in it. Jane Ellen Lewis and Peter S. Onuf edited a collection of writings by a dozen prestigious authors in *Sally Hemings & Thomas Jefferson: History, Memory, and Civic Culture* (1999). All the articles in this book are fascinating, particularly those by Gordon S. Wood (19-74), Winthrop D. Jordan (35-51), Philip D. Morgan (52-84), Rhys Isaac (114-126), and of course Jan Ellen Lewis's "The White Jeffersons" (127-160). On the same subject, Annette Gordon Reed, a Harvard graduate and law professor at the New York Law School has written a scholarly study entitled *Thomas Jefferson and Sally Hemings: an American Controversy* (1997).

Barbara Chase-Riboud, sculptor, poet, and historical novelist.

This story is typical of Jefferson, a man as complex as he was surprising. In 1772 he married a thirty-three-year-old widow, Martha Skelton, who died on September 6, 1782. She had bitter memories of her two stepmothers. Apparently, on her deathbed she asked her husband to give up any idea of remarrying. Her father, John Wayles, not only had three wives, but also a mistress, Betty Hemings, by whom he had six children. One of them was Sally Hemings, who became Jefferson's mistress. The least one can say is that these two Virginians were enduring in their liaisons!

Martha Skelton was a good match; historians readily state that it was as much a love match as a marriage of expediency. What, then, are we to make of his relationship with Sally Hemings? *(See note on previous page.)* 🌱

First and foremost, it must be pointed out that the young Sally who arrived in Paris in 1787, where Thomas Jefferson was the new American minister plenipotentiary, was very pretty. Her skin was light-coloured, evidence of her heredity. Sally's mother Betty was a mulatto, born of the union between an English sailor and an African woman. Sally's father was also the father of Jefferson's wife Martha, and quite possibly there was a family resemblance. However that may be, Jefferson despised blacks,✳ although he most certainly loved Sally, a slave whom he didn't see as being really black.

In Jefferson's mind, the presence of blacks in America was an accident of history, whereas the exotic Indians belonged to the natural order of things. Whatever his racial prejudices, however, Jefferson needed space—lots of space—to implement his views. The façade of his residence at Monticello looked westward—and so did his dreams.☙

When Jefferson began building his great manor house at the time of his marriage, "the West" meant the Ohio Valley. Gradually, through his reading and passion for geography, especially North American geography, he began to look beyond the Mississippi and toward the Pacific Ocean.

✳ In his "Notes of the State of Virginia," Jefferson states that blacks, by their very nature, were incapable of rivalling whites. In his eyes they were intrinsically inferior. (Dorigny, 2001: 55)

❧ "By education and temperament Thomas Jefferson faced east. His chosen roads … led him to places like Philadelphia, Paris, and London. … For Jefferson and other Virginians of his generation there was not one West but many Wests—each representing challenge and opportunity, adventure and advancement." (Ronda, 2000: 19)

Three Successive Projects: Clark, Ledyard, Michaux

Jefferson's mind was always in a state of effervescence, but it was even more active when stimulated. In the fall of 1783 he heard a rumour to the effect that British capitalists had subscribed a large sum of money to finance exploration of the region between the Mississippi and California. "They pretend it is only to promote knolege," railed Jefferson in a letter of December 4, 1783, to George Rogers Clark, a good friend and frontier hero. "I am afraid they have thoughts of colonising into that quarter." Jefferson himself was thinking seriously about organizing an expedition. "How would you like to lead such a party?" he asked his illustrious correspondent. Somewhat bitterly, Clark refused to envisage such a possibility. He had already done more than his share of "sacrifice to the Publick Interest" (Jackson, 1993: 43).✱

✱ George Rogers Clark had already given much, in the full sense of the word. He was never to see the day when Virginia would agree to recompense him for the expenses he had incurred on behalf of the nation and the losses that he had sustained (Jackson, 1993: 43 and 62; also Ambrose, 1996: 68, and Ronda, 2000: 21-22).

Jefferson tried to organize an expedition toward the Pacific more than once. He finally succeeded, thanks to William Clark, George Rogers Clark's younger brother, who was recruited by his friend Meriwether Lewis. A coincidence? More or less. It was a small society in which everyone knew each other, and where a man's experience and competence were generally public knowledge. Jefferson had first asked George Rogers Clark to head an expedition, but the latter had replied that he had already made his share of "sacrifice to the Publick Interest" (Jackson, 1993: 23).

In May 1784, a few weeks after receiving Clark's answer, Jefferson was named United States minister to France, succeeding Benjamin Franklin. If the splendours of Paris, the delights of France, and the charms of French women caused him to forget his American dreams somewhat, the accounts of James Cook, the brilliant British navigator, would have revived his interest. Three volumes of Cook's writings appeared in 1784, containing many maps of North America's west coast. The French responded to the challenge with expeditions led by Jean-François de Lapérouse. Still motivated by the search for the famous Northwest Passage, Louis XVI asked Lapérouse to go beyond the regions explored by Cook, "to see whether there be not some river or some narrow gulph, forming a communication, by means of the interior lakes, with some parts of Hudson's bay" (Jackson, 1993: 48).

Jefferson was so preoccupied and excited by this question that he let himself be convinced by a scheme proposed by John Ledyard, a young American adventurer who had been a member of Cook's crew between 1776 and 1780. Ledyard planned to cross North America from west to east, more or less following what we now know as the route of the Paleo-Amerindians. He left St. Petersburg in 1787, crossed

At the mouth of the Columbia

Captain Robert Gray was from Boston. He was the first navigator to cross the bar of the Columbia with his ship, the *Columbia*. About five months later, George Vancouver also reached the mouth of this impressive river. He thought it wise to use a smaller ship, the brig *Chatham*, to venture upriver, rather than his ship, the *Discovery*. It was therefore Lt. William R. Broughton commanding the *Chatham* who went up the Columbia for nearly a hundred miles (about 150 kilometres), until he reached the Cascades, a series of rapids that prevented further navigation.

the Ural Mountains, and started across Siberia by carriage, horseback, and boat. Ledyard clearly had plenty of pluck! He seemed to be at ease wherever he was—even a little provoking. On February 24, 1787, he was arrested at Irkutsk on the orders of Empress Catherine the Great, possibly because he appeared interested in the Russians' Alaskan colony and its fur trade (Appleman, 1975: 19).

Did Jefferson seriously believe in Ledyard's project? Probably just enough to give him concrete— that is, financial—backing on several occasions.

Information transmitted by Captain Robert Gray, a Boston trader, stimulated Jefferson's interest anew. In 1792 Gray had recognized the mouth of a great river already noted by the Spaniard, Bruno de Heceta, in 1775. The daring American captain crossed the bar of the river to explore the estuary for a short distance. Five months later, a party of British sailors under Lieutenant William R. Broughton (second in command of Captain George Vancouver's expedition) went 100 miles (about 150 kilometres) up the river. Gray had named the river after his ship, the *Columbia Rediviva*

(Appleman, 1975: 355). His most important act, however, was to establish a fairly accurate reading of the longitude and latitude of the river's mouth: 124° west by 46° north.

This information had been public knowledge since Cook's voyages, but it was confirmed by both Robert Gray and George Vancouver. Jefferson could now calculate the distance between Washington (77° west by 39° north) and the mouth of the Columbia, a distance of about 3100 miles (5,000 kilometres). He was among those who believed that the sources of the Columbia and the Missouri must be almost at the same latitude.

While Vancouver's men were exploring the Columbia, Jefferson, with the backing of the American Philosophical Society of Philadelphia, proposed that the French botanist André Michaux search for "the shortest & most convenient route of

Article 7 of the Treaty of Paris (1763)

"VII. In order to re-establish peace on solid and durable foundations, and to remove for ever all subject of dispute with regard to the limits of the British and French territories on the continent of America; it is agreed, that, for the future, the confines between the dominions of his Britannick Majesty and those of his Most Christian Majesty, in that part of the world, shall be fixed irrevocably by a line drawn along the middle of the River Mississippi, from its source to the river Iberville, and from thence, by a line drawn along the middle of this river, and the lakes Maurepas and Pontchartrain to the sea; and for this purpose, the Most Christian King cedes in full right, and guaranties to his Britannick Majesty the river and port of the Mobile, and every thing which he possesses, or ought to possess, on the left side of the river Mississippi, except the town of New Orleans and the island in which it is situated, which shall remain to France, provided that the navigation of the river Mississippi shall be equally free, as well to the subjects of Great Britain as to those of France, in its whole breadth and length, from its source to the sea, and expressly that part which is between the said island of New Orleans and the right bank of that river, as well as the passage both in and out of its mouth. It is farther stipulated, that the vessels belonging to the subjects of either nation shall not be stopped, visited, or subjected to the payment of any duty whatsoever. The stipulations inserted in the IVth article, in favour of the inhabitants of Canada shall also take place with regard to the inhabitants of the countries ceded by this article." ☛ *(see note on next page)*

This article is fairly ambiguous. It has been passed over by historians, although it deserved close analysis. In it "His Most Christian Majesty," in other words France, cedes to "His Britannick Majesty": "every thing which he possesses, or ought to possess, on the left (i.e., east) side of the river Mississippi, except the town of New Orleans and the island in which it is situated, which shall remain to France." New Orleans lies at a spot where the Mississippi divides in two. Article 7 clearly says that the demarcation in question is "a line drawn along the middle of the River Mississippi, from its source to the river Iberville, *and from thence, by a line drawn along the middle of this river,* [the Iberville] and the lakes Maurepas and Pontchartrain to the sea" (italics mine).

The essence of this article is in the recognition that there shall be free navigation on the Mississippi for the subjects of both Great Britain and France. After 1783, however, when U.S. independence was recognized, Americans were no long subjects of the British crown.

communication between the U.S. and the Pacific ocean" (Jackson, 1993: 76). Alas, this mission in which Jefferson believed so strongly got bogged down in political intrigue and was cancelled. Jefferson resigned himself to its failure, hoping that the British or French would not dislodge the comparatively quiescent Spanish who occupied the territory west of the Mississippi.✳

✳ The territorial boundaries of the United States did not extend west of the Mississippi at that time.

ⓒ Note that Article 7 of the Treaty of Paris makes no mention of His Catholic Majesty, the king of Spain, to whom His Most Christian Majesty, the king of France, had ceded the western shore of the Mississippi but a few months earlier. This article also implies that the city of New Orleans is on an island. In fact, New Orleans was built on the east side of the Mississippi, but on a huge strip of land surrounded by water. To the west of this strip was the Mississippi; to the east, the Iberville River that flowed into lakes Maurepas and Pontchartrain, then into the sea. River traffic to the Gulf of Mexico passed along the Mississippi, not the Iberville.

In lieu of quickly finding a river route to the Pacific, the Americans had to make sure that, at the very least, traffic could circulate freely on the Mississippi. It had been provided for in the Treaty of Paris (Article 7) in 1763, but was challenged in 1784 by the Spanish, to whom the drainage basin west of the Mississippi "belonged," as did the small town of New Orleans on the eastern side of the river. The Spanish played a cat-and-mouse game with the Americans for about a decade. Finally, with the Treaty of San Lorenzo in 1795, they agreed to give the United States the right to navigate on the Mississippi free of charge, a privilege subject to periodic renewal.

Jefferson was somewhat reassured, but—with good reason—he doubted whether Spain was strong enough to resist French ambitions. He could only hope that the Spanish would maintain their position until the United States was ready to dismantle their possessions for its own benefit.

In March 1797 the alarm was sounded in the mildest manner. Jefferson was present during a meeting of the American Philosophical Society, when the members had a chance to examine a sea-otter pelt brought from the Pacific by a young and enterprising fur trader, Alexander Mackenzie (Jackson, 1993: 95).

Jefferson already knew a fair amount about the Pacific coast. His wide reading included *Voyage to the Pacific Ocean. . . . Performed under the direction of Captains Cook, Clerke and Gore, in the years 1776, 1777, 1778, 1779, and 1780*, published in London in 1784. He had also read Captain Gray's most recent reports. This knowledge was rounded out by George Vancouver's authoritative *Voyage of Discovery to the North Pacific Ocean* (three volumes and an atlas), published in London in 1798.

Mackenzie's Exploit

The Scotsman Alexander Mackenzie, working out of Montreal for the North West Company, had accomplished an exploit of quite another order. He had crossed the entire width of the immense continent of North America.✳

The Scotch were omnipresent in the fur trade where they did extraordinarily well. They often spoke French and willingly joined forces with French Canadians for whom the long and perilous expeditions held no secrets. Both groups got along well with the Indians—male and female. This was the secret of their prowess and their success.

Alexander Mackenzie was a fairly educated, well-built man of unflinching determination who became a famous voyager. In 1789 he left Fort Chipewyan on the southern shore of Lake Athabasca and travelled along the Slave River. He then entered the magnificent river that bears his name and began floating downstream, filled with optimism about reaching the Pacific. Alas, five days later, on July 2, high mountains rose up on the horizon and the river forked unmistakably northward. Undaunted, Mackenzie went the whole way. The mountains marched steadily to the west of his route, while before him lay the delta of a

✳ See the excellent biographical article on Alexander Mackenzie by W. Kaye Lamb in *DCB*, 5: 537-543.

great river where he could see the ebb and flow of the tide. The Arctic Ocean awaited him. He calculated his latitude: 67° 45' north. In less than two months he was back at Fort Chipewyan—disappointed but not defeated. The discovery of a route to the Pacific would be for next time!

Aware of the difficulties of calculating his position, Mackenzie visited London (1791-1792) to perfect his training and to buy better instruments. In the fall of 1792 he set off for the Pacific, again from Fort Chipewyan, with, among others, Joseph Landry and Charles Ducette, two French Canadians who had been with him on his journey of 1789.

After wintering on the Peace River, he set off again in May 1793, travelling on the Parsnip River running southward, then navigating through a maze of lakes and rivers. He reached the Fraser, believing or hoping it was the Columbia. At this point the Indians advised him to continue by land. Mackenzie resigned himself to following well-travelled trails that would take him over what became the Mackenzie Pass at 6,500 feet (2,000 metres) to reach the Bella Coola Gorge, where the Indians would carry him downriver by canoe. *(See note on next page.)* ♛

On July 19, two weeks after leaving the Fraser, Mackenzie glimpsed "the termination of the river, and its discharge into a narrow arm of the sea" (Mackenzie: 430). Two days

⚘ "We proceeded at a very great rate. ... I had imagined that the Canadians who accompanied me were the most expert canoemen in the world, but they are very inferior to these people [the Indians], as they themselves acknowledged, in conducting those vessels" (Mackenzie: 417).

✳ In 1795 British mapmaker Aaron Arrowsmith published his famous *Map Exhibiting all the New Discoveries in the Interior Parts of North America*. He updated it a number of times. See Goetzmann and Williams, 1992: 116.

later he and his crew slept on a large rock in the Dean Channel, where Mackenzie left a record of their exploit inscribed on the rock face (Mackenzie: 438). Six weeks earlier, on June 5, George Vancouver had been there: Vancouver by sea, Mackenzie by land.

Jefferson had been president of the United States for about a year when he at last got hold of Mackenzie's *Voyages from Montreal on the River St. Lawrence through the Continent of North America to the Frozen and Pacific Oceans in the Years 1789 and 1793*. In the summer of 1802 the president was also gazing intently at Aaron Arrowsmith's latest map of the United States,✳ enhanced by new observations from British travellers, including Alexander Mackenzie. The latter was not only a trader and explorer, but a businessman and a visionary.

"The following general, but short, geographical view of the country may not be improper to close this work," wrote Mackenzie at the end of his book (Mackenzie: 482).

His brief geographical roundup is in itself intriguing. "By supposing a line from the Atlantic, East, to the Pacific, West, in the parallel of forty-five degrees of North latitude, it will, I think, nearly describe the British territories in North America." Mackenzie knew as well as Jefferson that the Columbia's mouth lay "in latitude 46. 20" (Mackenzie: 493) and had no qualms about putting forward hypotheses for establishing the British "to the South of the Columbia" (Mackenzie 484). He had also realized that the Columbia's source lay to the north and that the extension of the "snow-clad mountains. . . . so far South on the sea coast... prevents the Columbia from finding a more direct course" (Mackenzie: 486). As a result of this observation and a number of others more complex in nature, he concluded that "the Columbia is the line of communication from the Pacific Ocean, pointed out by nature, as it is the only navigable river in the whole extent of Vancouver's minute survey of that coast; . . . and consequently, the most Northern situation fit for colonization and suitable to the residence of a civilized people" (Mackenzie: 493).

The possibilities were there. The Pacific was the gateway to China—an enormous market. In Mackenzie's view, the time had come for three great enterprises—the North West, Hudson's Bay, and East India companies—to combine their efforts. To this complete control of the fur trade "may be added the fishing in both seas, and the markets of the four quarters of the globe. Such would be the field for commercial enterprise, and incalculable would be the produce of it, when supported by the operations of that credit and capital which Great Britain so pre-eminently possesses" (Mackenzie: 493).

Lewis—Jefferson's Choice

Mackenzie's *Voyages from Montreal* "was the spark," writes James Ronda, "but the fuel had been gathering for more than two decades" (Ronda, 2000: 27).

On February 23, 1801, less than a week after becoming president, Jefferson wrote to Meriwether Lewis, the young soldier who had already volunteered to lead an expedition to the West. He stated that he needed "a private secretary," and that "your knolege of the Western country, of the army and of all its interests & relations has rendered it desirable ... that you should be engaged in that office" (Jackson, 1978, 1: 2).

In recruiting Lewis, was Jefferson thinking of putting him in charge of the famous expedition of 1804-1806? Historian Donald Jackson objects to the importance and the meaning generally attributed to the expression "your knolege of the country in the West." For him "the West" refers to the Ohio Valley, which in fact Lewis knew well. It is Jefferson's allusion to the army that deserves attention. The president had made an election promise to reduce military expenses, and he would need an assistant to help do this. *(See note on next page.)* ✳

Alexander Mackenzie hadn't in fact found a truly practicable route to the Pacific, but he had at least

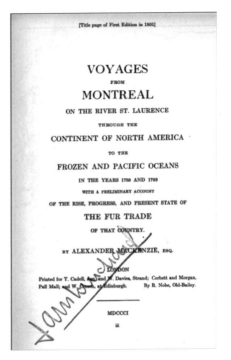

[Title page of First Edition in 1801]

VOYAGES
FROM
MONTREAL
ON THE RIVER ST. LAURENCE
THROUGH THE
CONTINENT OF NORTH AMERICA
TO THE
FROZEN AND PACIFIC OCEANS
IN THE YEARS 1789 AND 1793
WITH A PRELIMINARY ACCOUNT
OF THE RISE, PROGRESS, AND PRESENT STATE OF
THE FUR TRADE
OF THAT COUNTRY.

BY ALEXANDER MACKENZIE, ESQ.

LONDON
Printed for T. Cadell, Jun. and W. Davies, Strand; Corbett and Morgan, Pall Mall; and W. Creech, at Edinburgh.   By R. Nobe, Old-Bailey.

MDCCCI
iii

Alexander Mackenzie's account of his explorations, *Voyages from Montreal*, was finally published in London in 1801. New editions began appearing the next year in London, New York, and Philadelphia, and French and German translations were published in that same year.

I used a 1927 edition of *Voyages from Montreal* published in the series *Master Works of Canadian Authors*. This edition, with a long introduction by Charles W. Colby, is illustrated with photographs, engravings, and a map. The title page of the first edition is reproduced above. Note the stamped signature of Paul Bouchard at the bottom.

Meriwether Lewis was born in Virginia in 1774. At the age of twenty he joined the army, where he made his career. When Jefferson was elected president in 1801, he recruited Lewis as his private secretary. Was it the president's intention to entrust an expedition to the West to Lewis at this point? Historians differ on this question. One thing is certain: Lewis had already shown interest in such an enterprise. Jefferson prepared Lewis for his task in a number of ways, one of which was to have him complete his training with scientists at the University of Pennsylvania. It was Lewis's idea to ask his friend William Clark, whom he had known since 1795-1796, to share the leadership. When the expedition returned, Jefferson appointed Lewis governor of the Louisiana Territory. To all appearances, the demands of this post and personal problems led Lewis to commit suicide (1809).

✳ Like any good politician, Jefferson had made a few electoral promises, including that of cutting the size of the army in half (and profiting discreetly from the occasion to eliminate some Federalist elements). Jefferson knew very little about the army, however. One of Lewis's first tasks was to examine the lists of officers. Here Jackson is no doubt right in all respects (Jackson, 1993: 117-121). Ambrose agrees with Jackson in his incomparable work, *Undaunted Courage*, (59-62), certainly the best book for anyone wishing to "discover" Lewis and Clark.

accomplished a genuine exploit and paved the way for new attempts. Jefferson felt there was no time to lose.

The Americans needed permission from the Spanish to travel west of the Mississippi. Jefferson requested this from the Spanish ambassador to the United States, Carlos Martìnez, Marqués de Casa Yrujo, who wrote to Spain's minister of foreign affairs that Jefferson was "a lover of glory" and that he might attempt to "perpetuate the fame of his administration not ony [sic] by the measures of frugality and economy ... but also by discovering or attempting at least to discover the way by which the

Americans may some day extend their population and their influence up to the coasts of the South Sea" (Jackson, 1978, 1: 5). Yrujo had perfectly understood the new president's intentions.

In December 1802, Jefferson introduced the matter to Congress cautiously. Then, in January 1803, he put it in a secret message to the House. Finally, on February 25, Congress approved an appropriation of $2,500 "for the purpose of extending the external commerce of the U.S."—in other words, to explore the land west of the Mississippi.

Chapter 3

Instructions and Vision

As soon as Jefferson was elected he chose Meriwether Lewis as his private secretary. He would make him a hero. When the day came, Jefferson would send Lewis his instructions. Detailed and precise though they were, these instructions revealed how vague and even surprisingly naïve was Jefferson's knowledge of the West.

The president warned Lewis that he would probably encounter mammoths and perhaps the Lost Tribe of Israel. If Lewis met any whites, he should urge them to return to the east.

Jefferson considered the possibility of sending blacks back to Africa, for were they not an accident of American history? It was very different for the Indians. Those who balked at his policies would see their territory exchanged for land west of the Mississippi. In Jefferson's mind, this region was destined to become an immense Indian reserve. A model was created in 1804. An unforeseen and unforeseeable move by Napoleon provided a rare opportunity.

Jefferson's instructions to Lewis form a keystone of American history. There is nothing improvised about them. Jefferson had already set forth his ideas on April 30, 1793, when instructing the botanist André Michaux for a similar but aborted expedition. One of "the chief objects of your journey," wrote Jefferson, was "to find the shortest & most convenient route of communication between the U.S. & the Pacific ocean" (Jackson, 1993: 76). Ten years later, on June 20, 1803, Jefferson asked Lewis to seek out the route "that may offer the most direct & practicable water communication across

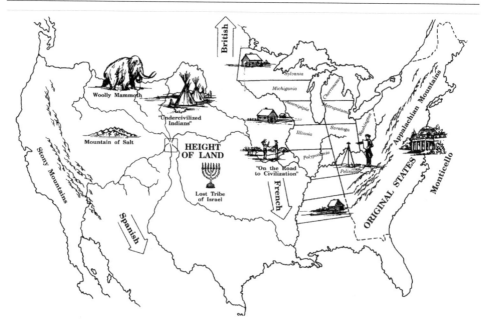

The map above shows the outline of today's mainland United States. Inserted in the interior are phenomena Jefferson and his contemporaries believed would be discovered there. Most important was the idea that a single mountain range existed on the Pacific side very similar to the Appalachians in the east in height and distance from the sea.

Not only did people believe in this symmetrical view of the continent's geography, they believed that there was a height of land somewhere to the north of present-day Wyoming from which flowed the great rivers of the west.

Jefferson had garnered from his reading the idea that a huge mountain of salt probably existed somewhere in the West, and wondered about the possibility of finding one of the Lost Tribes of Israel there. He did not believe in species becoming extinct, and supposed that the last of the prehistoric animals might be found. As to Indians who had never met the white man, they were necessarily "undercivilized." East of the Mississippi everything was ready for setting up new American states.

Clay Straus Jenkinson is well known in the United States for his speaking tours on Thomas Jefferson and Meriwether Lewis, subjects he approaches in a critical and occasionally mocking spirit. In 1991 the North Dakota Humanities Council published one of his articles entitled "The West of Jefferson's Imagination," accompanied by the map on this page that illustrates his subject (Woksape: 16-17).

What explains these notions about the Lost Tribe of Israel, the woolly mammoth, and the "undercivilized Indians"? We are looking at ideas current shortly before 1803, since there are still French in the southern Mississippi River area. The United States began its existence on the Atlantic seaboard. By 1800 French Canadians had been travelling south of the Great Lakes and down the length of the Mississippi for many years, whereas the Americans still had only a vague knowledge of these regions. Even Jefferson, although an extremely well–informed man, nonetheless had surprising ideas about the West.

this continent" (Jackson, 1978, 1: 61). On the following November 16, after the Louisiana Purchase had been ratified, Jefferson repeated this goal: "The object of your mission is single, the direct water communication from sea to sea formed by the bed of the Missouri & perhaps the Oregon [Columbia]" (Jackson, 1978, 1: 137).

It wasn't entirely this objective that made the president's project so original—after all, Europeans had been mesmerized by it for three centuries—but rather the accompanying instructions.

In writing to Michaux, Jefferson had insisted on the need for getting precise results and proof of the various stages covered. The American Philosophical Society had undertaken engagements with the expedition's subscribers and intended to honour them. In the case of failure, Michaux would have to repay what had been given him. He was strongly advised to be prudent in all circumstances and not to take any needless risk that might threaten his life, thereby depriving science of new knowledge and the inhabitants of the United States of "new fields & subjects of Commerce, Intercourse, & Observation" (Jackson, 1993: 77).

Jefferson had high expectations for the geographical side of the venture. "It would seem by the latest maps as if a river called Oregan interlocked with the Missouri for a considerable distance, & entered the Pacific ocean, not far Southward of Nootka Sound" (Jackson, 1993: 76). Jefferson liked to display his vast knowledge, but at the same time knew its limitations. His many warnings to Michaux included advice that "these maps are not to be trusted so far as to be the ground of any positive instruction to you" (Jackson 1993: 76).

Jefferson was keenly interested in palaeontology and much influenced by recent discoveries. He warned Michaux that he might encounter the mammoth or "the Lama, or paca of Peru" (Appleman, 2000: 21). About the Indians he knew practically nothing and merely

In a long letter of June 20, 1803, Jefferson outlined his instructions to Lewis, in part as follows (Jackson, 1978, 1: 61-66): "The object of your mission is to explore the Missouri river, & such principal stream of it, as, by it's course and communication with the waters of the Pacific ocean . . . may offer the most direct & practicable water communication across this continent for the purposes of commerce. Beginning at the mouth of the Missouri, you will take observations of latitude & longitude, at all remarkeable points on the river, & especially at the mouths of rivers. . . . Your observations are to be taken with great pains & accuracy, to be entered distinctly & intelligibly for others as well as yourself. . . . Several copies of these . . . should be made. . . . The commerce which may be carried on with the people inhabiting the line you will pursue, renders a knolege of those people important including their relations with other tribes . . . and articles of commerce they may need or furnish as well as productions of every kind."
Everything concerning the geography topography, flora, fauna, and mineral resources was to be carefully noted. The natives were to be treated "in the most friendly & conciliatory manner. . . . If a few of their influential chiefs . . . wish to visit us, arrange such a visit. . . . If any . . . wish to have some of their young people brought up with us . . . we will receive, instruct & take care of them. . . . Carry with you some matter of the kinepox; inform . . . them . . . of it's efficacy as a preservative from the smallpox. . . . Should [you] be of opinion that the return of your party by the way they went will be eminently dangerous, then ship the whole, & return by sea, by the way either of cape Horn, or the cape of good Hope." The president's letter included "my sincere prayer for your safe return."

suggested taking a census. In this respect the instructions to Lewis of June 20, 1803, are distinctly different from those to Michaux in 1793. Jefferson's emphasis was clear. "The commerce which may be carried on with the people inhabiting the line you will pursue, renders a knolege of those people important," he told Lewis (Jackson, 1978, 1: 61). Now Jefferson wanted to know far more about the Indians and about their relations with the "English" and "Canadian" traders (63). Lewis was to make every effort to inspire confidence and to avoid arousing the Indians' distrust. In passing, Jefferson strongly recommended telling them about the effectiveness of the smallpox vaccine (64).

Finally, Jefferson exhorted Lewis to exercise extreme prudence in all circumstances. He also raised the subject of future means of communication and of the return journey, including the possibility of coming home by sea (65). Obviously he neglected nothing.

The recent Louisiana Purchase led Jefferson to ask for accurate geographical data about the Americans' new acquisition. In a letter to Lewis dated November 16, 1803, he wrote, "As the boundaries of interior Louisiana are the *high lands inclosing all the waters which run into the Missis[s]ippi or Missouri directly or indirectly,* with a greater breadth on the gulph of Mexico, it becomes interesting to fix with precision by celestial observations the longitude & latitude of the sources of these rivers, and furnishing points in the contour of our new limits" (Jackson, 1978, 1: 137).

The United States had in effect acquired the western drainage basin of the Mississippi. It was a matter of some urgency to know the extent of this basin. What would it be used for? Jefferson had his own idea—an idea that seems like an enormity today.

During his long sojourn in France as American minister, Jefferson had scoured the bookshops, buying everything he could find on North America. The epic adventure of the French had caught his attention, especially its ramifications south of the Great Lakes in the Ohio Valley, Illinois country, and Louisiana. He had reread the accounts of La Salle, Joutel, Hennepin, Charlevoix, Lahontan, and the more recent one by Jean Bossu. He had delved into the *Histoire de la Louisiane* by Le Page du Pratz (Ronda, 1998: 54, n. 13). Once back in the United States he had kept up to date with everything written about the Mississippi and its tributaries. *(See note on next page)* ✳ He came across a copy of the journal of Jean-Baptiste Trudeau (or "Truteau") before it was even published and felt it advisable to send several extracts to Lewis, along with "copies of the Treaties for Louisiana, [and] the act for taking possession" (Jackson, 1978, 1: 136). His instructions to Lewis of June 20, 1803, were to go "As far

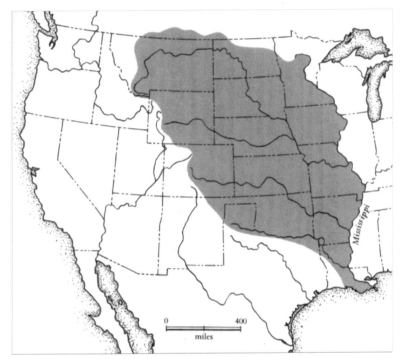

The territory of the Louisiana Purchase, which Napoleon ceded to the United States, covers the western drainage basin of the Mississippi.

up the Missouri as white settlements extend" (64)—but the Louisiana Purchase changed the basic premise. The Indians in this territory became American subjects, as did the whites.

Cahokia and Kaskaskia on the Mississippi's east bank were already part of American territory in 1803. St. Louis and Ste. Geneviève on the west bank now joined them. Since Britain's victory over the French in 1763, the population of these communities had grown while the villages on the east bank had shrunk as French Canadians chose to move to the Spanish side. In almost no time, St. Louis had become a thoroughly respectable, even comfortable place. It was the hub of the fur trade and a growing variety of commercial activities.

Lewis and Clark wintered over in 1803-1804 on the east bank at a spot called Camp Dubois. They spent

✳ Jefferson offered to sell his own book collection to Congress to replace some three thousand volumes lost when the British burned Washington's Capitol in 1814, during the War of 1812. Congress bought this encyclopaedic collection, although his political opponents were outraged at the move. "The bill would put $23,900 into Jefferson's pocket for about 6,000 books, good, bad, and indifferent, old, new, and worthless, in languages which many can not read, and most ought not," fulminated Cyrus King in a speech on January 26, 1815 (Jackson, 1993: 284-285).

a good deal of their time in St. Louis, gathering information about the Missouri.

Lewis was also mindful of a desire expressed by Jefferson. He wrote the president on December 28, 1803, to say, "I am fully persuaded, that your wish to withdraw the inhabitants of Louisiana, may in every necessary degree be affected in the course of a few years, provided the government of the U. States is justly liberal in it's donations" (Jackson, 1978, 1: 153). What had Jefferson meant? Was he afraid of the French Canadians? He probably distrusted the "Canadian traders from the Mississippi" (63) and intended to keep a sharp eye open on the Spanish side. However, his true intention was quite different: he intended to make part of Louisiana into an immense Indian reserve.

Throughout the expedition, Lewis had instructions to note carefully the number of whites settled west of the Mississippi. Jefferson foresaw that they would be few in number and hoped they would readily agree to move to the east. At the same time, all the Indians of the Ohio Valley would have to choose between abandoning their territories or changing their mode of life and becoming farmers among the white settlers.✳ The traditionalists (or diehards, if you will) could simply move to the territories west of the Mississippi.

✳ Jefferson envisioned finding a navigable route to the Pacific — which meant the Orient. It was a vision that had more than a touch of fantasy about it. He dreamed of making the Indians east of the Mississippi into a sedentary society and turning them into farmers, in line with his political ideals. Those who refused to comply with this plan could move west of the Mississippi. He encouraged what he thought were the few whites west of the Mississippi to return to the eastern shore. Jefferson looked ahead, but he didn't always see the reality of things. His election to the presidency in 1801 enabled him, at least, to get an expedition to the West under way. It was the start of an extraordinary adventure that became one of the founding myths of American history.

Jefferson's Indian Policy: Definitely Not a Theoretical Plan

Native resettlement was certainly not a purely theoretical plan. On March 30, 1802, Congress passed legislation designed to regulate relations with the Indians. The act described the territories occupied by various tribes and laid down rules for having boundaries respected.

Rumours about the possible transfer of Louisiana to France had made Jefferson nervous. As a result, he gave the order to intensify and speed up negotiations with the Indians. He feared that under French influence they would be less disposed to give up their lands. "We had better therefore do at once what can now be done," he wrote on February 27, 1803, to William Henry Harrison, governor of Indiana (Jackson, 1993: 210). He felt there was an urgent need to fortify American positions, not only to the south and west, but to the north, the source of British-backed traders.

In the late summer of 1804 three whites were murdered by a band of Sauks and Foxes. This put these nations in a defensive position. Harrison pushed them to the wall and, in a treaty of November 3, 1804, obtained the progressive cession of fifteen million acres (six million hectares) along the Mississippi—mainly on the east bank between the Illinois and Wisconsin rivers, but also on the west bank between the Missouri and Salt rivers.

According to the treaty, signed by three Sauk and two Fox chiefs, the territories in question remained in Indian hands until purchased by whites. In exchange, the Indians would receive an annual rent of $1,000, as well as the services of a trader, a blacksmith, and someone to teach them about farming.

The following summer a new Sauk and Fox delegation presented itself to the authorities. The meeting was pitifully ineffective. "We were desirous to oblige the United States," said the group at the outset, "but we had never before Sold Land, and we did not know the value of it." The new delegation maintained that the chiefs who signed the treaty had been disavowed by their people. Even so, they would stand by the treaty because, "We never take back what we have given, but we hope that our Great Father . . . will allow us Something in addition, to what Governor Harrison has promised us" (Jackson, 1993: 213).◉

What would Harrison have done? History doesn't tell us. "The late purchase is important," explained Jefferson to his secretary of war, Henry Dearborn, on December 16, 1804, "as it fortifies our right to keep the British off from the Mississippi" (Jackson, 1993: 220).

The 1804 treaty heralded the ruthless policy of Madison, Monroe, Adams, and Jackson applied to the Indians (Jackson, 1993: 220). It was completely in line with Jefferson's master plan regarding the fate of Native

◉ Sauk and Fox delegates came to St. Louis in 1805 to complain about the land deal, saying, "We were desirous to oblige the United States, but we had never before Sold Land, and we did not know the value of it, we trusted our beloved white men traders and interpreters to Speak for us, and we have given away a great Country to Governor Harrison for a little thing, we do not say we were cheated, but we made a bad bargain and the Chiefs who made it are all dead, deposed, yet the bargain Stands, for we never take back what we have given, but we hope our Great Father will . . . allow us Something in addition, to what Governor Harrison has promised us" (Jackson, 1993: 214).

⚜ "Cultivators of the earth are the most valuable citizens, they are the most vigorous, the most independent, the most virtuous," wrote Jefferson to John Jay in 1785 (Ronda, 2000: 29). In February, 1803, Jefferson had further thoughts. "In this way, our settlements will gradually circumscribe and approach the Indians, and they will in time either incorporate with us as citizens of the United States or remove beyond the Missisipi. The former is certainly the termination of this history most happy for themselves. But in the whole course of this, it is essential to cultivate their love. As to their fear, we presume that our strength and their weakness is now so visible that they must see we have only to shut our hand to crush them" (Jackson, 1993: 217).

The Removal Bill, providing for the deportation of all eastern Indians to the west bank of the Mississippi, was signed by President Jackson on May 28, 1830 (Jacquin, 2000: 139).

In 1804, fifteen million acres (six million hectares) of territory were ceded to the United States by the Sauks and Foxes in the Treaty of 1804. Map based on Jackson, 1993: 209.

Americans, who he hoped would "incorporate with us as citizens of the United States," or otherwise "remove beyond the Mississippi" (Jackson, 1978, 1: 155, n. 1). Jefferson didn't mince words: he believed in a rural society devoted to farming. *(See note on previous page.)* ☙ What was true for whites was all the more so for Indians: "When they withdraw themselves to the culture of a small piece of land, they will perceive how useless to them are their extensive forests." They must be made to yield. All means were fair—or almost. "We shall . . . be glad to see the good and influential individuals among them run into debt, because we observe that when these debts get beyond what the individuals can pay, they become willing to lop them off by a cession of lands" (Jackson, 1993: 216-217).

Jefferson later described the Indians as "our brethren, our neighbors" when speaking to the Society of Friends of Pennsylvania on November 13, 1807. "They may be valuable friends, & troublesome enemies. Both duty and interest then enjoin, that we should extend to them the blessings of civilized life, & prepare their minds for becoming useful members of the American family" (Jackson, 1993: 217 and 222, n. 19).

The gateway to the West opened to Americans between 1803 and 1806. They headed there in massive numbers. The immense Indian reserve of Jefferson's dreams would not materialize, for the land would be taken over by whites. The Indians' share would be intangible: feelings of melancholy, sadness, frustration, revolt—and a sense of injustice. Their survival would lie in the half-breed.

Chapter 4

The Louisiana Purchase

What Americans today call the Louisiana Purchase was one of the pivotal moments in the history of the United States.

By an amazing stroke of luck—unless Providence really had a hand in it—the departure of the Lewis and Clark Expedition coincided with the acquisition of France's "territory or province" of Louisiana. While Jefferson had dreamed of the expedition, he had never imagined his government gaining control of this huge tract of land.

What accounted for Napoleon's decision? Explanations such as his need for money or his wish to annoy Great Britain are legitimate, but behind these lay his enormous failure in St. Domingue.

In offering the Americans French Louisiana, Napoleon realized he was making possible the birth of a new power, but it is doubtful that he grasped just how great this power would become. With the signing of the Louisiana Purchase in 1803, the history of the United States took on a clearly expansionist focus—some would say imperialistic.

Toussaint L'Ouverture and Toussaint Charbonneau were both born in a French North American colony, the first in St. Domingue, the second in Canada. What did they have in common, apart from their given name and the French language? Probably nothing. And yet if Toussaint Charbonneau's name

Napoleon attacked Spain early in his rise to power, probably with an eye to possible spoils from Spain's colonial empire.

The young consul, attributed to Dutertre (1799) (de Villiers, 1903).

✳ In a 1791 decree the French Convention proclaimed, "Inhabitants of St. Domingue, whatever your colour or origin, you are all free and equal in the eyes of God and the Republic" (Hubert-Robert: 315). Slavery, which was partially re-established under Napoleon, once more stirred the Haitians' revolutionary zeal.

Toussaint L'Ouverture

François Dominique Toussaint was born May 20, 1743. According to tradition, he was the son of Gaou-Guinou, who had royal blood, and a black woman named Pauline. Freed in 1777, he married Suzanne Simon Baptiste, who had also been freed. About 1794 he joined revolutionary France, which had abolished slavery. He commanded his own troops and proved very courageous in battle. "L'Ouverture" became his last name in recognition of the openings ("les ouvertures") that he was able to breach in enemy ranks. He nevertheless kept his distance from the French. He had himself installed in office and promoted worthy measures, particularly in agriculture. He encouraged the repatriation of the former French colonists, and made commercial treaties with the United States and Great Britain. Taking advantage of a quiet period in Europe, Napoleon dispatched troops to St. Domingue to re-establish control. Early in 1802, the French fleet arrived. Toussaint L'Ouverture retired to the highlands after burning the towns. His strategy was to wage a war of attrition, relying on the deadly climate. Nevertheless, after a few weeks of heroic resistance, he surrendered with several of his lieutenants. The French, however, did not keep their promises and they put Toussaint L'Ouverture in jail. He died in a French prison at Fort Joux near Pontarlier in 1803, less than a year after General Leclerc succumbed to yellow fever.

is known to us today, and if his Indian wife Sacagawea and his son Jean-Baptiste are on the American dollar coin, it is perhaps indirectly due to Toussaint L'Ouverture.

St. Domingue Becomes Haiti

Toussaint L'Ouverture was born in 1743 on a plantation in St. Domingue. He was lucky enough to learn to read, and it is told that he eagerly scanned the writings of the French revolutionaries. He was among the slaves who rose up against their French masters. François Dominique Toussaint, as he was first known, made himself the champion not only of freedom for the slaves, but also of independence for his country. He became Toussaint L'Ouverture, and in 1798 the Haitians named him governor for life (Hine and Faragher: 135-136).✳

Revolutionary France abolished slavery in 1794, in keeping with its ideal of liberty, equality, and fraternity. However, it had no intention of giving up its colony. Napoleon, the young consul, was rising rapidly and keeping a sharp eye on every opportunity to enhance French power. He considered the

Haitian revolt unacceptable. St. Domingue was under French control at this time and could make an excellent base of operations if France wanted to re-establish a foothold on continental North America.

Louisiana had already been a French possession. "Tell me about Louisiana," Napoleon asked his entourage. It fell to Louisiana-born Joseph Delfau de Pontalba, who had come to study in France, to familiarize Napoleon with the colony. Pontalba's account was so compelling that the consul didn't wait for his written report before asking His Catholic Majesty, Carlos IV of Spain, "to retrocede to the French Republic . . . the colony or province of Louisiana, with the same extent that it now has in the hands of Spain and that it had when France possessed it," as stated in the Treaty of San Ildefonso, a secret agreement concluded on October 1, 1800 (Hubert-Robert: 326). Napoleon wanted to gain time, for he first had to quell black revolt in St. Domingue. He gave this mission to his brother-in-law, General Charles Leclerc. Guerrilla warfare and yellow fever proved too much for the general and his army of some twenty-three thousand men (Schoelder: 316-318). The French lost the war, although Toussaint L'Ouverture was taken prisoner and ended his days in a French jail.🌿 For the time being, however, the black population controlled the island.ⓔ

🌿 Although I write that the French lost the war, others will say that they won it.

ⓔ One of L'Ouverture's lieutenants, Jean Jacques Dessalines, did not surrender. He and other leaders held out against the Marquis de Rochambeau, a descendant of the hero of the American War of Independence, who succeeded General Leclerc. On May 18, 1803, Dessalines made a symbolic gesture by giving the rebels a flag with the white band in France's tricolour removed. On January 1, 1804, he proclaimed Haiti's independence, and St. Domingue once more took on its native name, Haiti. The history of the world's first black republic was to be a turbulent one.

Napoleon hesitated, perplexed. The picture sketched by Pontalba had stimulated his interest in Louisiana. Rumours circulated. The Americans wanted to know what was in the wind. The French dissembled as long as possible, but on October 15, 1802, the Americans finally obtained confirmation of Spain's transfer of Louisiana to France. The Spanish had stipulated that France must never turn over the territory to a third party, but in less than a year, on April 30, 1803, Napoleon sold Louisiana to the United States. The consul's dreams about Louisiana had suddenly evaporated under the combined effect of his European ambitions and the loss of Haiti.

Free Navigation on the Mississippi

When Jefferson heard of the Franco-Spanish dealings he was enraged. In 1795 the United States had signed the Treaty of San Lorenzo with the Spaniards, then

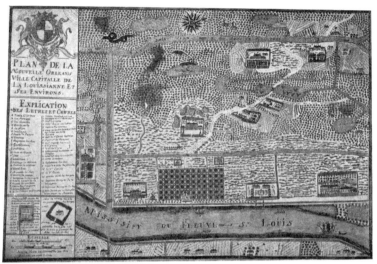

This map of "New Orleans, Capital City of Louisiana and of the Environs" dates from the mid–eighteenth century and is in the Dépôt des Cartes du Ministère de la Guerre, France (Villiers du Terrage, 1903).

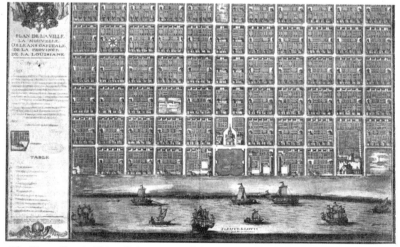

The Vieux Carré of New Orleans, site of the original French settlement. This map of "The City of New Orleans, Capital of the Province of Louisiana," attributed to Thierry and dated 1756, is in the Dépôt des Cartes du Ministère de la Guerre, France (Villiers du Terrage, 1903).

masters of Louisiana, thereby confirming arrangements that the U.S. considered essential (Weber: 289). The treaty had provisionally opened up the Mississippi and New Orleans to American trade, subject to periodic renewal. If rumours of Spain ceding the territory back to France proved to be true, what position would the French take? In Jefferson's view, access to the Gulf of Mexico via the Mississippi was vital. The 1763 Treaty of Paris✳ had provided for free passage on the great river, but this still depended on the goodwill of France or Spain, whichever held the territory. When this treaty was drawn up, the British had no idea that France had ceded to Spain "all the country known by the name of Louisiana," including New Orleans, by the secret Treaty of Fontainebleau signed on November 2, 1762.

The contents of the Treaty of Paris reached New Orleans in April 1763. The British gradually took possession of the Mississippi's eastern shore, but only in September 1764 did people living in Louisiana learn that the western shore had been ceded to Spain. The Spanish were even slower than the British to assume control of their newly-acquired territory and take advantage of the exceptional position of the city of New Orleans.❷ Meanwhile the French Canadians were moving out of what had become British territory, abandoning Fort de Chartres, Prairie du Rocher, Cahokia, and Kaskaskia to settle in Ste. Geneviève and especially in St. Louis, a community founded by Pierre Laclède and the young Auguste Chouteau on the west bank of the Mississippi at the mouth of the Missouri (Balesi: 280).

As soon as Jefferson became president he began negotiating for the purchase of New Orleans. Rumours as to which power possessed the city were still unconfirmed. Despite his francophile sentiments, Jefferson felt France would become an intolerable

✳ Spain only came into the Seven Years' War on the French side in January 1762. Almost immediately it lost Manila and Havana. At Fontainebleau on November 3, 1762, the French king offered his cousin, Carlos III, the western drainage basin of the Mississippi. After some hesitation Carlos accepted the offer, seeing it as an opportunity to protect Spanish colonies against possible British American invasion.

❷ At the same time, the British took over what was left of the former New France: the eastern bank of the Mississippi, the Great Lakes, and the St. Lawrence Valley. It took the opportunity of claiming the Floridas, agreeing to give up Havana to Spain in exchange. With a few strokes of the pen, the Spanish, after years of valiantly defending Pensacola, San Marcos, and St. Augustine, lost them without a shot being fired, while the French presence in Louisiana, which they had so often feared, simply evaporated.

It is worth noting that the Spanish residents were urged to leave the Floridas whereas the French, on the contrary, were encouraged to stay in Louisiana, a fact that greatly influenced the course of history in these regions.

Thomas Jefferson,
(Edme Quenedey, 1756-1830)

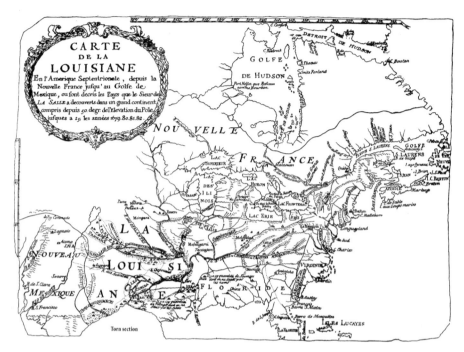

Map of Louisiana and New France under the French. The inscription reads: "In North America, from New France to the Gulf of Mexico, is shown the country discovered by the Sieur de La Salle in a great continent, between latitudes 50° and 25° north, in the years 1679, 80, 81, 82."

Robert R. Livingston
(Vanderlyn)

James Monroe
(Vanderlyn)

Robert R. Livingston had been sent to France by secretary of state James Madison to inquire about the payment of indemnities, and particularly about the nature of the agreements made between Spain and France. Did Louisiana still belong to Spain? Following a stormy debate on February 16, 1803, regarding navigation on the Mississippi, President Jefferson decided to send James Monroe to join Livingston. If the United States did not acquire New Orleans, Jefferson foresaw that war could not be far off and it would be better to prepare for it. When Monroe later became president, he formulated the Monroe Doctrine (1823), which stated as a matter of policy that outsiders were not to interfere in matters involving the Americas.

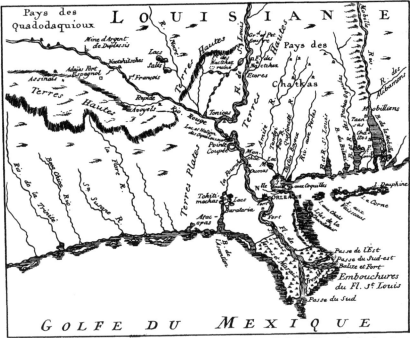

Early French map of the Lower Mississippi, then called the Fleuve de St. Louis
(LePage du Pratz, 1: 139).

"What will you give for the whole?" Talleyrand asked Livingston and Monroe, the American negotiators. Napoleon's minister was referring to the western drainage basin of the Mississippi, that part of the former Louisiana ceded by the French to Spain in 1762 and ceded back to France in 1803. Final negotiations were conducted with French treasury minister François de Barbé-Marbois. It is often said that the United States doubled its size by making this purchase. DeVoto (397) estimated the surface measurement of the United States in 1803 at 869,735 square miles (2,252,614 square kilometres). The territory acquired in the Louisiana Purchase measured 909,130 square miles (2,354,647 square kilometres)—a very arbitrary figure, perhaps, but it gives an idea of the size and importance of the acquisition. The official purchase price was $15 million. David Lavender (52) calculates the territory at 828,000 square miles (2,144,520 square kilometres). At 640 acres per square

François de Barbé-Marbois
(Maurin)

mile, this works out to a little less than three cents an acre. Lavender notes that at this time the American government was selling land at two dollars an acre (an acre being 5,200 square metres). Morris (1996: 572) calculates the size of the United States in 1783 at 541,364,480 acres (2,081,633 square kilometres), and the size of the Louisiana Purchase of 1803 at 529,911,680 acres (2,144,553 square kilometres). Some commentators include the basin of the Red River south of the forty-ninth parallel, an area of 29,601,920 acres (119,799 square kilometres).

Fox Indian
(Karl Bodmer)

Medal for the Indians of Louisiana, inscribed "Bonaparte, first consul of the French Republic." Engraved by Andrieu.

threat should it retain or acquire control of the city and, by extension, of navigation on the Mississippi. When it was officially confirmed that Spain had handed back Louisiana to France, Jefferson moved quickly. He was even ready to renew relations with his erstwhile enemy, Great Britain

A Surprise Move

Napoleon took everyone by surprise by deciding to sell the whole territory. He knew that by encouraging the growing influence of the United States he would be creating a powerful rival for Britain. "The sale assures forever the Power of the United States, and I have given England a rival who, sooner or later, will humble her pride," said Napoleon (Ambrose, 1996: 101).

The French of Louisiana watching an Illinois peace-pipe dance.

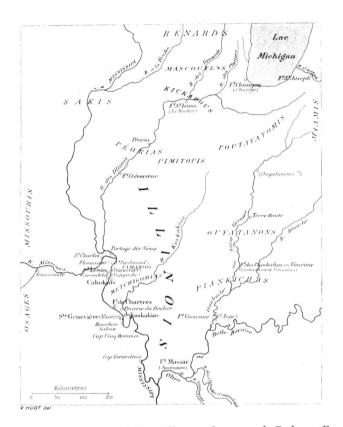

The French Directory supplied weapons to the privateers who infested American waters and Caribbean ports (Hubert-Robert: 324). The Americans naturally protested. President Adams issued a solemn denunciation on May 28, 1798, and finally Congress voted to suspend trade with France. On September 30 of the same year, France signed an agreement whereby it consented to pay indemnities. For how much? And when would this debt by paid? That was left to be negotiated.

In reality the transaction amounted to eighty million francs, of which twenty million were to be set aside for debts and paid directly to the ship-owners and businessmen who had suffered (Hubert-Robert: 343). The Americans had just concluded the deal of the century! Protestations were heard in the United States, where most people had little or no idea of the extent of the territories west of the Mississippi. What a lot of money for a desert! But Jefferson considered the price ridiculously cheap for this completely unexpected windfall (he even felt certain scruples about how low it was). The Louisiana Purchase changed the course of history and opened the way for the famous U.S. tenet of "manifest destiny" (see Ronda, 1998: 41).

In August 1803 Talleyrand greeted Robert R. Livingston, the American emissary, with the bald question, "Do you have money?" Talleyrand had lived in exile in the United States during the French Revolution and was completely at ease in English. He was equally comfortable in any transaction involving large sums of money. The Americans wanted New Orleans? Very well. "What will you give for the whole?" he asked the astounded Livingston. The American bore in mind the fact that France had officially recognized debts to the United States as reparation for French acts of piracy in American waters at the time of the Directory. No sum or date for payment had yet been fixed (Hubert-Robert: 324). Talleyrand was definitely not thinking of this, but rather of the fifty million francs that Napoleon wanted. No doubt he was already wondering

✳ In his remarkable work, *The Course of Empire* (397), Bernard DeVoto attempts to establish clearly the amount of the transaction, which he sets at $23,213,567.73. This comprises $3,747,268.96 for indemnities, and $11,250,000 corresponding to the sixty million francs agreed upon for the actual purchase. To this latter amount must be added $8,221,320.50 in interest, while subtracting $5,021.75 for debts that were graciously waived. The business of reparations dragged on until 1925.

just how he would take his commission. Livingston was caught short. He had no mandate to purchase the entire territory of Louisiana.

The French had been told that Jefferson was sending James Monroe with more vigorous instructions. Napoleon insisted that negotiations proceed before Monroe arrived in France. When the second emissary reached Paris on April 12, Livingston reported that the French were apparently ready to sell all of the Louisiana territory, lock, stock, and barrel. The two men acted without a mandate and without authorization. They could offer up to $9,375,000 for New Orleans; they ended by agreeing to pay $15,000,000 "for the whole" of Louisiana.✳

Lewis Gets Ready

While the Louisiana Purchase was being concluded in Paris (it was finalized on April 30, 1803), Lewis was buying provisions of "Portable Soup"! He planned to pay a dollar a pound for this dried soup, a mixture of various beans and vegetables that he heartily endorsed. In the end he spent $289.50 for 193 pounds of portable soup—"one of the most essential articles in the preparation [for the expedition]" (Ambrose, 1996: 86). Arms and ammunition were not forgotten, nor presents for the Indians and other items. Lewis also thought about recruitment and finally suggested that President Jefferson appoint William Clark as co-captain of the expedition. "The president," wrote Lewis to his friend Clark, "expresses an anxious wish that you would consent to join me in this enterprise; he has authorized me to say that in the event of your accepting this proposition he will grant you a Captain's commission" (Jackson, 1978, 1: 60). Counting on "the long and uninterrupted friendship and confidence which has subsisted between us," Lewis hoped his friend would respond favourably, at least for part of the journey (Jackson 1978, 1: 57-60). He waited for over five weeks. On July 18 Clark sent his acceptance. "I will chearfully join you in an 'official Charrector' *as mentioned in your letter*," [italics mine] he wrote, although in an initial draft he used the words "on equal footing &c." In the name of an unfailing friendship, he continued, "My friend, I do assure you that no man lives whith whome I would perfur to undertake Such a Trip &c. as your self" (Jackson, 1978, 1: 110, 111, n. 1). *(See note on next page.)* ♛

Lewis was in luck: Clark would be the perfect partner. Paradoxically, fortune would smile on him again when he was forced to wait for his main vessel, the keelboat that had been initially promised for July 20. If it had been ready, he would probably have started up the Missouri before Louisiana had been transferred to the United States. In fact it wasn't ready until August 31. This delayed his arrival at the mouth of the Missouri until early December—too late to start up the river before the onset of winter.

Lewis and Clark were denied access to the Missouri in any case. Colonel Carlos Dehault Delassus, lieutenant governor of Upper Louisiana, politely suggested that they cool their heels until the spring, despite the French and British passports that Lewis presented. Delassus preferred to wait for instructions about the transfer of Louisiana. The Purchase had only been public knowledge for a few weeks (Appleman, 2000: 364, n. 27). Jefferson had been told of it at the end of June and received a copy of the treaty on July 14, 1803. He immediately wrote to inform Lewis, who was then stuck in Pittsburgh waiting for the keelboat. Lewis wrote back to acknowledge receipt of the news on July 22 (Jackson, 1978, 1: 109, 111).

William Clark
(Charles Willson Peale)

☙ In his letter of June 19, 1803, addressed to William Clark, Lewis stated that the president was ready to give him a captain's commission. Clark did not receive this commission, however. Ambrose (1996: 99) notes that Secretary Dearborn had provided for the rank of lieutenant, and that Jefferson did not correct this.

On January 22, 1804, the president wrote Lewis in St. Louis to announce the official transfer of New Orleans to the United States on December 20, 1803, adding that the transfer of "the Upper posts" would soon follow (Jackson, 1978, 1: 165). Earlier, on November 30, 1803, the French flag had replaced the Spanish at a ceremony in New Orleans. Everyone knew this was merely a transition stage. The crowd remained silent. The inhabitants were now neither Spanish nor French: they were *Louisianais* (Hubert-Robert, 357). Twenty days later the tricolour was lowered and the American flag raised. Citizens and residents who wished to remain and obey American laws were absolved from their oath to the French Republic as of that moment (363).

In St. Louis a similar ceremony, this time for Upper Louisiana, lasted for two days. On March 9, 1804, Colonel Delassus, in the name of Spain, and Captain

This mural by Ezra Winter is
in the George Rogers Clark
Memorial in Vincennes, Indiana.
The history of Vincennes is rather
special. It was one of the last
pockets of French resistance at
the time of the British Conquest
of New France, and one of
the last places to be taken by
the Americans in the War of
Independence. George Rogers
Clark had to overcome British
forces there twice (in 1778 and
1779). The people of Vincennes
have kept alive the memory of
their French origins and are very
aware of the great moments of
North American history. The
taking of Vincennes in 1779
marked a phase in the move
west, as did the transfer of Upper
Louisiana to the Americans in St.
Louis in 1804.

Amos Stoddard, acting on behalf of France, pre-
sided over an initial ceremony that ended with
the tricolour being hoisted aloft. The St. Louis
populace was mostly French-speaking at the time,
and their spokesmen had expressed the wish to see
the French colours flying for at least one night—a
wish that was granted. Next day the stars and stripes
rose in its place.

Two weeks later Lewis and Clark entered Indian
country where the Americans now considered themselves masters. During the winter months of 1803-
1804 the St. Louis merchants had felt free to brief

The Affair of the Century

A new treaty was signed in Paris on "the tenth day of Floreal
in the eleventh year of the French Republic; and the 30th of
April 1803" by "Citizen Francis Barbé Marbois," Robert R.
Livingston, and James Monroe.

Article 1 reads: "The First Consul of the French Republic
desiring to give to the United States a strong proof of his
friendship doth hereby cede to the United States in the name
of the French Republic for ever and in full Sovereignty the
said territory the Colony or Province of Louisiana with all its
rights and appurtenances as fully and in the Same manner as
they have been acquired by the French Republic in virtue of
the above mentioned Treaty of San Ildefonso, October 1, 1800
concluded with his Catholic Majesty." When the treaty for
the Louisiana Purchase reached Washington on July 14, 1803,
Spain had already made known its objections to President
Jefferson. Had not France undertaken never to cede Louisiana
to another power (Weber: 291)? Not only did the United States
scoff at these objections; the American government claimed
that the transaction included part of Florida in the east and
extended west as far as the Rio Grande.

The year 1803 became a key date in American history.
At the time, Jefferson's political opponents weren't ready to
accept this sudden acquisition. Like almost everyone, they
knew nothing about the territories west of the Mississippi,
and as in any political debate, harsh words were said. But one
consideration made even the president pause. Did the United
States Constitution provide for acquiring a foreign territory by
purchasing it? The answer came in the form of ratification of
the Louisiana Purchase Treaty in October 1803.

the two captains for the adventure that awaited them. Antoine Soulard, a French citizen employed by the Spanish authorities, had opened his files and spread out his most recent maps of Upper Louisiana. French Canadians who no doubt felt that they had been doubly deprived of their nationality agreed to join the expedition as boatmen in one of the two pirogues. Three Métis, born of Indian mothers and Canadian fathers, were also recruited. Georges Drouillard was hired as an interpreter. Pierre Cruzatte and François Labiche were taken on as pilots of the keelboat and sworn in as privates in the U.S. Army (Thwaites, 1: 12). Other French Canadians, including Toussaint Charbonneau, would join the expedition along the way.

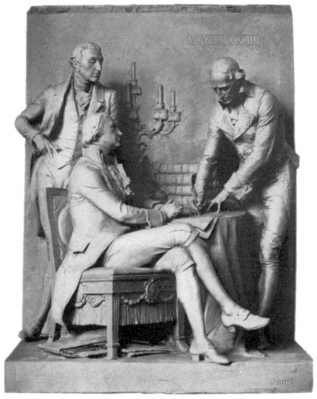

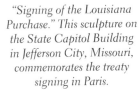

"Signing of the Louisiana Purchase." This sculpture on the State Capitol Building in Jefferson City, Missouri, commemorates the treaty signing in Paris.

Chapter 5

Guides and Interpreters, Little-known "Frenchmen"

The Mississippi had been travelled continually by the French and the *Canadiens* of old for over a century when Lewis and Clark arrived there in the fall of 1803. They would have to winter over at the mouth of the Missouri, which they planned to navigate to its source.

It was a lucky circumstance that forced them to wait. It gave them time to get information and documentation from people in and around St. Louis, and above all to recruit men who were familiar with the Missouri country and its inhabitants—especially boatmen, modest hired hands or "engagés" as they were routinely called, even in English. Their contribution was limited but very real. They would travel upriver with the expedition as far as the Mandan and Hidatsa country, where the white man's diseases had already arrived.

Let there be no misunderstanding: the aim of the present work is not to rehabilitate the expedition's boatmen. Bringing them out of the shadows doesn't mean making heroes of them. These "Frenchmen," as Lewis and Clark usually labelled them, were simply left over from a failed colonial attempt. Their presence served as a reminder that the new Province of Quebec created along the St. Lawrence in 1763 was but a small part of a former colonial empire. Their ties with the Indians were also a reminder of the nature of the relationship between the French and Indians.

History is written not only in great events, but in the bits and pieces of lives and destinies, even those of minor players—indeed, sometimes mainly in the fate of minor players.

Y ou used pole and rope to get up the Missouri and oars or paddles to go down-river. Lewis and Clark learned this soon enough. The French Canadians had known it for generations.

In January 1803 President Jefferson had asked Congress for the sum of $2,500 to explore the course of the Missouri. In his view, "An intelligent officer with ten or twelve chosen men . . . might explore the whole line, even to the Western ocean, have conferences with the natives on the subject of commercial intercourse, get admission among them for our traders as others are admitted" (Jackson, 1978, 1: 12). What others? Why, British traders, of course!

Jefferson's fears had crystallized during the preceding months. To understand why, it must be remembered that the president was one of the heroes of American independence—an event that was certainly not ancient history. A scant twenty years had elapsed since Great Britain had resigned itself to recognizing the independence of some of its North American colonies. But the British had kept a solid base to the north, principally what was now called the Province of Quebec. Since 1774 its frontiers had reached as far south as the junction of the Ohio and Mississippi rivers. In Montreal a new fur trade venture had been founded a few years after the British takeover in 1763. This was the North West Company. Its flotillas of canoes now glided along the routes opened by the *Canadiens* of New France. Their descendants had quite naturally passed into service with these new masters, once more travelling the Ottawa River toward Sault Ste. Marie and Fort Michilimackinac, respectively the gateways from Lake Huron into Lake Superior and Lake Michigan.

The North West Company had a rival: the Hudson's Bay Company operating in the Canadian north. The rivers of the Hudson Bay drainage basin led to Lake Winnipeg and Lake Manitoba in the heart of the continent (Wood and Thiesen: 2). French Canadians also knew these waterways. Pierre Gaultier de La Vérendrye had set up a chain of trading posts from Kaministiquia, at the far western end of Lake Superior, to the Lake of the Woods. Father and son had pushed on as far as the Red River, then built Fort La Reine on the Assiniboine in 1738. The Missouri was at their doorstep. By December 1738 they had reached a Mandan village consisting of one hundred and fifty dwellings surrounded by a stockade. The inhabitants were undeniably Indian, not white as the Assiniboins had jokingly suggested (Combet: 104, 106). On meeting the Mandans for the first time, La Vérendrye wrote that he was surprised, as he had expected to find people who differed from other Indians. He made a note to take everything he'd been told with a large grain of salt from

St. Louis and the Surrounding Region

In 1762, when the French handed over the territory covering the Mississippi's western drainage basin to Spain, there was already a French trading post, Ste. Geneviève, on that side of the great river. In August 1763, Pierre Laclède left New Orleans with his young clerk of thirteen, Auguste Chouteau, to open a post on the Mississippi at the mouth of the Missouri. People still didn't know about the transfer of Louisiana to Spain or the terms of the Treaty of Paris. The French authorities had just granted trading privileges on the Missouri River to a trader named Gilbert Antoine Maxent for a period of six years, hence the mission entrusted to Laclède, a young man of good family. He was an educated man, judging by the library of 200 volumes that he took with him. At the end of 1764, when Louisiana's inhabitants learned that it had been ceded to Spain and that the Mississippi's eastern shore was now under British rule, the village of St. Louis was already well established.

During the forty years under Spanish rule that followed, the Missouri remained wholly French in appearance, language, customs, and a certain view of life (Foley: 19). A number of French Canadians who had originally settled on the eastern shore preferred to live under Spanish rule rather than British. On the western shore life continued in French. The Spanish administration was slow to get organized. Little "French-Canadian" villages continued to spring up. Louis Blanchette, for example, went a few kilometres up he Missouri and founded "Les Petites Côtes," which became St. Charles in 1784. A little further north, François Saucier founded Portage des Sioux; to the south Mine à Breton and Nouveau Bourbon appeared, followed by L'Anse à la Graisse, established in 1783 by François and Joseph Le Sieur opposite the mouth of the Ohio. The story of Louis Lorimier, who lost his trading post on the Ohio to Americans, is a fairly revealing indication of the tensions arising in the wake of the British takeover in 1763 and the American Revolution. Lorimier settled at Cape Girardeau, where the Spanish granted him land in 1795 (Foley: 49-50).

Partial View of St. Louis

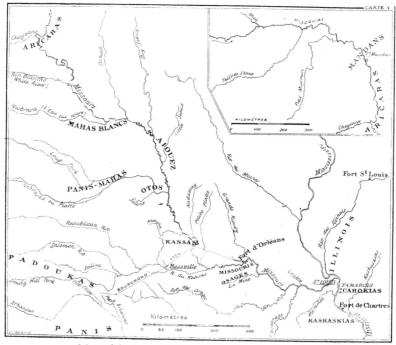

Map of the Lower Missouri River (de Villiers, 1925).

✳ Mandan territory was some 1,600 miles (2,600 kilometres) upriver from the mouth of the Missouri. When the explorer Louis Jolliet and the Jesuit missionary Jacques Marquette went down the Mississippi in 1673, they noted this wide tributary coming in from the west. Étienne de Véniard, sieur de Bourgmont, settled for a while along the Missouri in the early eighteenth century, although he did not reach Mandan territory. The first whites to reach it were probably the La Vérendryes (Wood and Thiessen: 298). Certain legends are tenacious, however, and it would not be surprising if the Mandans had welcomed a few whites at an earlier date.

then on. The Mandan women may not have had white skins, but they liked white men. All accounts agree on this point (Wood and Thiessen: 69, 117).

Since time immemorial the Mandans, like a number of other nations along the Missouri, had been well aware of the advantages of their geographical position.✳ They had established themselves as middle-men. The French who visited them in 1738 were followed by many others, some of whom settled among the Mandans or neighbouring tribes.

The Presence of *Canadiens* —So-called "Frenchmen"

During this same period, *Canadiens* began to settle farther down the Mississippi, particularly near Indian villages such as Cahokia and Kaskaskia on the eastern shore. This shore came under British control with the Treaty of Paris in 1763, while the western bank fell to Spain as a result of the secret Treaty of Fontainebleau in 1762. When the news of these crucial accords finally reached the region, the village of St. Louis had just been founded at the mouth of the Missouri.

Canadien settlers—soon to be distinguished as French Canadians—abandoned the Mississippi's eastern bank to settle in the existing communities of St. Louis or Ste. Geneviève. Other posts quickly sprang up around these two core villages, including St. Charles and La Charette along the Missouri.

⊘ The pirogue, commonly used to transport small loads, was made from a tree trunk that was hollowed out and carved in the shape of a canoe. (Foley: 51).

All the settlers in these communities were directly or indirectly involved in trade. They were old hands at navigating the Ohio, the Mississippi, and even the Missouri. It was from these settlers that Lewis recruited the team for one of the two pirogues intended to escort the vessel under construction at Elizabeth near Pittsburgh—a keelboat fifty-five feet (eighteen metres) long.

Lewis himself had worked out the specifications for this boat. In theory it could be navigated in four ways: by oar, by sail, by being poled, or by being hauled with a rope. The same held true for the pirogues,⊘ one of which could be manned by six paddlers, the other by seven or eight. The latter, nicknamed the red pirogue, was entrusted to a team entirely made up of French Canadians, piloted by Jean-Baptiste Deschamps.✳

At ten in the morning on August 31, 1803, just three hours after taking possession of his keelboat, the impatient Lewis cast off the moorings and set out on

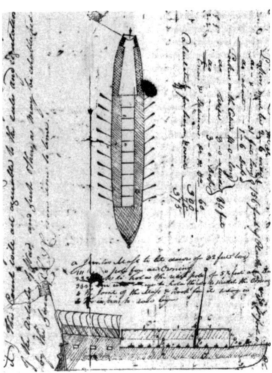

Clark's sketch of the keelboat.

✳ Deschamps wintered over among the Mandans and returned to St. Louis in the spring of 1805 with the keelboat, which was laden with specimens for President Jefferson.

Missouri River Boats

One of the vessels used in the area was the flatboat—a type of raft made of immense tree trunks. It could carry loads of great size. Once it reached its destination, the boat was broken up and the wood sold.

The flatboat could also carry heavy loads of great weight. A cabin was put up in the stern, or at least one of its sections was covered with a roof. "This covered freight boat with a keel could be propelled upstream in a variety of fashions," explains the historian of the Missouri, William E. Foley. "Sometimes it was poled along the shallow waters close to the shore, but when deep waters or soft bottoms made this impossible, the boat was literally pulled up the river by men walking along the bank tugging at the cordelle, a piece of rope attached to the mast. If neither of these methods proved feasible, then the boat had to be rowed. Only occasionally did favourable winds make it possible to hoist the square-rigged sail located on the center mast to relieve temporarily the struggling boatmen. In this backbreaking fashion the rugged boatmen painfully moved the sturdy keelboats laden with merchandise upstream to their destination at a rate of between ten and fifteen miles a day" (Foley: 51).

The handling of flatboats, pirogues, and other craft was done by Creoles from the south or French Canadians from the north called engagés. Initially recruited as boatmen, they had to be ready to take on a number of other jobs. These were sturdy men, bon vivants, and good singers. They were especially fond of call and response songs that cemented group solidarity and raised their spirits when needed.

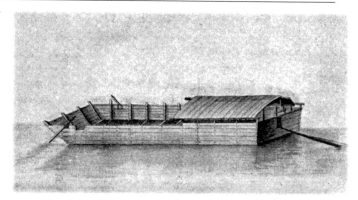

A typical Missouri flatboat.

the little Youghiogheny River. From there he passed on to the Monongahela and into the Ohio, which soon taught him a lesson about the difficulty of navigating in these parts. At summer's end the water was especially low, in places no more than six inches (fifteen centimetres) deep. The men had to unload the boat. Lewis rented horses and oxen to haul it along, literally sliding on the sandy bottom. All sorts of obstacles blocked the channel—piles of stones and driftwood, or simply the ever-shifting sandbars.

The red pirogue had been purchased in Pittsburgh, but the second, manned by six paddlers and nicknamed the white pirogue, was bought en route at Wheeling, West Virginia. On October 14 the three vessels came within sight of the falls of the Ohio, in reality a series of rapids some two miles long that Lewis and his party negotiated with the help of local pilots. A month later the group finally reached the Mississippi and began travelling upriver toward St. Louis. Lewis had now given up any thought of starting up the Missouri before winter. Even if he had wanted to, the Spanish authorities wouldn't have allowed it, as the transfer of Louisiana first to France and then to the United States hadn't been completed. Clark had now joined Lewis, and the Corps of Discovery set up its winter camp at the mouth of the Dubois River on the Mississippi's east bank, opposite St. Louis.

As previously mentioned, this delay was a piece of luck that contributed significantly to the expedition's success. By being in touch with the local settlers, especially St. Louis residents such as the Chouteau family, Lewis and Clark gleaned all the available information about the Missouri and its inhabitants.

The delay also provided the captains with a chance to complete their complement of manpower. They had recruited all the soldiers needed, but realized that the expedition would benefit by having some French Canadians who were familiar with the territory. At Fort Massac Lewis had already met Georges Drouillard, son of a French-Canadian father and a Shawnee mother. At St. Charles he took on Pierre Cruzatte and François Labiche, two Métis born of Omaha mothers from a tribe on the Missouri above the Platte River. Pierre's father had apparently lived for some time among the Omahas, but the Cruzatte family was now living in St. Louis. Young Cruzatte turned out to be an exceptional recruit, not only because he knew the Omaha tongue and the sign language common to the nations of the Missouri, but also thanks to his talents as a fiddler. His violin playing not only provided a pleasant distraction for the expedition's members along the way, but often amazed and entranced the Indians.

François Labiche, like Cruzatte, was well versed in the navigational snares lying in wait on the Missouri. Lewis entrusted him with the keelboat, alternating with Cruzatte. Labiche could turn his hand at almost anything. Lewis learned that he could depend on him, as also on Drouillard. Both men spoke French and English fairly well and became links in the translation chain, along with Sacagawea and Toussaint Charbonneau, who spoke no English. For example, when the expedition met the Wallawallas on April 27, 1806, Sacagawea was able to talk to a young Shoshone adopted by this tribe; she then translated the conversation into Hidatsa for her husband, Charbonneau, who in turn translated the message into French for Labiche or Drouillard, who finally rendered it in English for Lewis.

The many tasks that fell to Drouillard, Cruzatte, and Labiche account for their being frequently mentioned in the officers' journals, but the same was not true of the *engagés* of the red pirogue.

Can We Reconcile These Two Lists?

We know nothing definite about Jean-Baptiste Deschamps, who was in charge of the red pirogue. He may have been the son of one Jean-Baptiste Deschamps, husband of Marie Pinot, and he may have married Marie-Anne Baguette, *dit* Langevin, by whom he had a son also called Jean-Baptiste and baptized in St. Charles on August 15, 1792. The seven or eight boatmen of the red pirogue are scarcely better known. Lewis and Clark both gave lists in their journals. Lewis's reads: "Patroon [boss] Baptist Deschamps, engag[é]s: Etienne Mabbauf, Paul Primaut, Charles Hébert, Baptist La Jeunesse, Peter Pinaut, Peter Roi and Joseph Collin" (Moulton, 2: 255). Clark's list mentions "Battist de Shone, ptrn [patroon], Joseph Le bartee, Lasoness, Paul Preemau, Chalo, E. Cann, Roie, Charlo Cougee, another le bartee, and Rivee" (Moulton, 2: 347).

✳ John Ordway rapidly gained the confidence of the captains, who put him in charge of Camp Dubois in their absence. Trustworthy and methodical, Ordway was able to keep his journal without missing a single day. On August 21, 1806, he wrote, "Ross joined us in order to go down with us."

How are we to reconcile these two lists? Apart from Deschamps ("de Shone"), the first list has seven names, the second nine. To further complicate matters, two other names are given elsewhere. On August 22, 1806, on the return trip Clark mentions "a french man by the name of Rokey who was one of our Engagees as high as the Mandans," now living with the Arikaras. He adds, "This man had Spend all of his wages, and requested to return with us we agreed to give him a passage down" (Thwaites, 5: 356). Sergeant John Ordway's journal for August 21 states that "Ross joined us in order to go down with us" (Moulton, 9: 352).✳ Ross and Rokey are one and the same. There is no doubt about this. Was he an engagé not mentioned in either Lewis or Clark's lists? In his notes on the engagés, Moulton (2: 529) is generally prudent and adheres mainly to commentaries by Charles G. Clarke in *The Men of the Lewis and Clark Expedition*. However, he contests the link that Clarke (70) makes between Rokey, Ross, and Rocque. The Ross of Ordway's journal, he feels, might well be read as Roie or even Roei, while Rokey could refer to Pierre Roi, as men named Pierre (stone) were often nicknamed Rock or Rocky. In other words Moulton feels that Rokey and Ross are one and the same person as Lewis's Peter Roi.

We are back to square one with two lists, Lewis's with seven names, Clark's with eight or possibly nine (excluding the patroons). This gap can be reduced from two to one if we agree that Rivee is certainly the soldier Francis Rivet (Thwaites, 1: 30). *(See note on next page.)* ♔

It is hopeless to try to reconcile the two lists without first finding out more about each of the engagés and—especially important—reconstructing spelling where possible.

Charlo Cougee and Chalo are mentioned only on Clark's list. We know nothing about them.

Joseph Collin is probably a former engagé of the North West Company, according to Patrick Gass's journal. He should not be confused with Private John Collins of Sergeant Nathaniel Pryor's squad in the Corps of Discovery. Possibly Joseph Collin came from the Montreal region. On July 15, 1818, at Portage des Sioux, a man of the same name married Marie Louis Denis *dit* La Pierre, widow of Louis Clermont.

Like Joseph Collin, Charles Hébert is only mentioned in Lewis's list—unless he is the Chalo of Clark's list. Hébert may be the son of Charles Hébert and Ursule Forest of Prairie-de-la-Madeleine, near Montreal. This Hébert married Julie Hubert *dit* La Croix in St. Louis on September 11, 1792.

Paul Primeau (Primaut according to Lewis, Preemau according to Clark), married Pélagie Bissonet in St. Louis on November 18, 1759, and was the son of Joseph Primeau and Louise Lalumière of Chateauguay near Montreal. It is thought that he went back to St. Louis when the expedition reached the Mandans in the fall of 1804, probably with Jean-Baptiste La Jeunesse (called Lasoness by Clark). The latter was also married and a father. His wife, Élisabeth Malbeuf, whom he married in St. Louis on July 9, 1797, was the sister of another engagé in the expedition, Étienne Malbeuf, whom Lewis calls Mabbauf—a name that perhaps became Mallat under Clark's pen and is mentioned alongside William La Beice (François Labiche) (Moulton, 2: 347). Élisabeth and Étienne were the children of François Malbeuf, a native of Lac-au-Sable. He had two or three Indian wives, including Angélique, a Mandan woman who was Élisabeth's mother. Élisabeth was baptized in St. Charles in 1797, two months before marrying La Jeunesse.

Peter Pinaut is possibly the son of Joseph Pineau and a Missouri Indian woman. He may have been baptized in St. Louis in 1790. As Lewis mentioned a

♛ The name of Rivet (Rivee) on the list of engagés is probably an error. He had been recruited as a soldier. Everything points to him being a jolly fellow, full of vitality. He spent his life in the fur trade as a trapper and interpreter, both for the North West Company and—at age seventy-five—for the Hudson's Bay Company. He died in 1852 at the age of ninety-five in the Willamette Valley (today part of Oregon). When wintering over with the Mandans, he thoroughly enjoyed himself. On New Year's Eve, 1805, he led the dancing to the sound of a little drum, a horn, and Cruzatte's violin, even performing on his hands. In the enthusiasm of the moment, some spectators thought he was "dancing on his head" (Thwaites 1: 243, n. 1).

Charles Pineau in his account book (August 5, 1807), it is possible that the latter is the Chalo (rather than Charles Hébert) in Clark's list.

Finally, who is this mysterious Le Bartee mentioned by Clark on July 4, 1804, who apparently became Liberty in August: "The man *Liberty* whome we sent for the Ottoes has not come up" (Thwaites, 1: 98)? Gary Moulton lingers over this individual whose name is not on Lewis's list of May 26, 1804. After envisaging a variety of possibilities, Moulton notes that Donald Jackson found an official document dated 1819 in Illinois that mentioned one "Joseph Callin said La Liberty of portage de Scioux." As mentioned earlier, a Joseph Collin was married in Portage des Sioux in 1818. It is therefore possible that Lewis's Joseph Collin is the Joseph Le bartee of Clark's list.

To summarize, in attempting to reconcile the two lists we find doubles for Primaut (Preemau), Hébert (perhaps Chalo), La Jeunesse (Lasoness), Pinaut (perhaps Chalo), Roi (Roie), Collin (Joseph Le Bartee), and Mabbauf (perhaps Mallat?). Clark's E. Cann and Charlo Cougee have no opposite number.

The Engagés: Little Known, but Extremely Useful

A few conclusions are in order. The two captains spoke only English and had great difficulty pronouncing French names. As well, perhaps, the people bearing these names may not have counted for much in their eyes. This is probably the case for the engagés, although not for Drouillard, Labiche, and Cruzatte.

Lewis and Clark left St. Charles on May 21, 1804, reaching the first Mandan village at the junction of the Knife and Missouri rivers one hundred and fifty-seven days later, on October 26. The first snow had fallen five days earlier, and the welcome offered by the Mandans convinced the captains that they had found a promising spot for a winter camp.

In the spring the keelboat returned downstream to St. Louis, filled with all kinds of specimens, reports, and maps. Pilot of the keelboat was Joseph Gravelines, described as an honest man and an excellent boatman, who had been recruited the previous October en route from the Arikaras, among whom he had lived for several years. The squad led by Corporal Richard Warfington also went home, as did the few engagés who had wintered over among the Mandans. The keelboat took a mere forty-four days to do the homeward journey, from April 7 to May 20, 1805.

Rod and rope weren't all that took you up the Missouri in those days. You needed strength and willpower, not to mention experience. The French Canadians had all this. Deschamps piloted the red pirogue, while Cruzatte and Labiche were

The Mandan Paradise

The expedition's winter quarters were not chosen at random. The Mandans' reputation was widespread. In January 1798, David Thompson realized that the main reason traders made the long voyage into Mandan country was because of the Mandan women. "I found it was almost their sole motive for their journey thereto," he wrote (Glover, 1962: 234). He felt the Mandan women "were all courtesans; a sett of handsome tempting women" (234) who did everything they could "to heighten the voluptiousness of Love"—at which they were experts, having little else to do, especially the dancers (Wood and Thiessen: 117). The descriptions by Jean-Baptiste Trudeau that Lewis and Clark had in hand were even more explicit.

On January 1, 1805, New Year's Day was celebrated. The soldiers mingled with the Indians. Everyone danced, including York, at Clark's suggestion. The Indians were "Somewhat astonished that So large man should be active" (Thwaites, 1: 243). Biddle, Lewis and Clark's first editor, emphasized that "one of the Frenchmen … danced on his head." In this connection Thwaites (243, n. 1) notes that "Coues here asserts … that Clark explained to Biddle that the Frenchman danced on his hands, head downward"!

On January 2, the Mandans took things in hand and organized a buffalo dance on three successive nights. The young men offered their wives to the old men. "The Girl then takes the Old Man … and leads him to a convenient place for the business, after which they return to the lodge;" (Thwaites, 1: 245). The ritual had to be performed on a buffalo robe that served as the girl's only clothing. This was a way of sending a message to the herd to come near so that the cycle of life could be completed.

At other times, the purpose of this manoeuvre was to transmit the experience of the older tribe members through sexual relations. For the Mandans, as for many other Indians, whites were seen as old men and believed to have great powers and a new wisdom. Lewis and Clark would have to treat several cases of syphilis that winter. Possibly they took care of the engagés camped nearby as well. Fort Mandan was reserved for military personnel.

In 1806 the members of the expedition travelled downriver using the white pirogue (which they had recovered from its hiding place) and any other craft they could find. They would cover the distance from the Mandan village to St. Charles in thirty-six days (from August 17 to September 21), taking time out to stop and greet various Indian chiefs and try to convince some of them to accompany the returning expedition. On some days they covered 70 to 80 miles (110 to 130 kilometres), compared to about 6 miles (10 kilometres) a day on the outward trip.

(◉ James Alexander Thom has an interesting note on the contribution of the engagés at the end of his romanticized biography of Georges Drouillard, *Sign Talker*.

the bowmen of the keelboat. One can imagine them hardened to tough labour since childhood, yet good-natured, easygoing, and satisfied with their life. They rarely complained or deserted their post.

The French Canadians of the Missouri are the forgotten figures of history, at least as it has been studied and taught in Canada or the United States. Lewis and Clark themselves paid little attention to the Frenchmen whom they recruited or met. Reuben Thwaites, Gary Moulton, Roy Appleman, and Charles G. Clarke all say they are unable to draw up an exact list of the engagés. In this connection, it is noticeable that the expressions "Canada" and "Canadian" don't figure in the vocabulary of the expedition's officers and most American historians. Moulton, for example, describes Labiche and Cruzatte as both "half Omaha," the "sons of French traders," and so on.

Although little information ◉ has been gathered on the engagés hired by Lewis and Clark, we can still glean links with the villages of St. Louis, St. Charles, Ste. Geneviève, Kaskaskia, and Portage des Sioux. A number of these engagés were Métis born in the region. They were skilled in the ways of the wilderness, obviously clever and capable men, resourceful and trustworthy in all circumstances. Without them the Lewis and Clark Expedition could probably not have reached the Mandans—or at least not in such good shape.

Chapter 6

A Crucial Decision
and a "Curious Adventure"

The purpose of this book is not to tell the story of the Lewis and Clark Expedition from start to finish. A number of authors have already done this successfully: in French such writers as Michel LeBris, Annick Foucrier, and Michel Chaloult; in English numerous writers, with Stephen Ambrose, James Ronda, and Roy Appleman at the head of the line.

An article by Dayton Duncan inspired this chapter (in *We Proceeded On*, November 1998, v. 24, no. 4: 9-13). Among the decisive phases of the expedition were the crossing of the Rocky Mountains and the descent of the Columbia. But before these came the long portage made necessary by the Great Falls of the Missouri. It was here, too, that the men of the expedition encountered a particularly dangerous beast: the grizzly. On the day that Lewis realized the true extent of the Great Falls he also got some idea of the perils that awaited the expedition in the form of a charging grizzly bear. His account of his "curious adventure" is a fine example of the lively style of his journal.

One of Clark's maps is reproduced here, offering a telling example of how the talents of the two captains complemented each other.

On the morning of June 3, 1805, the members of the Lewis and Clark Expedition set up camp at the junction of two great rivers. Which should they follow—the north or south fork? Which was the true Missouri that would lead them to the foot of the Rocky Mountains, not too far, they hoped, from the source of the Columbia River, the route to the Pacific? The captains' only information had come from the Hidatsas, who insisted that there would be great falls on the

✳ Lewis had the greatest faith in Cruzatte, an old Missouri hand, noting on June 9, 1805, that "his integrity knowledge and skill as a waterman had acquired the confidence of every individual of the party" (Moulton, 4:27). However, Lewis chose the south fork, being strongly influenced by the maps of Fidler and the Indians, and the fact that the latter had described the Upper Missouri waters as "nearly transparent." An interesting detail is that "Big Muddy," as the Lower Missouri is nicknamed, gets this way because of the Marias River. Lewis's first description of the north fork, which he encountered on June 3, 1805, stressed the fact that "the north fork is deeper than the other but it's courant not so swift … ; it's waters are of a whitish brown colour very thick and terbid, also characteristic of the Missouri; while the South fork is perfectly transparent" (Moulton, 4: 248). See map.

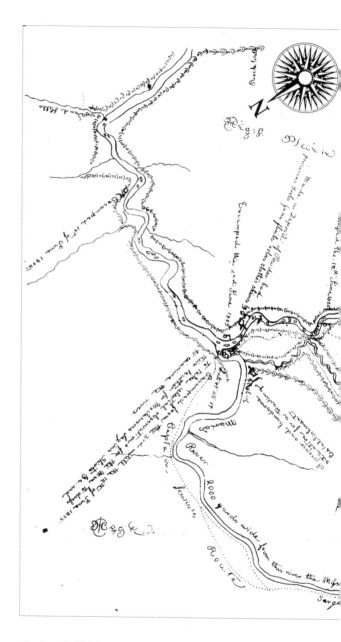

On June 3, 1805, Lewis and Clark reached a fork in the Missouri (see above, centre). The northwest branch ("north fork") would be known as the Marias River. The southwest branch ("south fork") would be

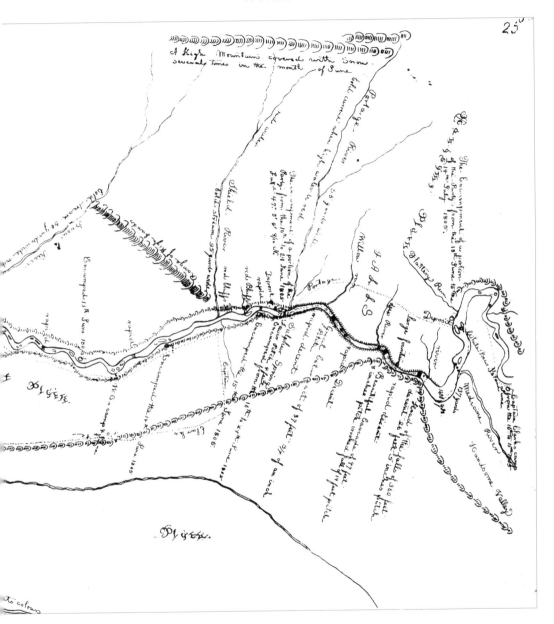

revealed as the true Missouri on which the explorers would find the great falls mentioned by the Indians. At the top right-hand side of this map, Clark has marked "High Mountains covered with Snow." The "Sulphur Spring" that healed Sacagawea is marked in the centre of the same page, beside the Missouri.

river they were seeking.

After some preliminary scouting, the captains decided to explore both routes for a short distance, each taking a small party. A few days' delay was a small price to pay compared to making the wrong choice. They set off the next day, Clark's party taking the south fork and returning on June 6. Lewis took his party up the north fork and returned on June 8, convinced that what he named "Maria's River" (after a cousin) was not the true Missouri. However most of the men in the expedition sided with the opinion expressed by Pierre Cruzatte, whose wide-ranging experience as a navigator was well known. He was sure they should take the north fork. He knew the Missouri well and the two captains held him in high esteem. *(See note on previous page.)* ✳

Nevertheless, Lewis and Clark were inclined to choose the south fork, based on their maps and

The Missouri Great Falls (two early views; Peterson, 1998). On Thursday, June 13, 1805, Lewis noted, "I had proceeded on this course about two miles with Goodrich at some distance behind me whin my ears were saluted with the agreeable sound of a fall of water and advancing a little further I saw a spray arrise above the plain like a collumn of smoke which would frequently disappear again in a instant caused I presume by the wind which blew pretty hard from the S.W. *(Note continues on next page)*

calculations (Moulton, 4: 271). The men accepted this decision, yet another indication of how much they respected their leaders' wisdom. That evening, June 9, they were "extreemly cheerfull" according to Lewis. Cruzatte brought out his violin, and before Lewis settled down for the night, somewhat recovered from a stomach ailment, he noted that the men had spent the evening dancing and singing. The next day they made preparations, hiding the red pirogue and burying a cache of supplies to be picked up on the return journey.

On June 11 Lewis and four men, including Drouillard, set off on foot beside the south fork. Clark and the main party would head up the south fork by water. On June 13 Lewis told his companions to hunt for game while he walked on alone to look for the falls. Soon his attention was caught "by the agreeable sound of a fall of water" and he "saw the spray arrise above the plain like a collumn of smoke ... which soon began to

"I did not however loose my direction to this point which soon began to make a roaring too tremendious to be mistaken for any cause short of the great falls of the Missouri. here I arrived about noon having traveled by estimate about 15 miles [24 kilometres]. I hurryed down the hill which was about 200 feet [60 metres] high and difficult of access, to gaze upon this sublimely grand specticle" (Moulton, 4: 283).

Crooked Falls (as Lewis named them) or Horseshoe Falls, for which Clark's estimated height of 19 feet (5.75 metres) is accurate. For the Great Falls, Clark calculated a height of 97 feet, 9 inches (29.75 metres), the actual height being 96 feet (29.25 metres)! His estimate of 42 feet, 8 inches (13 metres) for the Rainbow Falls is 4 feet, 4 inches (1.3 metres) too high. Clark estimated Colter Falls at 14 feet (4.25 metres). The actual height is 12 feet (3.65 metres).

make a roaring too tremendious to be mistaken for any cause short of the great falls of the Missouri." By noon, the spectacle of "a perfect white foam" greeted his eyes. Lewis was spellbound by the sight and described the falls in detail. Moved by its splendour, he wrote, "From the reflection of the sun on the spray or mist which arrises from these falls there is a beatifull rainbow produced which adds not a little to the beauty of this majestically grand scenery" (Moulton, 4: 283-284).

Lewis read over what he had just written. He decided to cross out everything and begin again, as his description did too little justice to the subject. He changed his mind, reflecting that perhaps he could do no better "than pening the first impressions of the mind" but "most sincerely regreted that I had not brought a crimee [camera] obscura with me." Instead, he decided to inspect the locale, hoping to find a place where "the canoes might arrive." Cliffs were everywhere, as though the water had "woarn a channel in the

process of time through a solid rock" (Moulton, 4: 286).

No matter: his companions had had good hunting. Later he wrote, "My fare is really sumptuous this evening; buffaloe's humps, tongues and marrowbones, fine trout✳ parched meal pepper and salt, and a good appetite; the last is not considered the least of the luxuries" (Moulton, 4:287). Lewis must have gone to bed that evening filled with a sense of euphoria, ready to meet any surprises the morrow might have in store for him—although certainly not the ones he expected.

June 14. Lewis rose before daybreak, no doubt still very excited. Joseph Field was ordered to take the good news to Clark. Drouillard, Gibson, and Goodrich were sent to gather the results of the previous day's hunt. Alone in their makeshift camp, Lewis savoured the moment. Around ten in the morning, nearly six hours after sunrise, he at last decided to explore the Missouri upstream in order to plan the inevitable portage.

Above: Black Eagle Falls, estimated by Clark at 26 feet, 5 inches (8 metres), actual height, 30 feet (9.14 metres). The dam later built here is called Black Eagle Dam. (The measurements are all Clark's because Lewis, while the better writer, bowed to his colleague's superior surveying abilities.)

A nearby promontory bears the name Indian Hill or Indian Butte because Indians used it as a lookout for observing buffalo herds or spotting enemies. (*Early views of Crooked and Black Eagle Falls, Peterson, 1998.*)

✳ "Cutthroat trout" or *Salmo clarkii* (Cutright, 1989: 157-158).

He had gone about five and a half miles (nine kilometres) when he came upon a second waterfall "about nineteen feet" (six metres) high, which he named "Crooked Falls." He wasn't much surprised, as he had been walking beside a continuous stretch of rapids with three small cataracts. As he stood musing, about

Buffalo. Catlin, 1913, pl.10.

to retrace his steps, he heard "a tremendious roaring above me." One of "the most beatifull objects in nature" awaited him—what is now called Rainbow Falls. "Here the river pitches over a shelving rock . . . without a nich or brake in it . . . in one even and uninterupted sheet." From a height of "about fifty feet" (fifteen metres; Lewis's estimate), this new fall stretched "at rightangles across the river from side to side" (Moulton, 4: 289-290). He compared it to a work of art, then thought of the first fall, but immediately gave up trying to decide which of these two great rivals was the more perfect, settling for "pleasingly beautifull" as a description of the one in front of him, and "sublimely grand" for the previous day's discovery. He hadn't gone a half-mile farther before a fourth, much lower fall rose in front of him (Colter Falls). Lewis "passed it by with little attention," by now at a loss for words!

Two and a half miles (four kilometres) upstream he found yet another waterfall that he estimated was of twenty-six feet (eight metres) high. A little below it lay a "beatifull little Island well timbered" in the middle of the river. Atop a cottonwood tree "an Eagle has placed her nest" (Moulton 4: 291). The Indians had spoken of this island, but hadn't made it clear that the "great falls" of the Missouri were in fact five successive falls. As Lewis contemplated the gruelling portage that faced the expedition, he was also very moved by the discovery of Black Eagle Falls, as the fifth became known. "It is certainly the greatest I ever beheld," he wrote, "greater . . . and more noble than the celebrated falls of Potomac or Soolkiln [probably Schuylkill]" (Moulton. 4: 291; 296, n. 5).

Beyond the fifth fall the river was calm. At last Lewis caught sight of "a most beautiful and extensive plain reaching from the river to the base of the Snowclad mountains to the S. and S. West." The Missouri itself, he noted, meandered toward the south. Another large river with well-wooded shores flowed into it from the west. Immense herds of buffalo grazed peacefully on the plain, while flocks of geese came to feed on the banks of the Missouri (Moulton, 4: 291).

Lewis thought it would be a good idea to kill a buffalo from the herd for later use. It was getting late and he still hadn't decided whether to return to camp that night. He chose "a very fat buffaloe and shot him

Grizzly.
Beth Berryman,
in Loftin, 73.

very well, through the lungs." He stood, silent and motionless, watching "the poor anamal discharging blood in streams from his mouth and nostrils, expecting him to fall every instant, and having entirely forgotten to reload my rifle" (Moulton, 4: 292).

Lewis looked up to find a grizzly watching him some twenty steps away. In a flash he remembered that his gun was empty. He was on open ground near the river, and he needed something to hide behind in order to reload.

Lewis considered "retreating in a brisk walk as fast as he was advancing untill I could reach a tree about 300 yards [275 metres] below me," but the bear "pitched at me, open mouthed and full speed, I ran about 80 yards [75 metres] and found he gained on me fast. . . . I ran hastily into the water about waist deep, and faced about and presented the point of my espontoon." The beast stopped at the water's edge, about twenty feet (six metres) from Lewis, then "suddenly wheeled about as if frightened, declined the combat on such unequal grounds, and retreated with quite as great precipitation as he had just before pursued me." Later that day, trying to understand this abrupt retreat, Lewis wrote that "the cause of his allarm still remains with me misterious and unaccountable" (Moulton, 4: 292-293).

Lewis's emotions were in for a further shock. Moments later he found himself face to face with an animal that he first took for a wolf before recognizing it as some sort of feline crouching near its den, ready to spring. Lewis fired, and the animal disappeared down its hole. Lewis felt "almost confident" that he had hit it (Moulton, 4: 293-294).

"It now seemed to me that all the beasts of the neighbourhood had made a league to distroy me," Lewis noted. That wasn't all. Shortly afterward, three "bull buffaloe" moved out from the herd and charged toward him. Was fate amusing itself at his expense, Lewis wondered? Instinctively he walked toward the three animals. They stopped in their tracks "within a hundred yards" before turning tail. Was he dreaming? "But the prickley pears which pierced my feet very severely . . . convinced me that I was really awake" (Moulton, 4: 294).

Despite the emotions of the day, Lewis took time to wonder about this animal that, at one point, "couched itself down like a cat looking immediately at me as if it designed to spring at me." He decided it "was of the tiger kind" (Moulton, 4: 293-294).

All in all, Lewis felt it was a good idea for him to rejoin the others, especially as they must be worried by his absence. Back in camp he found that Drouillard had decided to organize a search at daybreak. When he went to bed late that night, he was still trying to understand what had happened.

Perhaps Lewis's yellow flannel shirt had frightened off the buffalo, or possibly he radiated a sense of joy and invincibility that day. One thing was certain: he would not soon forget the events of this extraordinary June 14, 1805 — "this curious adventure," as he described it (Moulton, 4: 292).

Chapter 7

Georges Drouillard
"A Man of Much Merit"

George Drouillard, alias "Drewyer," is the true hero of the expeditionary corps and deserves special attention.

Drouillard, a Métis, appears to have retained the best of both worlds. He was in perfect harmony with man and nature. Without this superb hunter, the Corps of Discovery would have gone nowhere. Lewis's "portable soup" would never have been enough for men who could each devour between six and nine pounds of meat a day.

But there was also Drouillard the interpreter, the scout, and the negotiator. This chapter not only demonstrates his merits, however, but also one of Lewis's serious errors in judgment made on the return journey—an error that the captain fully realized. It would cost Drouillard his life a few years later.

The artist George Catlin took an interest in the Indians, whereas Alfred Jacob Miller was fascinated by the French-Canadian Métis. This and subsequent chapters

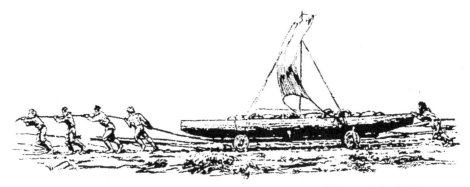

To portage past the great falls on the Missouri, the men of the expedition built makeshift trailers to carry their dugout canoes, loaded with supplies.

provide an opportunity to include samples of their work, among those of other artists who portrayed the American West.

As an illustration of the dangers arising from Lewis's error, I have included the story of John Colter, a member of the expedition who later became one of the legendary "mountain men." The story is interesting in itself, but also for John Bradbury's commentary on the probable cause of Blackfoot hostility.

Hired as an interpreter, Drouillard quickly revealed himself as the best hunter in the group. How many times did Lewis and Clark send Drouillard and the two Fields brothers "to kill some meat"? Historian Arlen J. Large counted mentions of hunting forays in the journals (*We Proceeded On*, Feb. 1, 1994). The Fields brothers were well ahead, Joseph with eighty-three mentions and Reuben with ninety-two. They beat John Shield (sixty-three mentions), John Collins (sixty-one), young George Shannon (fifty-three), and François Labiche (forty-two). Georges Drouillard took the palm, however, with one hundred and fifty-three mentions! During the winter spent at Fort Clatsop Clark noted that the expedition would have survived badly, if at all, without the efforts of this excellent hunter (Moulton, 6: 200).

Hunting pronghorn. (Harpers Weekly, May 23, 1873).

"To kill some meat"

Such was Lewis's expression when he sent his best hunters to shoot some game. How many animals were killed by Drouillard and the Fields brothers, Reubin and Joseph? It's impossible to tell, obviously, but the records show that on occasion Drouillard killed seven or eight animals in a single outing—these being various members of the deer family. Early in the expedition, during the journey from St. Charles to the Mandan villages, there were over forty men each eating between six to nine pounds of meat a day. This translates into four or five deer a day. We know that between the Mississippi and the Kansas River the expedition's hunters killed at least seventy deer. Sometimes Drouillard would also kill bear and beaver. Not only was he a good shot; he knew how to track game. He had endurance and strength. He was also a master at finding his bearings and lost no time getting back to the main party. Often he would leave the game lying along the expedition's route. In a single day, January 12, 1806, Drouillard and another hunter, unidentified by Clark, killed "7 Elk." Clark was truly impressed, and took time to make the following comment: "Maney others also exert themselves, but not being acquainted with the best method of finding and killing the elk and no other wild animals is to be found in this quarter, they are unsucksessfull in their exertions" (Moulton, 6: 200). Lewis and Clark spoke of deer and elk. On the Pacific coast they encountered an unfamiliar type (Moulton, 3: 237). It was the Columbian black-tailed deer (*dama hemionus columbianus*) rather than the white-tailed variety (*dama virginianus*) (Cutright, 1989: 52 and 242). West coast Indians told them that elk were abundant, larger than deer, easy to hunt, and provided better meat (Moulton, 3: 249). This was to be an important factor in choosing their winter camp.

The handkerchief trick: Luring pronghorn was easy, according to artist George Catlin (1796-1872). They were very curious animals, he explained—a trait that sometimes cost them their lives. Hunters who knew this would attract them by simply tying a handkerchief to the end of a stick. This enabled them to kill two or three animals at one go (Catlin, 1913, 1, fig. 40: 145).

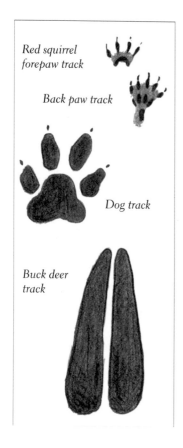

Red squirrel
forepaw track

Back paw track

Dog track

Buck deer
track

✳ Lewis got his low opinion of
the Blackfeet from their enemies,
the Shoshones and Nez Percés.
Possibly he had a premonition, or
perhaps this passage was rewritten
in an attempt to justify, if not
explain, the subsequent blunder.
(See Moulton 8: 115, n. 7.)

Drouillard was called upon constantly—whether to recover escaped or stolen horses, pursue a deserter (Private Moses B. Reed), bring Indians around to a more receptive way of thinking (such as two quarrelling Nez Percés chiefs), or to serve as a guide. When the expedition was returning along the Lolo Trail, Lewis wrote of "Drewyer our principal dependence as a woods-man and guide" (Moulton, 8: 31).

Lewis took Drouillard with him when looking for the Missouri falls, scouting for the Shoshones, and exploring the Marias River country on the return journey.

For this important excursion into dangerous Blackfoot territory, Lewis chose the Fields brothers as well as Drouillard—the three best shots in the expedition. Lewis anxiously confided to his journal, "The blackfoot indians rove through this quarter of the country and as they are a vicious lawless and reather an abandoned set of wretches✳ I wish to avoid an interview with them if possible" (Moulton, 8: 113).

A Regrettable Incident

The Blackfeet turned up nine days later. Eight of them were visible, but others were probably hiding, since Lewis noticed saddled but riderless horses. He was on the alert and determined "to resist to the last extremity, prefering death to that of being deprived of my papers instruments and gun" (Moulton, 8: 129).

After exchanging greetings and distributing the usual gifts of medals and flags, Lewis suggested to the Indians—apparently Piegans of the Blackfoot nation— that they camp together for the night. This was a supreme error on his part. In the morning, an Indian grabbed the Field brothers' guns and made off at top speed. The Indian was out of luck, for Reubin Field was one of the two best runners in the Corps of Discovery, Drouillard being the other. Field caught up with the warrior within fifty paces, grabbed his gun, and stabbed the Indian in the heart.

The tumult awoke Drouillard and Lewis who found two other Indians in the act of stealing their guns. Drouillard wrested one weapon away. Meanwhile, the second Indian was fleeing with Lewis's rifle. Lewis pulled out a pistol and "bid him lay down my gun." The Fields brothers "drew up their guns to shoot," but the Blackfoot dropped the weapon, and Lewis asked everyone to keep calm. In the confusion, the Indians tried to make off with all the horses. Lewis states that after several warnings he raised his gun to his shoulder and shot one of the Indians in the stomach. "He fell on his knees … and fired at me," then "crawled in behind a rock." Was he mortally wounded? Lewis would never know. The man stabbed by Reubin Field lay dead. Lewis had given this man a medal the day before. In a rage, he decided to leave the medal around the dead man's neck, "that they might be informed who we were" (Moulton, 8: 134-135).✳

Lewis and his men burned the weapons abandoned by the Indians, rounded up four of the latter's horses, and set off. This flight—the word is apt—is recounted in the next chapter. By the next day they had rejoined the rest of the expedition on the Missouri.

Lewis's journal entries show that he was well aware of the gravity of this incident. Despite his careful narration of the affair, however, the fact remained that one Indian and possibly two had been killed.

An Eye for an Eye

Nearly four years later, early in 1810, Blackfeet attacked two former members of the Lewis and Clark Expedition, John Potts and John Colter, near a place called Three Forks. Potts was killed, and Colter, who chose to surrender, managed to get out of this tight spot alive. A month later he told people in St. Louis of his astonishing adventure.

Drouillard was among the next victims of the Blackfeet, who gave him no quarter. They had been prowling about an area where a number of trappers were

✳ The Piegans belonged to the Blackfoot Confederation and were Algonkians. French-Canadian trappers were on good terms with the Blackfeet and gave them guns. Some commentators feel that Blackfoot animosity toward Americans originated in the incident of July 27, 1806—the result of a grave error on Lewis's part. The care he took to give a detailed account of the incident reveals his anxiety in this regard. It is also true that, as far as the Blackfeet were concerned, the arrival of the Americans in these regions meant that their enemies—the Shoshone, Crow, Flatheads, and Nez Percés—could get guns (Moulton, 8: 132, n. 8).

This American medal, similar to the one left on the body, was as good as a signature. The Blackfeet understood, and were fired with a desire for vengeance.

working for Kaskaskia merchant Pierre Ménard, the partner of St. Louis fur trader Manuel Lisa. On April 12, 1810, five trappers were killed. Ménard's men, some twenty in all, hesitated to do the rounds of their traps. Drouillard decided to keep on working and did so without difficulty until a band of Blackfeet attacked him.

Thomas James, in *Three Years Among the Indians*, described the scene that met his eyes when he discovered Drouillard and the two Indians who had been with him. M.O. Skarsten, in an interesting biography devoted to Drouillard, reconstituted the scene based on James's description. One shudders on reading it. It is sickening to think that a man of Drouillard's stamp should die such a

---

Colter's Story

The Indians disarmed John Colter and stripped him naked. To amuse themselves at his expense, they allowed him a slight head start and then ran after him. Colter killed his closest pursuer, then plunged into the Jefferson River where he was able to hide until the Indians gave up trying to find him. After taking care of his feet, which were full of thorns from prickly pears, he hurried to Fort Lisa.

Thomas James, a trapper for the Missouri Fur Company of St. Louis, recounted Colter's adventure in *Three Years Among the Indians and Mexicans* (1846). John Bradbury, a St. Louis botanist, gave his version of the story in *Travels in the Interior of America in the Years 1809, 1810, and 1811*, published in Liverpool in 1817. Bradbury's version seems more likely, although it hardly matters, seeing that Colter's adventure has now become the stuff of legend. Bradbury's account, however, contains a very telling comment with regard to the consequences of Lewis's act: "Aware of the hostility of the Blackfoot Indians, one of whom had been killed by Capt. Lewis, they [Potts and Colter] set their traps at night and took them up early in the morning, remaining concealed during the day" (Colter-Frick: 16).

Charles Russell. Amon Carter Museum.

horrible death. Lewis's blunder comes to mind. That medal laid on the corpse was a signature. The Blackfeet understood perfectly and were filled with a desire for vengeance.

Drouillard's attackers weren't content merely to kill him. "Druyer and his horse lay dead," James recounted, "the former mangled in a horrible manner; his head was cut off, his entrails torn out, and his body hacked to pieces. We saw from the marks on the ground that he must have fought in a circle on horseback, and probably killed some of his enemies, being a brave man, and well armed with a rifle, pistol, knife and toma -hawk" (Skarsten: 310).

On returning to St. Louis, Pierre Ménard recounted the misadventures of his trappers. The *Louisiana Gazette* of July 26, 1810, reminded readers of the Blackfeet's anger regarding the Americans' trade relations with their enemies, the Crows. The paper recalled the massacre of April 12 and gave the names of the victims before detailing the circumstances of Drouillard's death. "He [Drouillard] was attacked by a party in ambush by whom himself and two of his men were literally cut to pieces. It seems from circumstances that Drouillard made a most obstinate resistance as he made a kind of breastwork of his horse, whom he made to turn in order to receive the enemy's fire, his bulwark, of course, soon failed and he became the next victim of their fury" (Holmberg: 11).✳

Sixty years later, Ménard's son, Pierre Jr., gave his version to historian Lyman C. Draper. According to this version, the mutilation of Drouillard's body by the Blackfeet suggested that they had scores to settle with him and that that they wanted to send a warning to the Americans (Holmberg: 12).

How old was Drouillard? And what do we know about his origins?

✳ "Early in May George Druilard accompanied by some Delawares, who were in the employ of the [Missouri Fur] Company, went out to hunt, contrary to the wishes of the rest of the party who were confident the Indians were in motion around them, and that from a hostile disposition they had already shewn it would be attended with danger, their presages were too true, he had not proceeded more than two miles from the camp before he was attacked by a party in ambush by which himself and two of his men were literally cut to pieces." (Pierre Menard, in his interview with the *Louisiana Gazette*, June 26, 1810, reprinted in Thomas James, *Three Years among the Indians and Mexicans*, St. Louis, Missouri Historical Society, 1916.) The riches in furs that made taking risks worthwhile can be judged from Menard's closing remarks: "Adding all those untoward circumstances the Fur Company have every prospect of success, although the majority of the season was occupied in distributing the hunting parties and exploring the foot of the mountains, ... yet they have been able to send down about fifty packs of Beaver, besides other Furs of a considerable amount and have taken measures to ensure more than double that quantity in the Spring."

Portrait of Antoine Clément

There is no existing portrait of Georges Drouillard. However, James Alexander Thom and Charles G. Clarke have both tried to describe this extraordinary man. A few years later, the artist Alfred Jacob Miller became interested in Indians and French Canadians as attractive subjects, and particularly Métis. In 1837, he accompanied the eccentric William Drummond Stewart to the Far West. Antoine Clément served as guide and hunter for this expedition. In his notebooks, Miller said of Clément: "The subject of the sketch is a half-breed (that is, his father was a Canadian, his mother an Indian) and one of the noblest specimens of a Western hunter: in the outward journey he killed for us about 120 buffalo." Drouillard must have had the look, stature, and proud bearing of Clément, although he was a more disciplined and more serious individual (see Ross: XIX, 2, 37, 155).

Georges Drouillard—"Drewyer," as Lewis and Clark referred to him—was known as a Shawnee Métis. His father, Pierre Drouillard, lived in Detroit where he married Angélique Descamps in 1776. Was Georges born before or after this marriage? We don't know, but a letter written to his half-sister, Marie-Louise, on May 23, 1809, seems to indicate that the family readily accepted their half-Indian brother. The very fact that Drouillard kept in touch with his relatives and the tone of the letter suggest good relations. He closed with these words: "My respects to our Mother who I embrace well, also all my brothers and sisters who I would like very much to see" (Skarsten: 19).

With his mixed heritage, Drouillard seems to have embodied the best of both cultures. Historians agree that he was the most important man in the expedition after the two leaders.

"A man of much merit," concluded Lewis in his report, "who has uniformly acquitted himself with honor" (Thwaites, 7: 359). This time, Lewis wrote "George Drulyard" and not "Drewyer" as was his habit—perhaps a sudden mark of respect. When the expedition started out, Lewis didn't have much esteem for the French Canadians. They were British subjects, and although Catholics, too inclined to have a good

Skarsten cites Drouillard's letter in English, but in what language was it written? Did Drouillard himself write it? One would like to know more about this key figure in the Lewis and Clark expedition.

Look

Tell me

Give

Much

"A Man of Much Merit"

"A man of much merit, he has been peculiarly useful from his knowledge of the common language of gesticulation, and his uncommon skill as a hunter and woodsman; those several duties he performed in good faith, and with an ardor which deserves the highest commendation. It is his fate also to have encountered on various occasions, with either Captain Clark or myself, all the most dangerous and trying scenes of the voyage, in which he uniformly acquitted himself with honor," wrote Lewis of Drouillard (Thwaites, 7: 359). Lewis would have liked him to receive the minimum salary of $30 per month. Drouillard actually received $833.33 for his thirty-three months and ten days' service, or $25 per month as an interpreter, like Toussaint Charbonneau. Note that the latter only served sixteen months, eleven days. Both men received five times as much pay as the soldiers (Thwaites, 7: 361).

time. Their ties with the Indians bothered him as well. Men with outstanding qualities such as Drouillard, Cruzatte, and Labiche no doubt led him to suppress a natural aversion.

Clark displayed a far more open mind in this respect, although this didn't prevent him, in later days, from initially refusing his slave York's request to be freed. Lewis and Clark were indeed men of their time and their country.

Chapter 8

Seaman's Fate

Lewis's dog Seaman was a Newfoundland—a breed developed by early fishermen on the island. This dog's most outstanding attribute is its habit of spontaneously jumping into the water to save anyone in trouble. The Newfoundland is also patient, hardy in cold weather, and devoted to its master. It is thought that Basque fishermen on the Grand Banks insisted on having a Newfoundland aboard their fishing boats. What gave me the idea of giving a chapter to Seaman? Tongue-in-cheek, my answer might be that he was a Canadian, but of course Newfoundland wasn't part of the fledgling Canada at the time.

I am discussing Seaman for two reasons. Analyses of the handwriting in the Lewis and Clark journals have produced two possible ways of deciphering the name of Lewis's dog: Seaman or Scannon. This offered an opportunity to show why, as with all documents of the past, a careful paleographic approach is necessary.

As well, I wished to point out that Seaman's fate has genuinely interested more than one researcher. Among them is James J. Holmberg, who has carried out a serious enquiry recorded in an article for *We Proceeded On*, the scholarly journal of studies on the Lewis and Clark Expedition. It is a model of its type.

After all, as Robert Delort has shown in *Les animaux ont une histoire* (Seuil, 1984), animals, too, have their history.

Lewis felt profound respect and great friendship for Clark. He soon acquired an equal appreciation for most of his men, Georges Drouillard in particular. Drouillard was the man for difficult missions, and Lewis was well pleased to have him along. This was the case on the return voyage, when he decided to explore the Marias River. This unfortunate phase of the expedition would have fatal consequences for Drouillard in the long run, as we saw in the preceding chapter.

✳ Seaman (referred to as "Scannon" by some) is rarely called by name in the explorers' journals. When mentioned by Clark or Ordway, some read Scannon, others Seaman. The "c" resembles an "e," the "m" could be read as "nn," and the final syllable is sometimes written as "on" or "an" in both versions. A comparison of the different handwriting leads me to think that the dog's true name is Seaman. This example demonstrates the difficulties inherent in transcribing the manuscripts of the Lewis and Clark Expedition.

◉ Lewis had less need of the Indians on the return journey. He was more impatient and sometimes even aggressive. According to Lewis, the Indians in question were the Wah-Clel-Lars. On April 9, 1806, Lewis talked of a village called Wah-Clel-Lah close to magnificent falls. These are probably either the Multnomah or the Horsetail Falls, suggests Moulton (7: 100, n. 4). As for Indians deemed "very unfriendly" by Lewis, these were probably the Watlala Chinookians (Moulton, 7: 100, n. 1).

Was the same true for another of Lewis's inseparable companions, his favourite after Clark and Drouillard?

More than once during his long mission, Lewis lost patience. He was not one to suffer a mistake gladly or be tolerant of what he considered peculiar behaviour. If it was a question of his dog Seaman, his temper could get the better of him. ✳

"Fire on them!" Lewis ordered when Indians made off with Seaman. For several days they had been circling around the expedition as it moved laboriously up the Columbia River. The Americans had been keeping a close watch on them. Attempts at theft became more frequent. On the evening of April 11, 1806 three Indians went too far. Lewis, mad with rage, sent three of his men "in pursuit of the theives with orders if they made the least resistence or difficulty in surrendering the dog to fire on them" (Moulton 7: 105). ◉ This was the first time in two years that Lewis had given an order to fire on Indians. The dognappers soon realized that they had better let Seaman go. Lewis's anger was not easily quelled, however. When another petty theft in the camp occurred—"an ax" this time—he put everyone on guard. The Indians were warned "by signs that if they made any further attempts to steal our property or insulted our men we should put them to instant death" (Moulton 7: 105).

As for Seaman, Lewis mentions him for the last time on July 15, 1806. On that day the poor dog was howling as mosquitoes tormented him. What became of Seaman after this? A number of writers have pondered the question, especially authors of children's books.

Seaman Enters Children's Literature

Film writer and director Roland Smith is especially interested in animals and made Seaman the hero of his short book, *The Captain's Dog* (Harcourt Brace, 1999). Smith suggests that Seaman was with Lewis during the exploration of the Marias River. The murderous skirmish of the morning of July 27, 1806 provoked a frantic flight by the Americans, who covered a distance of some 120 miles (200 kilometres) in just over twenty-four hours. According to Smith, Seaman could not have kept up such a pace. Was Lewis so terrified that he was ready to abandon his dog? It is difficult to believe. And why didn't Seaman raise the alarm at the

Newfoundlands are known for their patience and devotion.
Montage of drawings by Uebing Cavender (*The Newfoundland Annual*, 1998, 66-67.)

attempted theft that led to the shooting of two Blackfeet?

Gail Karkoski, in *Seaman the Dog Who Helped Lewis & Clark Explore the West* (1999), simply lets the reader believe that Seaman ended his days running free somewhere in the Upper Missouri region.

A few months earlier, in 1998, veterinary R.W. Gustafson took a more romantic view in a little book for children, *The Dog Who Helped Explore America*. If Seaman was very attached to his master, we may also suppose that the Newfoundland made it his duty to keep an eye on Sacagawea's child. Gustafson imagines Seaman spending peaceful days with Clark and little Jean-Baptiste Charbonneau after the child had been entrusted to the captain, who had offered to supervise his education.

An Intriguing Search

The fate of Seaman would have remained a complete mystery without the insightful research of James J. Holmberg, published in the magazine *We Proceeded On*. Holmberg has written extensively on the Lewis and Clark Expedition and is curator of special collections at the Filson Historical Society in Louisville, Kentucky. At first reading, his story seems almost unbelievable, and yet . . .

In 1814, when the first edition of Lewis and Clark's journals under the direction of Nicholas Biddle appeared, Timothy Alden published a series of five books (apparently at his own expense) entitled *A Collection of American Epitaphs and Inscriptions with Occasional Notes*. Alden was a man of letters, as well as a respected pastor and educator who was passionately interested in history. He had begun modestly by noting down epitaphs on monuments and tombstones and methodically recording every inscription that he encountered. Among these were the following words inscribed on a dog collar: "The greatest traveller of my species. My name is Seaman, the dog of captain Meriwether Lewis whom I accompanied to the pacifick ocean through the interior of the continent of North America" (Holmberg: 8).

It is generally admitted that the Viking explorer Lief Ericsson was accompanied by an enormous dog called Oolum, and that this dog and others were crossed with dogs on the island of Newfoundland when Europeans returned around 1500, or perhaps before.

Where did Alden see this collar? In the Alexandria Museum, he noted—and nothing more. Jim Holmberg, despite taking Alden very seriously, felt he owed it to himself to explore further. Here is what he was able to establish.

In 1812, a Masonic Lodge in Alexandria, Virginia, decided to open a museum. On August 21 one of the lodge's officers, Thomas Sanford, wrote Clark to thank him for the gifts he had made to their budding institution. The letter didn't provide a descriptive list of the gifts, but its author stated that they were curiosities worthy of being ranked among the most important exhibits of the new museum.

If we take the words of the inscription noted by Alden seriously, it is possible to imagine Seaman's last days, something Alden has obligingly done for his readers, evoking the dog's remarkable loyalty and affection after what was probably Lewis's suicide. "The fidelity and attachment of this animal were remarkable. After the melancholy exit of gov. Lewis, his dog would not depart for a moment from his lifeless remains; and when they were deposited in the earth no gentle means could draw him from the spot of interment. He refused to take every kind of food, which was offered him, and actually pined away and died with grief upon his master's grave!" (Holmberg : 8).

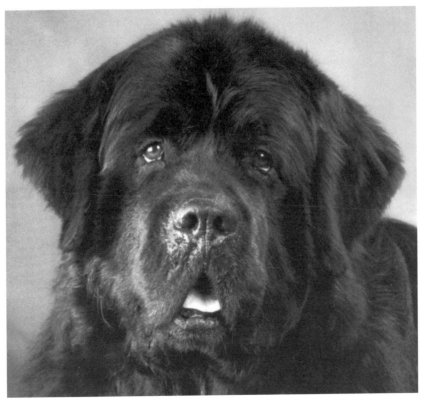

According to Lewis and Clark scholar Ernest S. Osgood, Newfoundland dogs may have come originally from the Pyrenees, brought to the New World by Basques who appreciated their strength and endurance, as well as their swimming prowess.

Timothy Alden was a member of a number of historical societies and clearly a conscientious worker. When he wrote about Seaman's death, Nicholas Biddle and William Clark were still alive and well and could have contradicted him. Of course, he might hope that they would never see these five volumes of epitaphs and inscriptions. On the other hand, he may well have contacted them before writing his commentary. This is the most plausible theory, and one that Holmberg supports. To check it out, he got in touch with the head of the new Alexandria lodge, Jack Riddell, who had preserved several precious documents, including the minutes and an incomplete catalogue of the former museum (most of its contents had been destroyed by a fire in 1871). The catalogue contains no mention of the collar. We are left with Sanford's letter to Clark of August 21, 1812, and above all with the credibility accorded Alden's statements.

Did Seaman return from the expedition with his master? We must believe that he did. It's hard to imagine that his disappearance would go unmentioned by Lewis, Clark, Ordway, Gass, or Whitehouse. Did Seaman die on Lewis's tomb? Why not? Is it not a Newfoundland's nature to show an abiding affection for its master?

In a sense, Seaman can be considered Canadian in origin, much as Drouillard, Charbonneau, Labiche, Lepage, Deschamps, and others. Like them, he contributed in his own way to the expedition's success. In that case, do not his role and his final days deserve to be recounted, especially as was done in Holmberg's intriguing and perfectly credible inquiry?

Chapter 9

Charting the Territory

Before setting off on their journey up the Missouri, Lewis and Clark were able to consult several maps drawn by, or based on the reports of, explorers who had preceded them. The most important of these was Aaron Arrowsmith's map, which provides a reminder of the astute and daring explorers who contributed to the data on which the map was based. Least known among these is probably Peter Fidler.

This is also the moment to emphasize the contribution made by the Indians. Apart from the coming and going of traders, the Missouri had been the target for exploratory missions such as those led by James Mackay and Jean-Baptiste Trudeau. Both men had kept their journals in French, something that would bother Lewis.

Lastly there was information to be gained from the Spanish authorities, who possessed the territory between 1762 and 1800 and often depended for personnel on French Canadians, or from French citizens such as Antoine Soulard, surveyor general of Louisiana at the moment when Lewis landed in St. Louis.

The goal of the Lewis and Clark expedition was clear: to reach the Pacific by a navigable waterway. But which one? The most likely itinerary, to all appearances, was to travel up the Missouri to its source, cross a mountain range, find the source of the Columbia, and follow it to the ocean. As the latitudes of these two major rivers seemed fairly close, this stood a good chance of being a practical route.

In fact, the mouth of the Missouri lay at 37° north, but at its Great Bend in Mandan country it reached 46° north, almost the same latitude as the mouth of the Columbia.

Lewis had little time to make many inquiries about the route. Once President Jefferson had obtained the approval of Congress, Lewis had to plunge into an intensive course of study covering a variety of subjects such as botany, medicine, and astronomy. He also had to prepare his list of equipment, food supplies, and munitions, design a keelboat according to particular specifications, and recruit the men needed for the expedition.

When everything was ready, or almost ready, it was too late in the season to start up the Missouri, especially as the American purchase of Louisiana had created a new context by changing the political situation. Lewis had to wait until the following spring to give the signal for departure. He and his teammate Clark then had time to wonder about the nature of the territory they would have to cross. They had some idea of the distance to be covered—but what was the terrain like? What kind of navigational conditions would the expedition encounter on the Missouri, for example, then on the Columbia? Would they be similar to those on the Ohio? Were there falls requiring portages?

The Theory of a Symmetrical Continent

Ever since the voyages of Father Jacques Marquette and the explorer Louis Jolliet, the Missouri had been considered the most probable route to the Pacific. It was thought that this imposing waterway had its source in mountains, and that on the other side of these mountains there were rivers flowing toward the Pacific. It was a normal supposition. In all logic, the same river couldn't run in two directions.

Somewhere between the Mississippi and the Pacific, therefore, there must be a mountain range creating a watershed similar to that in eastern North America, according to the theory that the continent was somewhat symmetrical. Just as rivers rising in the Appalachians flowed either toward the Atlantic or the Mississippi, others must rise in the western range to empty into the Mississippi, as did the Missouri, or into the Pacific, as did the Columbia. Naturally, geographic depictions of the time suggested the presence of a western range similar to the low eastern range in terms of both altitude and topography. It was a theory that remained to be proven.

Peter Fidler Pushes Back the Frontiers of the Unknown

In the same way that European explorers had learned to use Indian, Métis, or French-Canadian guides, land surveyors thought of getting information from the Indians. One of them was Peter Fidler of the Hudson's Bay Company, working out of Chesterfield House at the confluence of the Red Deer and South Saskatchewan rivers. In September 1800 this trading post lay at the frontier of territories known to Europeans. Here Fidler was visited by Blackfeet, Kootenays, Snakes, and Nez

Percés who were familiar with the regions to the north, south, and west. A number of these Indians circulated over vast stretches of land, crossing the Rockies and following routes toward the Pacific.

Fidler was at ease among Indians, being married to a Cree named Mary, and spoke Chipewyan, Piegan, and possibly other Indian languages. A man of an enquiring mind, Fidler was always keen to know more about native North American peoples and their territories. He asked questions and, even more important, took notes. Fidler was an educated man who never stopped enlarging his knowledge, especially when he came in contact with the surveyor Philip Turnor. This was how

Thompson among the Mandans

In 1797 David Thompson reached the Mandan village with a group of French-Canadian traders. He questioned two visitors who had arrived from the Upper Missouri. They told him of sizeable tributaries such as the Yellowstone, of enormous falls near the sources of the Missouri, and above all of the existence of three mountain ranges. This information contradicted the generally accepted idea of a single range that could be crossed with a short portage. Thompson was inclined to believe his informants, remarking that "they appeared to be very intelligent, as almost all Natives of the Mountain area" (Nisbet: 45).

The illustration shows a Mandan village on the Missouri
by Charles Russell, Amon Carter Museum.

Philip Turnor, "surveyor and astronomer" in the service of the Hudson's Bay Company, taught Peter Fidler and David Thompson surveying techniques at Cumberland House, Saskatchewan, during the winter of 1789-1790. Since Thompson was slowly recovering from a serious leg wound, it was Fidler who later accompanied Turnor on an expedition to Fort Chipewyan on Lake Athabasca. The party was made up of Turnor, Fidler, Malchom Ross with his Indian wife and two children, and "four Orkney servants" (Nisbet, 1995: 33-35, and E.E. Rich, *DCB*, 4: 740-742).

Like David Thompson, Peter Fidler married an Indian woman, first according to "the custom of the country," then formally. She survived Fidler and eleven of their fourteen children. See the excellent biography by Robert S. Allen in *DCB*, 6: 249-252. Above: Indian woman depicted by Alfred Jacob Miller (Ross, 1951, no. 11).

he learned the rudiments of cartography.

When Old Swan, the second Blackfoot chief of that name, agreed to describe the western part of the Prairies occupied by his people, Fidler hastened to draw maps. He was therefore the first white man to depict the Missouri drainage basin, at the same time showing new information about the Rockies and their extent.

In London, mapmaker Aaron Arrowsmith prepared a new version of his 1795 map of North America. He quickly included the information supplied by Fidler and his Indian informants. A few months later his new map, published in 1802, was in the hands of President Jefferson, and then Lewis and Clark.

On the day that the expedition came upon the mouth of the Marias River, Lewis began to doubt "the varacity of Mr. Fidler or the correctness of his instruments" (Moulton, 4: 266)—a remark that proves that Lewis, who had in hand Arrowsmith's most recent map of North America, knew that the information in question came from Fidler. Given his present latitude of 47° 24' 12.8" and the assumption that "we are now within a hundred miles of the Rocky Mountains," Lewis was puzzled. "[T]he [Missouri] river must therefore turn much to the South, between this and the rocky Mountain to have permitted Mr. Fidler to have passed along the Eastern border of these mountains as far S. as nearly 45° without even seeing it" (Moulton, 4: 266-267). Both Lewis and Clark noted that they would have to make corrections to Fidler's data and to the information they themselves had sent to Washington the preceding spring, when they had trusted to descriptions provided by Indians to estimate the course of the Missouri and its point of contact with the Rockies. "I think therefore that we shall find that the Missouri enters the rocky mountains to the North of 45°," concluded Lewis in his entry for June 8, 1805, noting that "I rather suspect that the actual observation will take him [Fidler] at least one other degree further North." (Moulton, 4: 267).

Unlike Fidler, Lewis and his men obviously had the advantage of being able to make observations on the terrain and complement the data supplied by the Indians.

Apart from Fidler's maps, Lewis and Clark took with them at least three others, attributable to Jean-Baptiste Trudeau (or Truteau), James Mackay, and Antoine Soulard.

Fidler, Mackenzie, and Thompson: Arrowsmith's Informants

In preparing his maps, Arrowsmith used data supplied by Peter Fidler and two other celebrated Canadian explorers, David Thompson and Alexander Mackenzie (Lavender: 33-34). Jack Nisbet in *Sources of the River* (1994: 76) states that when Lewis and Clark set off on the Missouri in 1804, they carried with them a map that David Thompson had prepared on his expedition among the Mandans seven years earlier. Lewis and Clark never mention Thompson. However, according to Masson (1889: 310-311), Larocque reported that Lewis and Clark "found all the longitudes estimated by David Thompson to be inaccurate" (Thwaites, 1: 246, n. 1).

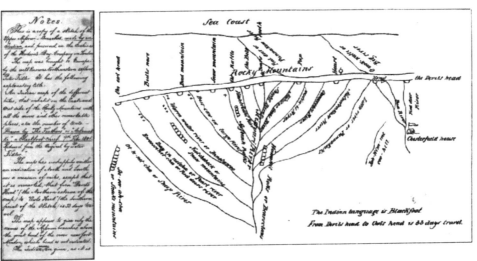

"This is a copy of a sketch of the Upper Missouri's Branches, made by an Indian and preserved in the Archives of the Hudson's Bay Company in London. ... Drawn by ... a Blackfoot chief... Feb. 1801. ... Pictured [i.e., copied] from the original by Peter Fidler."

Three Tentative Expeditions

Trudeau and Mackay met on the Mississippi in the spring of 1796. Each had been put in charge of an expedition to the Mandan country by the Upper Missouri Company, a new enterprise formed in St. Louis in May 1794. The company's directors faced several challenges. Their main task was to organize or rather regulate trade on the Missouri and to back up Spanish authority against inroads by British traders coming from the north, in particular via the Assiniboine River. The ultimate objective was to find the sources of the Missouri and somehow get to the Pacific coast, with a view to gaining access to the Chinese market as well as preventing the spread of Russian traders. No small mission!

As of June 1794, several months before receiving royal sanction (Parks: 50), the Upper Missouri Company organized a first expedition led by Jean-Baptiste Trudeau of St. Louis. Born in Montreal on December 11, 1748, Trudeau apparently went into the fur trade at a young age, since he stated in 1794 that he had twenty-six years' experience with tribes both east and west of the Mississippi.

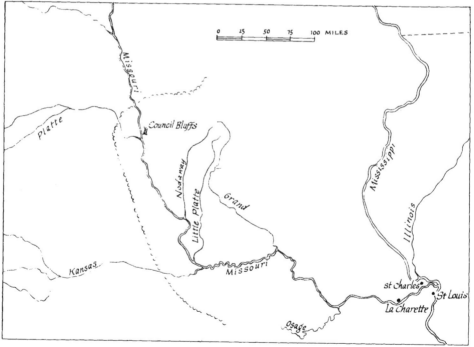

The Missouri from St. Louis to the Platte River
(John Logan Allen, 1991).

The expedition's financial backers had high expectations. Trudeau, with his wide background of experience, was determined to succeed. His instructions were precise. Once among the Mandans, he was to build a fort containing two buildings surrounded by a garden. He must also establish good relations with the Indians, check on their needs, and settle the conditions of future trade. He had to keep a journal containing all information gathered, both about the Indians and the geography of the

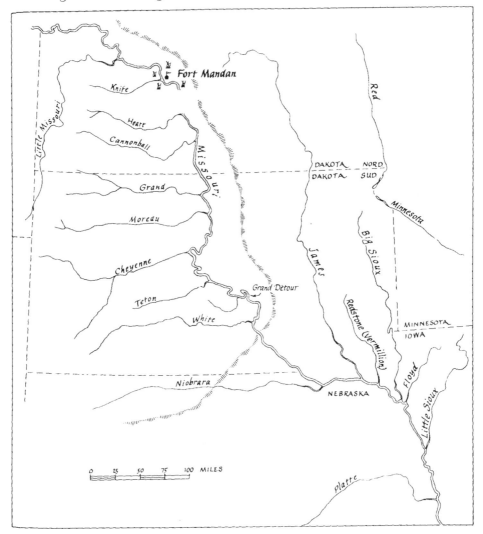

The Missouri from the Platte River to the Mandan village
(John Logan Allen, 1991).

land he passed through. In this regard, he fulfilled his instructions assiduously.

Before Trudeau's return, however, the Upper Missouri Company sent out a second expedition in June 1795, headed by a man named Lécuyer. Despite the large sums invested, this expedition got off to a very bad start. News of its difficulties soon reached St. Louis. The stakes were too great for the company to resign itself to failure, and a third expedition was immediately got ready. It was entrusted to a former agent of the North West Company, a man by the name of James Mackay who had taken Spanish nationality two years earlier. By the end of August 1795 he was on his way and had stopped to winter over among the Omahas. He had a fort built, which he named St. Charles in honour of the king of Spain. Mackay made a rather unusual choice of lieutenant—one John Thomas Evans, a native of Wales, who had been instructed by a Welsh association to look for an Indian tribe with Welsh origins in North America. The Spanish authorities were leery about such a mission and had put Evans in jail as soon as he reached St. Louis in the spring of 1793. He had just been freed when Mackay recruited him. Both men were idealists and got on well. Mackay's aim was far-reaching. Evans would go as a scout among the Mandans and from there would push on to the source of the Missouri in order to find a navigable waterway to the Pacific, no less!

In the summer of 1797 Mackay and Evans ✳ returned separately to St. Louis,

---

The Journal of Jean-Baptiste Trudeau or Truteau

In a letter of November 16, 1803, Jefferson wrote, "I inclose you also copies of the Treaties for Louisiana, the act for taking possession . . . & some information collected by myself from Truteau's journal." Attached to the letter was a document entitled, "Extracts from the Journal of M. Truteau, Agent for the Illinois trading company, residing at the village of Ricara, up the Missouri." As the president wrote, these weren't actual extracts, but various bits of information taken from the journal. Together, they give a thumbnail sketch of the Indians of the Missouri, their numbers, contribution to the fur trade, rivalries, and so on. The enclosure states, for example, that "the Sioux inhabit the Northern part of the Missisipi . . . and are hostile to the Ricaras, Mendanes, big-bellies and others. . . . They have from 30. to 60.000 men, and abound in fire-arms. They are the greatest beaver hunters; and could furnish more beavers than all the nations besides." Some of the information concerns the Ricaras, Grands Osages, Petits Osages, Kansas, Mahas, Poncas, and Panis, among other nations (Jackson, 1978, 1: 136-140).

The "Journal tenu par J Bte truteau agent de la compagnie du haut Missouri" was complemented by a "Description abrégée du haut missouris adressée à Monsieur don Zenon trudeau ... par j Bte truteau voyageur." These two documents exist in several versions. The most complete version is in the Quebec Seminary in the Viger-Verreau Collection. It was transcribed by historian-geographer Fernand Grenier and was the basis for a new English translation by Mildred Mott Wedel for the University of Nebraska Press. A new edition is being prepared under the direction of anthropologist Douglas R. Parks.

---

clearly unable to say they had accomplished their mission. Each man had kept a journal, however, and Evans had even drawn a map of his journey from Fort St. Charles to the Mandan villages.

"I now inclose you a map of the Missouri as far as the Mendans," wrote Jefferson to Lewis on January 13, 1804. "[I]t is said to be very accurate having been done by a mr Evans by order of the Spanish government" (Thwaites, 7: 291).

One week later, on January 22, Jefferson recalled recently sending Lewis extracts of Trudeau's journal, adding, "I now inclose a translation of that journal in full for your information" (Thwaites, 7: 292). On his side, Lewis was also having translation problems. "I have also obtained Ivins's and MacKay's journal up the Missouri, it is in French & is at present in the hands of Mr. Hay, who has promised to translate it for me," Lewis told Jefferson in a letter of December 28, 1803 (Jackson, 1978, 1: 155). The Mr. Hay in question was then in charge of the trading post at Cahokia. During the winter of 1803-1804 he performed many services for Lewis and acted as interpreter with the St. Louis authorities.☙

In any event, Lewis and Clark had the so-called Mackay-Evans map and journal with them. They referred to it on occasion in their own journals, each time misspelling the name Evans, which became Ivans, Evens, Ivin, Ivins, or Evins.

Antoine Soulard's Map

Finally, Lewis and Clark also had a map attributed to Antoine Soulard, "a Frenchman, a man of good information" (Jackson, 1978, 1: 149). Like many others, he had fled revolutionary France. In the winter of 1803-1804 he was uncertain where his allegiance lay. He was a Spanish civil servant, and the United States had just acquired the territory for which he was responsible as surveyor-general.

Among the many maps of Louisiana was "A Topographical Sketch of the Upper

✷ According to Gordon Speck (76), Evans escaped a double assassination attempt during his stay with the Mandans. René Jussaume, a trader living with the Mandans and Hidatsas, plotted with some Indians to enter Evans's living quarters in order to rob and kill him. Evans was considered a Spanish trader, although in fact a Welshman. When the plot was discovered, Jussaume tried to shoot Evans in the back. The quick intervention of Evans's interpreter saved his life. The exasperated Jussaume took off in the direction of the Souris River before Evans could exact his revenge. What accounts for this act? Jussaume was probably employed by the North West Company at the time and may have wanted to get rid of a competitor.

☙ It may seem surprising at first glance that Mackay's journal was written in French, but it is indeed the case. Historian Raymond Wood, an expert on the Mackay-Evans expedition, confirms this by recalling Mackay's antecedents and also the fact that the journal was destined for Spanish administrators, not the American authorities.

Mississippi and the Missouri." Such a map (see below, with detailed discussion on p. 153) must have excited Lewis's interest, for it showed the Missouri running clearly from west to east, with its source at the foot of the Rockies, not far from another river called "Oregan or R. of the West," flowing into the Pacific. Since this river appeared to be much shorter than the Missouri, Lewis was able to draw very encouraging conclusions.

Lewis visited Soulard, who agreed to give him "any information of which he was possessed," in particular the contents of the 1800 census. The surveyor-general even supplied "pen, ink & paper" so that Lewis could make an extract. Soulard then had second thoughts. "'Perhaps some person may come in,' [he said,] and taking hold of my hand with much apparent agitation, [he] beged that I would desist, adding that when he had granted me permission to take an extract from that paper, the impropriety of such permission did not occur to him," and that it would "injure him with his government," as Lewis told Jefferson in a lengthy letter of December

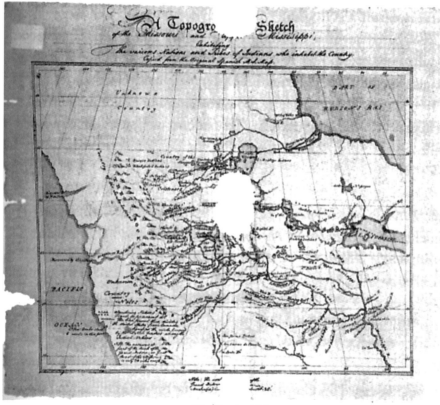

The Soulard Map

The Soulard Map

As its title shows, the Soulard Map is "A Topographical Sketch of the Upper Mississippi and the Missouri, Exhibiting the various Nations and Tribes of Indians who inhabit the Country, copied from the Original Spanish M.S. Map." In fact it is an English version based on a Spanish map by Antoine Soulard. It was found among Clark's manuscript papers (Allen: 148, n. 60) and is worth looking at, even though the present reproduction is not very good.

The best method is to follow the Mississippi from the lower right corner of the map. The villages of Kaskaskia and Cahokia are clearly shown on the east bank, below the Illinois and Ouisconsin (Wisconsin) rivers. The "Fox R." shown here must refer to a branch of the Wisconsin connecting with the Fox River that leads to Lake Michigan via Green Bay.

On the west bank we see New Bourbon, Ste. Geneviève, and St. Louis. Moving up the Mississippi, we come successively to the Ausage (Osage), Kansaz (Kansas), Plate (Platte), and the Little Missouri rivers. The Grand Detour (Great or Big Bend) is clearly marked, although much exaggerated in the sense that it veers too sharply toward the south. Various Indian tribes are mentioned, including the Ausages (Osages), Kansaz (Kansas), Panees (Pawnees), Mahas, Mandans, Chayeniens (Cheyennes), and Sioux. Turning to the Mississippi north of St. Louis, we find the Des Moines River and other Indians, including the Sioux, Osonaboins (Assiniboins), and Sauteux (Salk). Further north are the Cristenoes and Blackfoot Indians.

Finally, to the far west, beyond the named Indians and waterways, lies a range of not very intimidating mountains, relatively close to the sea. The latitude of the Missouri's source is shown very close to the mouth of the Oregon (Columbia). According to the map, the sources of these two rivers are a short distance apart. Optimism was the order of the day.

Despite its poor condition, the Soulard map attracts a lot of interest. It is frequently reproduced, but in an almost unreadable format. Both Thwaites and Moulton included it in the atlases that accompanied their respective editions of the Lewis and Clark journals. Note the similarity of the hole in the centre of the map and the missing pieces above and below—a sign that the map was folded for a long time. It is now in Yale University's Beinecke Rare Book and Manuscript Library, Collection of Western Americana.

28, 1803, written from Cahokia. Naturally, Lewis "instantly desisted," but even so he finally learned that the non-Indian population of Upper Louisiana numbered about ten thousand souls, of which two thousand were "slaves & people of colour, and of the remaining 8,000, two thirds of them at least were emigrants from the U'States; that the remaining third, were either French or Canadian descendants, the Spaniards and their descendants being so few in number, that they deserved no particular notice as a class of people" (Jackson, 1978, 1: 149-150).

Lewis no doubt became still more interested when Soulard showed him "a manuscript map" that included a portion of the Mississippi and "the Missouri … in it's whole extent." Could he make a copy? Soulard wanted to please the American, and may have been urged to do so by John Hay, who was acting as interpreter for the occasion. The surveyor-general, still nervous, explained that he needed the authorization of the Spanish commandant as well as the permission of the merchant

Unknown

Country

Chippewian
Indians

Country of the

Beaver Indians

Black footed Indians

Sturgeon
L.

Wintering
Place of the
English

Brochet
L.

Dupas R.

Swan R.

An English
Fort

Ojenabin
Ind.

The Saques

The Bow

Cristenoes

Beôntan M.

Discovered
by J. de Fuca

THE

of the Snake Indians

Flatfoot Indians

Grande Ind.

Mountain of Pines
or the Piney Mountains

The Osnaboins

Schabôin Ind.

Turtle M.

Red Cote L.

Crapoo
River

R O C K Y

Elk Mount.

Chat Cat Ind.

The
Grand
Detour

Discovered by L'Aguillard

oregan, or R. of the West.

Action
Indians

Bouche
Ind.

M O

River Missouri

Mandan

Sioux Ind.

Arar
Ind.

Archechote Ind.

Chaviene Ind.

Crow feather

Richard Ind.

Chevienne R.

The Little Missouri R.

Red Bead Ind.

The River

PACIFIC

Unknown

Country

Red Bow

U N

T A I N S

N. Fork of the Plate

OCEAN

St Fra: Drake staid
6 weeks in this port

The Plate Mountain

North River

Notes.

○○○○○ Wandering Nations
○○○○○ Fixed & permanent d.
― ― ― The line formed thus, divides
the United States from Canada
.... significes the route pursued
by the English traders among the
Indian Nations.

N.B. The narrowest
part of the Neck of the
Grand Detour, or Great
Bend of the Missouri
is only 20 miles across.

PART OF

HUDSON'S BAY

Ft P. of Wales
Churchill R.

Bungi Nation   Ft York
York   River

Ld Lake
Winnepeek   Muskego Indians

L. Bourbon
Oupas

Lake   N°ipeyon

Winnepeek R.   Sauloux Indians

L. of the   Woods.

Rainy lake

English Ft   Grand Portage

Sauloux Indians

L.   SUPERIOR

Red L.

Sioux Ind.s

Pine   Sioux Ind.f

Maha   Red R.   Quicconsin R.

Ind.f   The   Upper Mississippi

Wolf Ind.s   Plate   St Peter's R.   Fox R.

250 leagues
from the Missouri   Oto   Mouth.

Little Nid Mad. R.   R.   Missouri

Republican   Blue R.   Great Nid Mad R.   R. des Moines

Fork   Kansey Ind.s   Illinois R.

Kansey River   Saline R.   Cahine R.

St Louis   Kaskaskia

North Fork   Great   Ausage

Little Ausages   Pichou R.   St Genevieve   New Bourbe

Ste Genevieve

Sau Jerome Detroit   Little Water R.   Mississippi R.

Sau Lorran de Picour?   So Fork of St Joseph

So Santa Fé   Great Boratho R.   La Tour

Sparoi R.

River   des

Arac

Antoine Soulard

who owned the map. It was a complicated business, and Lewis concluded that everything would be far more aboveboard "as soon as the American government takes effect in Louisiana" (Jackson, 1978, 1: 150-151). Nevertheless, if this map resembled the one shown on the preceding pages, which there is every reason to believe, Lewis must have been delighted to have had a chance to look at it.

Lewis viewed the British as rivals if not enemies. The French Canadians who worked for them aroused his mistrust, but those who had gone over to the Spanish turned out to be precious assets. The French Canadians and Creoles of St. Louis, St. Charles, and La Charrette provided abundant information. Apart from the travel journals and maps that they showed the two captains, they passed on their extensive knowledge of the Missouri region and its inhabitants. Not only were the French Canadians very familiar with the tribes; they were their trading partners, and some had lived among the Indians. Lewis and Clark recruited a number during this time, and others during the voyage.

Gradually the west bank of the Missouri emerged from the mists of the unknown. Otos, Omahas, Sioux, Arikaras, and Mandans took shape and acquired a face. In the spring of 1804, Lewis and Clark set forth into a land unknown—but a little less mysterious than they had imagined.

To the theory of continental symmetry, with a high zone from which powerful rivers flowed, was added information provided by Fidler, Trudeau, Mackay, and Soulard. Americans keep, if not the memory, at least numerous traces of these men's passage that, sooner or later, will lead to some recognition of their contribution to the exploration of North America.

Chapter 10

Guides, Interpreters, and Hunters: The Backbone of an Expedition

Drouillard, Labiche, Cruzatte, and Charbonneau played an important but little-recognized role in the success of the Lewis and Clark Expedition. Was this a unique case, or a common phenomenon of the time?

We have already looked at the contribution of French Canadians as guides and voyageurs in relation to two other truly remarkable explorers, Alexander Mackenzie and David Thompson. The naturalist John James Audubon and the historian Francis Parkman also wrote about their famous expeditions and their helpers.

Audubon and Parkman write of two larger-than-life figures: their respective guides Étienne Provost and Henri Chatillon.

Provost subsequently inspired the painter, Alfred Jacob Miller. The artist included the portly guide and his distinctive mule in illustrations of a later expedition (1837) with Sir William Drummond Stewart, the Scottish laird who spent nearly ten years of his life in Canada and the American West. It is with a sense of pure joy that one delves into Miller's astonishing *oeuvre*.

Miller, a man of kindly disposition, didn't have a special sense of mission or of his role—unlike his contemporary George Catlin, who created a precious pictorial record of American Indians of the Great Plains in the early and mid-1830s. Audubon met these Indians slightly later than Catlin and often criticized the artist, in what seems a mean-spirited way, for romanticizing Native Americans. Parkman rather resembles him on occasion, offering numerous severe judgments on Indians, Mexicans, and Mormons. Sometimes he even finds the wilderness itself unbearable.

However, Parkman could also be sensitive and understanding, as can be seen in his first volume of history, *The Oregon Trail*. This was the route that would eventually be followed by thousands of pioneers to reach the Pacific coast.

Upon meeting the Indians, the French quickly adapted to life in the North American continent. They became *Canadiens*. Some turned their hand at being farmers or artisans, others chose the fur trade. They spread in all directions, promoting the development of a vast network of French-Indian alliances and enabling France to extend its influence over almost the entire continent.

Molly (Mary) Brant became William Johnson's companion in 1759, when he was successfully working to weaken, if not destroy, the French-Indian alliances. People in the British-American colonies referred to several successive conflicts as "the French and Indian Wars," which reveals the importance of these alliances. Their end meant the end of New France. Mary Brant is described by Barbara Graymont in her *Dictionary of Canadian Biography* article (4: 416-419) listed under the Indian name, Konwatsi Tsiaienni. She belonged to the Mohawk nation, known to the French as *les agniers*.

In contrast, Anglo-American settlers were more interested in acquiring actual territory. Whereas the *Canadiens* usually lived among the Indians, British colonists took a confrontational approach. There were exceptions, of course, such as William Johnson, the wealthy landowner and landlord in the Albany area. He had married an Indian and understood the need to break or at least weaken French-Indian alliances. He succeeded in doing this in 1759-1760, enabling British settlers to gain the upper hand in the final French and Indian War (1754-1760).

Immediately after the signing of the Treaty of Paris in 1763, the British drew the borders of the Province of Quebec along the St. Lawrence. In theory, the *Canadiens*, descendants of the French, were confined to this new colony.

This assumption ignored the existence of the inhabitants of the Louisiana territory as well as the French Canadians to the north in the *Pays d'en Haut* (the Great Lakes region) including Detroit and Michilimackinac, and those in Illinois country, including Vincennes on the Wabash and Kaskaskia and St. Geneviève on the Mississippi.

Before losing all their North American possessions, France had made a little present to Spain in 1762—part of what was called Louisiana, in reality the western drainage basin of the Mississippi. In the winter of 1763-1764 two Louisianians, Pierre Laclède and Auguste Chouteau, founded the village of Saint-Louis on the river's west bank, near the mouth of the Missouri.

French Canadians on the east bank had come under British rule with the Treaty of Paris of 1763. They quickly moved with their possessions to the new settlement, and French Canadians from the Province of Quebec followed suit, arriving in a steady trickle. *(See note on next page.)* ✳

When the frontiers of this province were suddenly extended in 1774 as far as the junction of the Ohio and the Mississippi, French Canadians felt at ease from the standpoint of their trading activities. Nevertheless, they looked even further

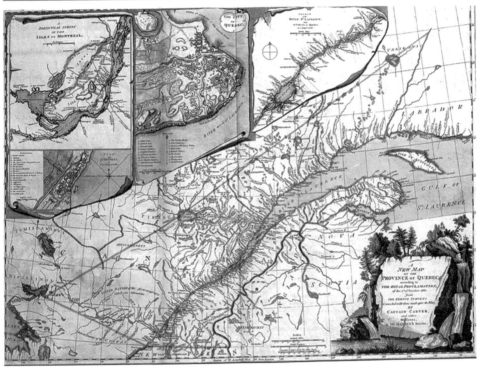

Carver's Map

A New Map of the Province of Quebec, according to the Royal Proclamation of the 7th of October 1763. On Jonathan Carver's map, what the proclamation referred to as the "Government of Quebec" forms a sort of trapezoid. Its northern border extends in a line from the source of the St. John River (upper right) to Lake Nipissing, turns to meet the St. Lawrence at the forty-fifth parallel, runs eastward toward Lake Champlain, and turns again to follow fairly closely the height of land south of the St. Lawrence, going toward the north shore of Chaleur Bay, and there crossing the St. Lawrence west of Anticosti Island, to follow the St. John back to its source.

The map was published in 1776 in London, and in 1777 in a French edition in Paris, "chez le Rouge, rue des Grands-Augustins." Note that the longitude was calculated from London.

✱ The expression "Province of Quebec" is the mark of the conqueror, as Quebec historian Maurice Séguin was fond of saying. Under the 1763 Treaty of Paris, what had until then been referred to as Canada ceased to exist—but there were still *Canadiens*, as Séguin's colleague Guy Frégault used to retort. The British already had fourteen colonies in North America, if we count Nova Scotia, acquired in 1713 under the Treaty of Utrecht. They created a fifteenth colony along the St. Lawrence. "Province" here means "colony." A very different Province of Quebec was born with Confederation in 1867, but for many the word "province" still has its old meaning.

ⓔ The experienced steersmen and bowmen were almost all descended from the French living around the forts and trading posts of the interior that were abandoned when the British took over New France. They came from Prairie du Chien, l'Arbre Croche, Butte des Morts, Côte sans Dessin, the Baie des Puants (Green Bay). These Frenchmen were taken into Indian tribes and supplied the first British traders with the best crews, guides, and interpreters. The prestige that these Frenchmen enjoyed among the Indians was extended to the British. (Léo-Paul Desrosiers, *Les Engagés du Grand Portage*, Fides, 1957: 49).

west toward Upper Louisiana. They became *voyageurs* in the service of the North West and Hudson's Bay companies, as well as guides, interpreters, or hunters for exploratory and scientific expeditions.ⓔ As a result, French Canadians were present in nearly all the great expeditions for almost a century. The Lewis and Clark Expedition, on all accounts the most important of these, was able to rely on men such as Georges Drouillard, an exceptional interpreter and hunter, as well as Pierre Cruzatte and François Labiche, Jean-Baptiste Deschamps and his engagés, and Toussaint Charbonneau, whose contribution has been eclipsed by the legend of his wife Sacagawea, the young Shoshone woman.

There is no denying that the expedition's success rested on the talents and discipline of the two captains, Meriwether Lewis and William Clark. They were sturdy, intelligent men, skilled at using the scientific instruments at their disposal. They were unbeatable at establishing their position or getting their bearings, as was the case on the return journey. However, faced with the choice between two converging rivers, their expertise faltered momentarily. When confronted by a mountain range rising up like a wall, they needed help. This could only come from the Indians, and interpreters were crucial. It was impossible to find one person who spoke all the languages encountered on their long journey. Georges Drouillard, being a Métis, had mastered sign language and the vital art of making contact and establishing a minimum of confidence with the Indians. His presence proved to be essential, and he was to be present on all delicate missions. Also, because he spoke French and English, he was able to alternate in the translation chain with François Labiche, another Métis who shared Drouillard's skills as a hunter and guide.

THE PROVINCE OF QUEBEC
1763

Sea of Labrador

Hudson's Bay

RUPERT'S LAND

NEWFOUNDLAND

QUEBEC

NOVA
SCOTIA

LOUISIANA

INDIAN
TERRITORY

THIRTEEN
COLONIES

ATLANTIC OCEAN

Gulf of Mexico   FLORIDA

THE PROVINCE OF QUEBEC
1774

Sea of Labrador

Hudson's Bay

RUPERT'S LAND

NEWFOUNDLAND

QUEBEC

NOVA
SCOTIA

LOUISIANA

INDIAN
TERRITORY

THIRTEEN
COLONIES

ATLANTIC OCEAN

Gulf of Mexico   FLORIDA

THE PROVINCE OF QUEBEC
1783

Sea of Labrador

Hudson's Bay

RUPERT'S LAND

NEWFOUNDLAND

QUEBEC

NOVA
SCOTIA

LOUISIANA

UNITED STATES

Under the control of:

Britain
Britain
Spain
United States
Contested territory

ATLANTIC OCEAN

Gulf of Mexico   FLORIDA

In the wake of the Quebec Act of 1774 the "Province of Quebec" was enlarged to cover parts of the territory of the former New France (Labrador, Anticosti Island, the Magdalen Islands), and territories temporarily reserved for the Indians that extended northward to the southern border of the Hudson's Bay Company's land and toward the southwest as far as the junction of the Ohio and the Mississippi.

The Thirteen Colonies that gave birth to the United States lay along the Atlantic coast between the Alleghenies and the sea. West of these mountains was an Indian territory under British control as far as the Mississippi. The Mississippi's western drainage basin was ceded to Spain in 1762, then taken back by France and sold to the United States in 1803. On gaining independence, the United States obtained all the territory north of the Floridas (which, after some juggling, also became part of the U.S.) up to the Great Lakes and the southern limits of the 1763 Province of Quebec, and from the Atlantic coast to the Mississippi, with the exception of the city of New Orleans, even though it lay on the river's eastern shore. New Orleans was under Spanish control, as indirectly confirmed by Article 7 of the 1763 Treaty of Paris. This small detail would make all the difference. The United States wanted to be able to navigate freely on the Mississippi, and Jefferson wanted to make sure this would happen by acquiring New Orleans, either by negotiation or by force.

Georges Drouillard was a man apart. He could keep a cool head, and his senses were constantly on the alert. No detail escaped him. Without him, without Cruzatte and Labiche or Toussaint Charbonneau and Sacagawea, would Lewis and Clark have succeeded in their mission? Probably not. Luck certainly played a part in the expedition's success. All the members of the expedition returned safely, except for Charles Floyd, who apparently died of acute appendicitis. The expedition was able to feed and care

John Senex's Map, 1771

A *New Map of the English Empire in America*, London, 1771. John Senex's map shows British North America. As though he had a premonition, Senex distinguishes the Thirteen Colonies from the rest. American ambitions were already clear: they wanted the south shore of the St. Lawrence and Lakes Ontario and Erie. Great Britain refused, sticking to the 1763 frontiers. Benjamin Franklin felt it was better not to insist at this time, pointing out that it would cost less to buy "Canada" (a term current between 1763 and 1791) than to send an army to conquer it.

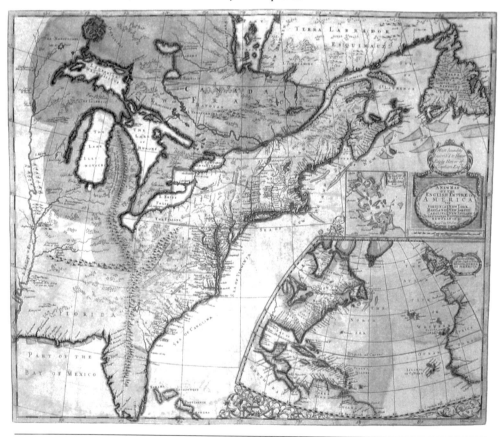

for itself; its members escaped drowning and survived grizzly attacks, being shot at by Piegans, and various other accidents. Chance brought them good fortune, but so did flair, intuition, intelligence, and initiative, qualities that Lewis and Clark possessed in abundance. Even so, they needed the support of a team of tough, disciplined men. Their handpicked group of soldiers provided this support, but if Lewis and Clark had set out prematurely in 1803 things would have been very different. The Pittsburgh drunkard who delivered the keelboat late is to be blessed: the delay allowed time for completing the Louisiana Purchase and for recruiting men who were familiar with Indians and their ways, as well as knowing the territory, with its resources and mysteries.

The case of Lewis and Clark is not an isolated one. The conquest of the Far West would rely for its success on guides, interpreters, and hunters who were French Canadians or of Canadian origin. We can get a good idea of their contribution by looking at a few of the major expeditions—those of two exceptional explorers: Alexander Mackenzie, the first European to cross North America, and David Thompson, one of the greatest North American explorers. And those of two other giants, each in his sphere—the naturalist John James Audubon and the historian Francis Parkman, both of whom had a very personal relationship with French Canadians.

Woodcut by Carl W. Bertsch taken from Grace Lee Nute's *The Voyageur*. The birchbark canoe is a marvellous craft, perfectly adapted to North American conditions. French-Canadian voyageurs had obviously learned from the Indians not only how to manoeuvre canoes, but how to build and repair them.

Alexander Mackenzie

"The canoe was put into the water: her dimensions were twenty-five feet [7.6 metres] long within, exclusive of the curves of stem and stern, twenty-six inches [66 centimetres] hold, and four feet nine inches [1.5 metres] beam," wrote Alexander Mackenzie on May 8, 1793, in his *Voyages from Montreal on the river St. Laurence, through the Continent of North America . . . in the Years 1789 and 1793*. "In this slender vessel, we shipped provisions, goods for presents, arms, ammunition, and baggage, to the weight of three thousand pounds [1360 kilograms], and an equipage of ten people; viz. Alexander Mackay, Joseph Landry, Charles Ducette, Francois Beaulieux, Baptist Bisson, François Courtois, and Jacques Beauchamp, with two Indians, as hunters and interpreters. . . . With these persons I embarked at seven in the evening" (Mackenzie: 265).

Beginning the following day, Thursday, May 9, 1793, they had to fight a strong current. A little before eight o'clock they stopped for the night. At three in the morning on Friday, May 10, they set off again. Around noon, Mackenzie recounted, "the canoe being strained from its having been very heavily laden, became so leaky, we were obliged to land, unload, and gum it" (266). Mackenzie profited by the occasion to calculate their latitude (55° 58' 48"), their point of departure being latitude 56° 9' north by longitude 117° 35' 15" west.

Mackenzie kept up this pace for five weeks. On June 18 he reached the Fraser River, confusing it with the Columbia. At this point the

Alexander Mackenzie
(Frontispiece, *Voyage from Montreal*, 1927).

Indians advised him to take the land route to the Pacific. "According to their account," he noted, "this way is so often travelled by them, that their path is visible throughout the whole journey, which lies along small lakes and rivers. It occupied them, they said, no more than six nights, to go to where they meet the people who barter iron, brass, copper, beads, &c., with them for dressed leather, and beaver, bear, lynx, fox, and marten skins" (356).

Mackenzie was perplexed. He very much wanted to believe his Indian informants but in order to follow their advice he would have to backtrack a considerable distance. "In a voyage of this kind, a retrograde motion could not fail to cool the ardour, slacken the zeal, and weaken the confidence of those, who have no greater inducement to the undertaking, than to follow the conductor of it" (357).

✳ *"My altitude, by an artificial horizon, gave 52° 20' 33"; that by the natural horizon was 52° 20' 48" North latitude"* (438).

In the event he trusted to his Indian guides. They led him to the Pacific. It took a whole month to reach what they called "the lake whose water is nauseous, and where they had heard that great canoes came two winters ago" (359).

Mackenzie reached the coast and calculated his latitude as 52° 20' 48" north. ✳ The weather was clear and he was able to take observations and calculate the longitude at 128° 2' "West of Greenwich" (440).

⊘ Mackenzie tells of the real fear exhibited by his young Indian guide: "his agitation was so violent, that he foamed at the mouth." Mackenzie himself admitted to being a little nervous, but he showed no emotion so as to not to add to the near panic of his men. However, he agreed that the canoe would be loaded and made ready for a quick getaway (437-438).

As his young Indian guide seemed very frightened by some local natives, Mackenzie and his party set up camp on an isolated rock (438).⊘ Just before leaving it in the morning, Mackenzie mixed a bit of vermilion with melted grease and wrote on the southeastern face of the rock: "Alexander Mackenzie, from Canada, by land, the twenty-second of July, one thousand seven hundred and ninety-three" (438). On the same day they began the return journey and progressed rapidly, "as my people were very anxious to get out of the reach of the inhabitants of this coast" (441). One month later, on August 24, 1793, they were back at Fort Chipewyan. All were safe and sound. In a little over three months they had covered 2,300 miles (3,833 kilometres). On the return journey they kept up an average pace of 36 miles (60 kilometres) a day for the segment on water (about 860 miles / 1,433 kilometres), including portages (*DCB*, 5: 541).

In 1793 Alexander Mackenzie was not yet thirty. He was a fearless,

☙ Mackenzie "had great physical strength, determination, and stamina," wrote W. Kaye Lamb (DCB 5: 538). He was said to be a tough leader of men. On returning from his disappointing trip to the Arctic Ocean, Mackenzie said of his men that he had never heard them grumble, and that they were on the contrary always in good humour, ready to accompany him always wherever he decided to take them. We know that two of these men, Joseph Landry and Charles Ducette, followed him to the Pacific. When Mackenzie returned from this voyage he had difficulty publishing his travel journal, as was the case with Meriwether Lewis. He had to wait until 1801 for it to appear. He seemed to be at loose ends after this and went into politics. He was elected to the Lower Canada House of Assembly in 1804 but attended only one session, admitting that he was "heartily tired of Legislation." (DCB, V, 542). In 1812, at the age of 48, he married Geddes Mackenzie, a fourteen-year-old heiress. In 1820 he died unexpectedly in an inn while returning from a visit to an Edinburgh doctor.

Lewis never succeeded in getting his journal published during his lifetime. He never married, found it difficult to carry out his administrative duties as governor of Upper Louisiana, and ended by committing suicide. He died alone during a trip—in an inn, like Mackenzie.

honourable man. In tight situations—and there were many—he was to be found in the forefront. *(See note on next page.)* ☙

On the return trip he had to face a most extraordinary situation: he couldn't get his men to climb into the canoe. "My steersman, who had been with me for five years in that capacity, instantly replied that he was ready to follow me wherever I should go, but that he would never again enter that canoe, as he had solemnly sworn he would not, while he was in the rapid. His example was followed by all the rest, except two, who embarked with Mr. Mackay, myself, and the sick Indian" (446-447).

Mackenzie readily admitted that the journey was extremely difficult. The party going by land was continually obliged to wait for those in the canoe. This time he didn't insist or try to convince his men, whereas in other situations he had been persuasive to the point of reminding them of the terms of their engagement.

Above all, Mackenzie appreciated his men, even if he wasn't very demonstrative. His low-key manner is especially evident in his laconic way of describing the first sign of the nearby ocean that they had travelled so far to see. *(See note on next page.)* ◉ When necessary, he willingly gave his companions "a warm eulogium on their fortitude, patience, and perseverance" (360). At the end of his voyage, "crowned with success" (481), he said, "The Canadians who accompanied me were the most expert canoe-men in the world," a compliment repeated by historian Grace Lee Nute in *The Voyageur* (Nute: 229).

His men had led him to the Pacific and back to his starting point. For the first time, Europeans had crossed the North American continent from east to west. Unfortunately the route had no practical value. Jefferson had surmised as much. The Pacific had been reached, but a navigable route remained to be found.

This was the challenge facing Lewis and Clark, but it would be David Thompson who would eventually find practical routes to the Pacific.

David Thompson

On December 30, 1797, David Thompson was visiting the Mandans along with René Jussaume, who was heading a party made up of Joseph Boisseau, Alexis Vivier, Pierre Gilbert, François Perrault, Toussin Vaudril (Vaudreuil), Louis-Jos Houl (Houle), and Jean-Baptiste Minie (Meunier).

> ☞ On July 19, 1793, Mackenzie "came upon six curious houses built on stilts. … 'From these houses … I could perceive the termination of the river, and its discharge into a narrow arm of the sea'" (DCB, 5: 540).

Thompson had come to North America as an apprentice for the Hudson's Bay Company in 1784, at the age of fourteen. He first worked for Samuel Hearne, the tireless explorer. It was the right school. Five years later Thompson took advantage of the presence of the surveyor Philip Turnor at Cumberland House, during the winter of 1789-1790, to learn surveying and astronomy. He had found his vocation.

In the spring of 1797 he thought of moving to the North West Company, where the directors took more interest in questions of frontiers and surveying, especially along the forty-ninth parallel west of Lake of the Woods (today in Ontario).

When the time came for Thompson to renew his contract with the Hudson's Bay Company and succeed Malchom Ross, who was in charge of trade north of Lake Athabasca, Thompson informed Ross that he considered himself "a freeborn subject and at liberty to choose any service he thought to be most to his advantage" (Nisbet: 40).✳ A few weeks later, he was at Grand Portage, the summer rendezvous of traders, agents, and company partners. Here he met French Canadians who were heading for Rainy Lake and joined up with some of them, "a fine, hardy, good humoured set of Men, fond of full feeding" (Nisbet: 43). He set off immediately, reaching the Assiniboine River (today in Manitoba) in November 1797.♛ It was

> ✳ Why did Thompson leave the Hudson's Bay Company so suddenly? Succeeding Ross would have been a promotion. Although he had complaints about his employer, the main reason for leaving seems to have been his dreams of being an explorer and surveyor. The North West Company was more active in this respect.

> ♛ His work at this time consisted of surveying the land westward along the forty-ninth parallel, considered as being the most likely frontier between British and American territories west of the Lake of the Woods.

from there that he undertook his journey to the Mandans. Bitter winter weather raged. Cold and wind paralyzed the party. It consoled itself with buffalo meat, a favourite of the French Canadians who were reportedly able to consume eight pounds of fresh meat a day. Thompson appreciated their company, their taste for good food, and their *joie de vivre*. He was amused by their patois, the *lingua franca* of the Northwest. He began studying French, just as he had learned Cree and Piegan earlier.

Thompson was twenty-nine and had chosen his way of life. His companion was to be Charlotte Small, the daughter of a Cree woman and Patrick Small, one of the founders of the North West Company. She was fourteen. They were married according to the custom of the country on June 10, 1799,✳ and spent the winter at Fort George on the Saskatchewan River, where Thompson began putting his notes in order. The following spring they settled at Rocky Mountain House, the company's westernmost post. Trading became Thompson's main activity, and this disappointed him, for he still dreamed of exploration and discovery.

In the autumn of 1806 Lewis and Clark returned to St. Louis. They had succeeded in reaching the Pacific at the mouth of the Columbia River. North West Company shareholders were worried. Could this river possibly reach far enough into the interior of the continent to provide access to their trading territories?

✳ In the fall of 1812, Thompson regularized his marriage and had his wife and four of their five children baptized in the Scotch Presbyterian Church of Montreal (*DCB*, 8: 882).

Paradoxically, Lewis and Clark had been able to use maps produced by Aaron Arrowsmith and others whose work owed much to Thompson, Mackenzie, and Fidler. Now it was up to the Montrealers to take up the challenge! Arrowsmith's map may not have been a great help, but it had been a sign that the British were pushing back frontiers. With the return of the Lewis and Clark Expedition, the situation was suddenly reversed. The directors of the North West Company had previously reduced their explorations; now they gave the signal to reactivate them. This was Thompson's chance. In 1804 he had become a partner in the company and was beginning to be seriously "dissatisfied … at not being able to pursue his interests in exploring and surveying" (Nicks, *DCB*, 8: 881; Belyea: 264-295).

Once again Thompson began exploring toward the Rockies. He took a party up the North Saskatchewan River and, in June 1807, finally crossed over the height of land to the upper reaches of the Columbia River, where he founded Kootenay House on the west bank. As the river ran northward at this point, he had no inkling of its real identity.

Thompson's progress upset the Piegans, who felt their position as middlemen between the Kootenays and Flatheads was being undermined. He had to be wary.

His men, especially Boisverd, Clément, Bercier, and Boulard, had much to do. All sorts of problems arose, including communication difficulties. Thompson complained that what he said in French had to be repeated in Blackfoot, then Kootenay, then Flathead, and so on, so that the meaning could be lost before the sentence reached its destination. He was surrounded by a veritable Tower of Babel—people speaking English, French, Piegan, Blackfoot, Kootenay, and Cree. Thompson sometimes found Boulard lazy, but he needed him as an interpreter and guide. "He is useful in many respects more than another & [in] many respects much less so—upon the whole he is a cheap bargain" (Nisbet: 89; Belyea: 225).

For three years, Thompson worked at enlarging his territory, but he set out for the mouth of the Columbia when American fur trader John Jacob Astor came to the Northwest with plans that included operating west of the Rockies through the Pacific Fur Company. Thompson probably went with a view to establishing the North West Company's

Woodcut by Carl W. Bertsch taken from Grace Lee Nute's *The Voyageur*. The artist portrayed the voyageur as described by the author, an energetic-looking man inseparable from his pipe. Distances were sometimes calculated by the time it took to smoke a pipe.

Nute's voyageur here seems tall and slim. In general, voyageurs were short, sturdy men, suited to the size of their canoes. He could paddle for twelve to eighteen hours a day and keep his good humour. During portages, he was capable of backpacking between 200 and 450 pounds (90-205 kilograms).

presence at the river's mouth—but that in itself wasn't enough. He had wanted to get there before the arrival of one of two expeditions sent by Astor: the overland Hunt Expedition, and Astor's ship, the *Tonkin*, coming via the tip of South America

(*DCB* 8, 881). Above all, Thompson wanted to find a relatively easy route to the Pacific. ✳

Gabriel Franchère, who had made the journey aboard the *Tonkin*, described Thompson's dignified arrival. It was July 15, 1811. Franchère and his companions were about to load the canoes when "toward midday, we saw a large canoe, carrying a flag. We did not know who it could be. . . . The flag she bore was British, and her crew was composed of nine boatmen in all. A well-dressed man, who appeared to be the commander, was the first to leap ashore; and addressing us without ceremony, [said] that he was one of the partners of the North West Company" (Nisbet: 210-211).

Seeing was believing. Thompson had to accept the evidence: the Pacific Fur Company's *Tonkin* had outstripped him, arriving in March. A contingent of men had already finished building Fort Astoria. Thompson consoled himself by saying that his explorations would make it possible to find a practicable route. In any case, he was under the impression that the North West Company held a third of the shares in Astor's enterprise. There was a certain sense of mistrust in the air. The land expedition sponsored by Astor and led by Wilson Price Hunt was expected before the winter. There was some question of going to meet it. Thompson stressed the dangers and difficulties to be expected. The Astorians were skeptical, saying that two of their Indian hosts had given them reassuring information in this regard.

Thompson was certainly amused upon encountering the two Indians in question, whom he knew well. Franchère reported that Thompson recognized the two Indians, and told the Astorians that they were two women. One, dressed as a man, was a Kootenay *berdache* (someone assuming the role of the opposite sex) called Qanqon, the former wife of Augustin Boisverd.

Thompson confided to his journal that she had become a prophet, then declared that she was now a man. She dressed as a man, carried weapons, and took a young girl as a wife. Qanqon was born to intrigue and she scented danger. Thompson was willing to protect her, but for a few days only, as he planned to return to Montreal. He agreed to accompany a party of Astorians up the Columbia as far as the Dalles (*DCB*, 8: 882). Here they parted ways. Thompson left Qanqon and her companion behind, as well as Michel Boulard, his travelling companion of eleven years. He had suggested that Boulard be exchanged for a Hawaiian named Coxe, *(see note on next page)* ♕ whom he considered more useful in fighting against

✳ In August 1809, Thompson explored as far south as Montana's Kootenai River region with a crew made up of Beaulieu, Bostonan, Boulard, Buché, Mousseau, and a Salk hunter (Belyea: 243).

the current on the journey upstream. Boulard, he noted, was "well versed in Indian affairs, but weak for the hard labor of ascending the River" (Nisbet: 224).

In fact, what Thompson needed most, after more than twenty-five years devoted to travelling extensively in the Northwest, surveying and mapping, were strong arms to take him back to Montreal. In all that time these arms had belonged to French Canadians, whose good humour, endurance, and carefree spirit he appreciated. But now he had only one idea: to return to Montreal.

In a letter written on December 21, 1810, at the foot of the Rockies ꙮ and addressed to his old friend Alexander Fraser, now settled in Montreal, Thompson gave way to nostalgia. "I am getting tired of such constant hard journeys," he wrote. "For the last 20 months I have spent only [a] bare two months under the shelter of a hut, all the rest has been in my tent, and there is little likelihood the next 12 months will be much otherwise" (Nisbet: 174).

However difficult these years of travelling may have been, they were not the most painful of his life. Thompson died in 1857. He had been blind for several years, and hadn't been able to finish the account of his travels. It was left to geographer and historian Joseph Burr Tyrrell to bring him out of the shadows. But the work published in 1916 under the auspices of the Champlain Society has an index that omits the French Canadians! This surprising neglect was corrected in 1962 when a second, enlarged edition was published under the direction of Richard Glover, who also supplied an introduction and annotations. This time Michel Boulard, Augustin Boisverd (Qanqon's former companion), and the other French Canadians were mentioned. On the other hand, the Hawaiian Coxe, whom Thompson considered "a prodigy of wit and humor" (Nisbet: 224) was ignored. Decidedly, the writing of history is something of a moveable feast. *(See note on next page.)* ✳

ꙮ How did a Hawaiian happen to be in the Columbia River region in 1811? Gabriel Franchère, a French Canadian who had made the trip on the *Tonkin* from New York to Fort Astoria, kept a journal. In it he recounts how the ship stopped at the Sandwich Islands (Hawaii) and hired twenty-four islanders, half as domestic servants, the other half as seamen. He noted that "These people, who make very good sailors, were eager to be taken into employment, and we might easily have carried off a much greater number" (Franchère: 227-228, and Thwaites, 1966, 6: 229). Another interesting point is that several whites were living on the islands, including "A young Frenchman from Bordeaux, preceptor of the king's sons, whom he taught to read" (Franchère: 227 and Thwaites, 1966, 6: 220).

ꙮ Thompson's letter of December 21, 1810, in which he expressly mentions being at "the foot of the Mountains," was written while travelling on the Athabasca River (Belyea: 227).

John James Audubon

Audubon: the name sounds French. And why the double-barrelled "John James?" Audubon himself took care to cover his tracks. At one point he said he was a Louisianian, at another Louis XVI's son—the dauphin whose fate remains a historical conundrum.

To complicate things, his granddaughter Maria R. Audubon, working with Elliott Coues, ♛ published an expurgated work entitled *Audubon and His Journals* in 1897. Did Coues know that Maria had censored the material? We have no idea.

Elliott Coues is a noteworthy name for anyone interested in Lewis and Clark. We owe the second edition (1892-1898) of the two explorers' journals to him. Coues was passionate about ornithology—which was probably what led him to Audubon—and added a large number of extremely useful natural history notes to this edition. Alas, he is also considered responsible for some rather astounding changes to the manuscripts. Reuben Gold Thwaites, the third editor of the journals, realized that Coues had taken it upon himself to make additions or clarifications designed (in his view) to improve the original text. Thwaites didn't hesitate to denounce such inexcusable practices and to show where they had occurred when preparing the text of his scholarly edition (Thwaites, 1: xlix, and 11, n. 1). Coues was a genuine scholar and a tireless researcher, but he was also capable of taking a few liberties with an original document (Cutright, 1976: 97).

Whether because of his temperament or perhaps through carelessness or ignorance, Coues allowed his co-editor, Maria, to cut, alter, and generally bowdlerize or even destroy some of the original text. Later she explained that she had wanted to stop family secrets and confidences about certain delicate subjects from falling into the wrong hands.

As Michel LeBris, another passionate devotee of the history of the West, has noted in his introduction to *Journal du Missouri*, the truth finally surfaced,

✻ McGill-Queen's University Press has at last brought out a truly complete edition, thanks to the work of Barbara Belyea. It contains Thompson's complete journal with his abundant notes on the longitude and latitude of various places, the hour, temperature, etc. As might be expected, the index is equally exhaustive.

♛ Elliott Coues (1842-1899) always displayed great interest in natural history. In 1872 he published *Key to North American Birds*, a classic of its kind. Audubon's works fascinated him, and he worked with the celebrated naturalist's granddaughter, Maria R. Audubon, on preparing Audubon's personal journals for publication. As well as an edition of the Lewis and Clark journals, Coues wrote a number of books on the birds of the American Northwest (Cutright, 1976: 79). Note that the first edition of the Lewis and Clark journals (1814) was the work of Nicholas Biddle (Cutright, 1976: 53-72).

The published Audubon plates by London engraver Robert Havell, Jr. are masterpieces. Often described as Audubon originals, these engravings are worth a fortune today. The last known sale was for some $U.S.4 million.

revealing to us an untamed, passionate Audubon, by turns sentimental, dissolute, or melancholic, given to whisky and women (Audubon, 1993: 29).

Today, thanks to the work of John Francis McDermott and Alice Ford, to various Audubon letters found over the years, and to numerous travel journals by his contemporaries, we can get a good idea of the origins and life of John James Audubon.

Audubon was born in Haiti (then St. Domingue) on August 26, 1785. His mother, Jeanne Rabin or Rabine, worked on the plantation of Captain Jean Audubon of the French navy. When she died soon after her son's birth, Captain Audubon decided to return to France. Here he married, and the new couple adopted the child. Legend has it that the parents entrusted him for a time to the celebrated artist Jacques Louis David, the painter of Napoleon.

In 1803, apparently to prevent young Audubon from being caught up in the future emperor's military conscription, his parents sent him to the United States

Catching Up.
Alfred Jacob Miller (Ross: No. 197).

on the pretext of entrusting the management of some family property to him. He settled first at Mill Grove near Philadelphia, where he lounged around doing very little, then in Cincinnati where he worked as a taxidermist. In 1820 he took part in a long excursion on the Mississippi. He had a passion for birds, which he studied and drew. It was in England that he finally found an engraver to publish his 435 plates of North American birds.

After his *Birds of America* appeared, Audubon embarked on the study of four-footed animals. It proved to be a subject even more vast than American birds and, in particular, more difficult to study. Many animals were nocturnal, others ranged from fairly hostile to ferocious. No matter: it would be his life's work, he decided. Around 1840 he began his task. He felt doubly pressured, first because of his age (although he thought he could live to be a hundred), but mainly

Étienne Provost—whom Miller described as "Mo'sieur P. adipose & rotund" (Ross: 97)—was born in Chambly in 1782 and emigrated to St. Louis around 1815. He guided several major expeditions, including those led by Joseph N. Nicollet and John C. Frémont. It was said that he was "the soul of the trappers of the Mountains." Provost was a legendary figure who has survived in Alfred Jacob Miller's watercolours. He specialized in the Missouri River region, the Platte, and the Santa Fe Trail, and was probably the first white man to visit Great Salt Lake.

because of the steady flow of Europeans and the so-called progress of civilization that was decimating the Indians and the buffalo, and covering the prairies with roads, trading posts, and towns. Audubon was a naturalist, fascinated by the wild splendour of America's heartland. He wanted to warn humans, to make them aware of the devastation they were causing, each day more detestable (Audubon, 1993: 18-19). Not only was the wilderness landscape threatened, but its peoples and wildlife as well.

His last great expedition was undertaken in 1843. His close colleagues (taxidermist John Bell, artist Isaac Sprague, and geologist Edward Harris) accompanied him, as did a number of French Canadians—men like Alexis Bombardier, Charles Primeau, and Bonaventure LeBrun, whom he observed with pleasure, admiring their resourcefulness and good humour. All were skilled hunters, particularly Étienne Provost, who also turned out to be an exceptional guide and companion. Audubon and Provost—what a pair of *bon vivants*!

Provost, referred to as *le vieux capitaine*, became Audubon's inseparable companion from early June to mid-October, 1843. He was an indefatigable hunter, always on the move, always on the lookout. He was also an inexhaustible mine of information.

"Old Provost" told Audubon a thousand things full of interest about beaver, once so abundant and then so rare, noted the naturalist on Wednesday, July 5, at the end of a rainy day that exhausted the hunters. Provost informed Audubon that a trapper needed nearly seventy beaver pelts to make up a hundred-pound (45 kilogram) pack. If the sale went well, this pack would bring in $500, and when the season was good a trapper sometimes earned as much as $4000 (Audubon, 1993: 184).

✳The following year (1844), Provost was a guide for Armand Fouché, one of the sons of Joseph Fouché, Napoleon's famous minister.

On Sunday, July 9, Audubon was working on a drawing representing the head of a wolf. "I drew at a Wolf's head," Audubon noted. "Provost tells me that Wolves are oftentimes destroyed by wild horses, which he has seen run at the Wolves head down, and when at a proper distance take them by the middle of the back with their teeth, and throw them several feet in the air, after which they stamp upon their bodies with the fore feet until quite dead" (Audubon, 1960, 2: 83).

"Provost told me" is a phrase that occurs more than once in Audubon's journal of this time. On another occasion, "Provost told me (and he is a respectable man) that, during the breeding season of the Mountain Ram, the battering of the horns is often heard as far as a mile away" (Audubon, 1960, 2: 67, 68). Above all, Audubon

Étienne Provost, Miller's Favourite Subject

Alfred Jacob Miller (1810-1874) started out as a portrait artist, but discovered the universe of the Indians and trappers thanks to Sir William Drummond Stewart, who hired him as an artist for a major expedition to the Far West. Later Miller dealt with the same subjects in various pictures. This was the case for *The Trapper's Bride*, of which several versions exist. Miller's work has only recently begun to attract attention, particularly for their documentary value. Miller's expedition notes have been preserved. He identified "Monsieur Proveau" on at least two occasions: one (seen above) entitled *Threatened Attack — approach of a large body of Indians* (Ross: No. 76), the other, *Catching up* (Ross: No. 197). By close examination of Miller's many paintings, and taking into account his portrayal of "Monsieur Proveau" (his corpulence, his hat, and his mule), it is possible to recognize him in the following scenes: *Indian Guide, Crossing the Kansas, Moonlight — camp scene, Storm: waiting for the caravan, Caravan taking to water*, and *Our Camp*. This list is based on works reproduced in Ross (1951).

added concerning Provost, he was a man to be trusted (Audubon, 1993: 174).

They parted on October 18, 1843, at the end of a two months' return journey down the Missouri from Fort Union to St. Louis. The boat, piloted by Provost, stopped at St. Charles. Here Provost received his salary for services rendered to Audubon: $214, or $50 per month ✻ (Tykal: 181).

Whereas Audubon had complete respect for Provost and his French-Canadian companions, he was less appreciative of all the "mixed-bloods" that he met day after day. On May 28, at Fort George (about thirty miles from Fort Pierre), he noticed more squaws and children than he had expected. But, he added, "as every

Caravan Taking to Water (Alfred Jacob Miller, Ross: No. 170). The painting shows the trappers entering a river to throw pursuers off the trail. Miller explains that "the varmints are on their tracts."

Indian Guide (Alfred Jacob Miller, Ross: No. 55). Miller didn't identify Provost here, but the trapper is unmistakable, sitting on his mule and listening attentively to the Indian guide.

clerk and agent belonging to the companies has *a wife*, as it is called, a spurious population soon exhibits itself around the wigwams" (Audubon, 1960, 1: 521). Audubon stressed the fact that he encountered many Métis. Clearly their numbers impressed him, and he made a point of distinguishing them from Indians and French Canadians. "Alas the half-breeds are so uncertain," he commented. He referred to the judgment of the "very beautiful" Mrs. Culbertson, "who has great pride in her pure Indian blood, [and who] told me with scorn that 'all such no-color fellows are lazy'" (Audubon,1960, 2: 112).

Mrs. Culbertson, the wife of the *bourgeois* or "boss" of the Fort Union trading post, may have found grace in Audubon's eyes — which isn't saying much — but this wasn't true of Indians in general. The naturalist found physical contact with them repugnant. The very act of shaking hands with them disgusted him. "Several great Warriors have condescended to shake me by the hand; their very touch is disgusting . . . and each and every one of those dirty wretches we had all to shake by the hand" (Audubon, 1960, 2: 16, 17). In fact, Audubon failed to recognize the Indians of his dreams, idealized by Europeans and portrayed by the prolific George Catlin who, like many others later on, including Edward S. Curtis, wanted to show Native Americans as they were before becoming corrupted by civilization or simply vanishing.

About a decade separates the major expeditions of Catlin and Audubon. Could such changes have come about in so little time? Audubon refers to Catlin at several points in his journal. "Ah! Mr. Catlin," he wrote on May 17, 1843, "I am now sorry

George Catlin (1796-1872), like E.S. Curtis, felt that the Indians were threatened with extinction. He decided to devote his career as an artist to them. In 1830, with the support of William Clark, then superintendent of Indian Affairs for the Missouri Territory, Catlin set to work. During the years that followed he made hundreds of what were basically descriptive watercolours. The red stone that several tribes used to make their pipes was called Catlinite.

The Author painting a Chief at the base of the Rocky Mountains

to see and to read your accounts of the Indians *you* saw — how very different they must have been from any that I have seen!" (Audubon, 1960, 1: 496).

Whatever the weather, Audubon fulminated against Catlin. On June 11, for example, he must have been in a good humour because "This day has been tolerably fine, though windy. ... We have seen much remarkably handsome scenery, but nothing at all comparing with Catlin's descriptions; his book must, after all, be altogether a humbug. Poor devil! I pity him from the bottom of my soul; had he studied, and kept up to the old French proverb that says: 'Bon renommé vaut mieux que ceinture doré,' (meaning 'A good name is worth its weight in gold') he might have become an honest man" (Audubon, 1960, 2: 26, 27).

☙ Edward Sheriff Curtis (1868-1952) was to Indians what John James Audubon was to ornithology. Over some thirty years, Curtis visited more than eighty tribes from Canada to Mexico. He took some 40,000 photographs that were the basis for a monumental publication, *The North American Indian*. In 1974 a French version was brought out by Éditions Denoël with a choice of texts and photographs prepared by T.C. McLuhan, entitled *Pieds nus sur la terre sacrée*.

On July 22, the atmosphere was heavy and oppressive. Provost and La Fleur, a half-breed who proved to be an excellent hunter, were looking for "antelopes," while Audubon and the others "remained looking at the Indians, all Assiniboins, and very dirty. When and where Mr. Catlin saw these Indians as he represented them, dressed in magnificent attire, with all sorts of extravagant accoutrements" was more than Audubon could guess, or that Mr. Culbertson could tell him (Audubon, 1960: 2: 108).

Was Audubon offended by Catlin's views? A little, no doubt, as he was a rival. But it is true that Catlin chose to give a positive image of the Indians of North America and to hold out a helping hand to a dying race. Catlin even objected to the word "savage" as applied to Indians, the meaning of which had been so distorted that few people understood Native Americans. In his writings he often preferred the expression "wild Indian," connoting the untamed or precolonial state of the Amerindian. Catlin was undeniably an unwavering supporter. Today he himself has his fervent admirers. While Audubon's drawings are precious tools in the study of the birds and mammals of North America, Catlin's work is equally so in researching the history of the American Indian.

Étienne Provost also had "his" painter. Alfred Jacob Miller depicted "Monsieur Proveau" in at least two of his canvases and named him in his notebooks (Ross, 76, 197). Apparently Miller captioned one picture "Monsieur Proveau, subleader, with a corpus round as a porpoise, revolving in his mind what was to be done."

٭ Detail from Miller's *Catching Up* (Ross: No. 197).

Thanks to Mormon genealogical records, we know that Étienne Provost, who died on July 7, 1850, at the age of 65, left a daughter, Mary, from his marriage with Marie-Rose Salle (Tykal: 93). Provost's union with a Crow Indian woman around 1828 is said to have produced a son, Nicolas, who in turn had a son, Michel, reportedly born in Canada. The existence of this branch was confirmed several times over the years.

These two paintings date from 1837. One, entitled "Threatened Attack," shows Provost beside the famous traveller, Sir William Drummond Stewart; the other, "Catching Up," shows his strapping, roly-poly figure in the left foreground, his hands cupped to his lips. In both cases the artist emphasizes his corpulence, giving him a highly original hat and a mule for a mount. This animal is clearly visible behind Provost in "Catching Up." The portliness, the hat, and the mule enable us to recognize him in several other paintings. Étienne Provost was well known for his strength and toughness, especially after the day in 1824 when he escaped an ambush by a band of Shoshones, which ended in the massacre of some ten whites.

Provost was a great drinker and owned a tavern in St. Louis. ٭ For historians of the Far West he was the quintessential "Man of the Mountains," and the Utah city of Provo was named after him—a paradox, considering the fact that alcohol and even coffee were prohibited by the pioneer Mormons. Provost was first and foremost a much sought-after guide. Some consider him the discoverer of South Pass, which became the key element in the Oregon Trail. This achievement is disputed today, but it takes nothing away from his fame. Perhaps it is enough that he was credited with its discovery for so many years.

Francis Parkman

Lewis and Clark reached the Pacific, but their route was virtually useless from the practical point of view. The Indians knew of and used various other passes through the Rockies, and European trappers found out about them one after another. By 1812 Canadians and Americans in Fort Astoria were already able to share such information. David Thompson, coming from the north, had finally found a possible route. Wilson Price Hunt, who started out following the trail of Lewis and Clark, veered southward on the advice of trappers.

Gradually a southern route took shape. It was to become the Oregon Trail. In the 1840s, thousands of settlers embarked on this trail, heading

Francis Parkman (1823-1839) was the type of historian that we no longer see today, in the sense that he could combine a captivating account with solid research. Despite his many health problems, he was a prolific writer. Parkman couldn't read for many hours at a stretch. As a result he stopped frequently to reflect on his documentation, exploring it, analyzing the context, questioning in his mind the people involved—the witnesses. He has been criticized for a partisan approach and his tendency to give excessively important roles to certain figures. At least Parkman is never boring, and he produced a considerable body of work.

for the Pacific coast. At the time the mouth of the Columbia River was still in disputed territory, principally between Americans and British.

The American strategy was to occupy the region. Its beauty and promise were much vaunted. The Oregon Trail immediately acquired symbolic value, becoming an intriguing, fascinating focus of people's dreams.

Until this period, young Francis Parkman's principal enthusiasm had been for horticulture. His health was frail and it was thought that fresh air would be the best cure. He went to live with a farming uncle and attended a school a mile away—not with great regularity, for he preferred the school of nature. He idealized it, turning toward the study of North America in all its primeval purity. Later, Parkman recalled that he had first thought of writing an American history "that would have the forest as its principal character" (Schama: 48).

In the summer of 1846, the future historian was in St. Louis with his friend Quincy Adams Shaw. The pair had decided to travel to a noble and pure land. "The Oregon Trail trip thus cost Parkman his health for life," wrote one of his first biographers, Charles Haight Farnham, "but so predominant was his ambition, so much did he value his Indian studies, and so little compassion had he for his physical being, that he never regretted this costly but fruitful experience" (Farnham: 136).

Apart from his health, Parkman lost some of his illusions on this expedition. As Simon Schama pointed out in his unforgiving comments on the great American historian, "He [Parkman] had thought to find some sort of wellspring for America and had discovered instead a barren thing; an antechamber, not of heaven, but of hell" (Schama: 55).

Francis Parkman is indeed a monument of American historiography.✳ Even

Karl Bodmer (Joslyn Museum, Omaha, Nebraska).
This watercolour sketch shows Minitari women, as described by Prince Maximilian on February 11, 1833, performing a scalp dance. Male musicians are shown at upper right (Thomas, 1976: 196, 215).

today, in the bookstores of American shopping centres where works of history are few and far between—there, beside the Lewis and Clark journals and the inevitable *Democracy in America* by de Tocqueville, stands the eternal Parkman. It is very rare that *The Oregon Trail*, *The Conspiracy of Pontiac*, and sometimes *A Half Century of Conflict* are not prominently displayed on the shelves—works one hundred and fifty years old! His books have been much criticized, but it makes no difference: Parkman's books are always there!

One of the first commentators to reproach Parkman was a friend who travelled with him on a European trip, Theodore Parker. In a long letter dated from Boston, December 22, 1851, two years after *The Oregon Trail* appeared, the Reverend Parker didn't mince words: "Yet I do not think you do the Indian quite justice; you side rather too strongly with the white man and against the red. I think you bring out the vices of the Indian into more prominence than those of the European—which were yet less excusable" (Farnham: 374). Treachery, cruelty, firewater, and the abuse of Indian women, Parker reminded him, were vices to be laid at the door of the whites.

In fact, very little found grace in Parkman's eyes, which, incidentally, were extremely weak. In *The Oregon Trail* he complained of the unbearable heat, violent storms, dung-covered buffalo, and venomous snakes. He scoffed at humans, too: the trappers and their bloated squaws, the Mexicans and their "brutish faces," the Mormons and their fanaticism (Parkman, 1899: 87, 376, 455). Above all, there were the Indians, including "the old women, ugly as Macbeth's witches, with hair streaming loose in the wind, and nothing but the tattered fragment of an old buffalo-robe to hide their shrivelled limbs. The day of their favoritism passed two generations ago; now the heaviest labors of the camp devolved upon them." And Parkman gives the list of these labours carried out amid the clamour of dogs and the cries of children, while the warriors lazed around in "listless tranquillity" (Parkman, 1899: 112-113).

These famous Plains Indians, the Indians of George Catlin and Karl Bodmer, were now but the shadow of their former selves. According to Parkman,

✳ In my many years of book hunting in the United States, I've always been astonished by the continual presence of Parkman's works. True, the classic work by de Tocqueville is almost always available, and of course one or more works on Lewis and Clark. My own interest began with reading Stephen Ambrose's *Undaunted Courage*. The fact that Thwaites, the renowned editor of the *Jesuit Relations*, had brought out a scholarly edition of the Lewis and Clark journals finally convinced me to follow the trail, so to speak, of the two American explorers. They led me well beyond the Pacific and brought me back to the heart of North America, as expressed in the title of Benoît Brouillette's fine work *La pénétration du continent nord-américain*.

🕮 Above all, they are the result of colossal research, much of it done in the marvellous Newberry Library of Chicago.

🐚 From these encounters and exchanges emerged a type of man that Parkman was unable to see—something for which his severe visual problems were in no way responsible. It was more likely due to his general state of physical and psychological health. Parkman unburdened himself in a letter to Quebec historian Abbé H.R. Casgrain, who was sending him documentation on New France. His doctors wondered if his problems came from "an abnormal state or partial paralysis of certain arteries of the brain" (Farnham: 136).

Omaha Indians. By George Catlin

these aristocrats of the forest had taken on the worst faults of the average American. Lazy, double-dealing, dependent on others, and perpetually warring among themselves, they were now doomed. As Schama so dryly remarked, "It was finished before it had begun, then, this romance with the West" (Schama: 55).

This extremely sombre portrait of the Indians drawn by Parkman in his works has a silver lining, nevertheless. It prompted one of America's foremost historians to choose his vocation.

In the preface to his first book, *The Invasion of America*, Francis Jennings wrote that "This book got itself started, unknown to me, when I picked up a used set of Francis Parkman's works in 1956 (at ten cents the volume). Having acquired them, I did the uncharacteristic thing of reading them all the way through, fascinated by the flow of dramatic, if sometimes turgid, prose, and increasingly plagued by a sense of something terribly wrong" (Jennings: v.).

Jennings' works are a real delight, filled with intelligent comment and also a generous spirit.🕮 He was able to see beyond the Indians' misfortunes and weaknesses and to appreciate their role and the valuable aspect of their alliances. Parkman looked for heroes: La Salle, Frontenac, and above all Wolfe— in whom he probably saw himself reflected in many respects. Contrary to this, Jennings offers cultural transfers, interbreeding, trade and commerce, peace and war.🐚

Wracked with pain, Parkman became inconsolable when a son died at the age of fourteen. He felt great bitterness. Did this make him unjust and morally blind?

Perhaps. But Parkman was also a man of his time and milieu. His immense popularity is understandable. His success was based on his talent, style, and literary gifts, but also on his sense of affinity and a certain communion of thought and feeling with contemporaries of similar interests and background.

For part of his travels on the Oregon Trail, Parkman reported only images of poverty and decline, although such images didn't include the French Canadians — the travelling companions whom he met throughout his gruelling expedition. He expressed curiosity and even pleasure in dealing with men like the trappers Bisonette, Boisverd (*sic*), Gingras, Morin, Rouleau, Saraphin, and Troché, or jacks-of-all-trades such as Bordeaux, Dorion, Lajeunesse, Le Rouge, Perrault, Rouville,

Henry Chatillon by Remington

Illustrator, painter, writer, and sculptor, Frederic Remington (1861-1909) is famous mainly for his sculptures, which glorify the horse. He illustrated the deluxe edition of Parkman's work published in 1899 by George N. Morang & Company.

"I have never, in the city or in the wilderness, met a better man than
my true-hearted friend Henry Chatillon" wrote Parkman.

Simoneau, and Sorel. He remembered their *joie de vivre* and their way of coming to terms with life, and especially with religion. One evening he was talking with two of them, Raymond and Reynal, whom he found "as indifferent to their future welfare as men whose lives are in constant peril are apt to be" (Parkman, 1899: 253). ✳ Strangely enough, he didn't make the link between these men and the French of New France, the subject of his later historical works. His attitude toward the former French colony was extremely harsh.

Parkman would always remember his companions of the Oregon Trail. In the preface to a fourth edition of his book (1872), he made a point of mentioning "the hunter Raymond" who "perished in the snow during [J.C.] Fremont's disastrous passage of the mountains in the winter of 1848." Immediately before this, he expressed the hope that "the faithful Deslauriers," his genial muleteer, was "still living on the frontier of Missouri" (Parkman, 1899: xvi).

Henry Chatillon, Parkman's guide, occupied a special place in the historian's memory. At the beginning of *The Oregon Trail* he had written admiringly of Chatillon—his generosity, skill as a guide, and "quiet good-nature" (Parkman, 1899: 17-18). At the end of the book Parkman repeated his admiration. It was the moment of saying goodbye at the Planter's House in St. Louis. "Chatillon came to our rooms to take leave of us. No one who met him in the streets of St. Louis would have taken him for a hunter fresh from the Rocky Mountains. He was very neatly and simply dressed in a suit of dark cloth. ... he had a native good taste which always led him to pay great attention to his personal appearance. His tall athletic figure with its easy flexible motions appeared to advantage in his present dress, and his fine face, though roughened by a thousand storms, was not at all out of keeping with it" (Parkman, 1899: 466).

Parkman would have liked to be Chatillon. To combat illness, the historian had increased his physical exercise in an attempt to strengthen his muscles, and had hiked for miles. It was no use. He was to be Francis Parkman, a man of rage and passion—but a man with a heart.

✳ In these delightful passages, Parkman freed himself somewhat from his demons. "Your Spanish woman?" Parkman asked Raymond. "I never heard of her before. Are you married to her?" "No," answered Raymond. "The priests don't marry their women, and why should I marry mine?" This was an "honorable mention of the Mexican clergy," Parkman made a point of saying. The conversation continued. Raynal, another French Canadian on the expedition, told of a priest who stopped at Fort Laramie about two years previously, who had heard confession from all the men there, and given them absolution. "I got a good clearing out myself, that time," added Raynal, "and I reckon that will do for me till I go down to the settlements again" (Parkman, 1899: 253).

Chatillon "had served us with a fidelity and zeal beyond all praise. We took leave of him with regret; and unless his changing features, as he shook us by the hand, belied him, the feeling on his part was no less than on ours" (Parkman, 1899: 466).

Parkman returned from his Oregon Trail journey weakened, lame, and disillusioned, but in Chatillon he had found proof of what nature, left to itself, can sometimes do. "I have never, in the city or the wilderness, met a better man than my true-hearted friend, Henry Chatillon" (Parkman, 1899: 18).

Chapter 11

Two Charbonneaus, Two Princes

The title of this chapter is ambiguous. Were the two Charbonneaus, father and son, princes in their own way? No indeed! Just the opposite? No again.

In general, American historians have said little about Toussaint Charbonneau, Sacagawea's husband, unless it was merely to censure him for being cowardly, violent, and oversexed.

And yet Sacagawea had an opportunity to leave Charbonneau and return to her own people. She didn't take it. A real prince, Maximilian of Wied-Neuwied, spent many hours in Charbonneau's company and drank in his words. But above all there is the testimony of William Clark who, at the end of the expedition, paid a truly touching homage to the interpreter.

The fact is that Toussaint Charbonneau was a man of his time, a man of the forest, a bon-vivant, a true *Canadien*. And a genuine man-without-a-country.

My aim is not to rehabilitate Charbonneau here, but to offer a more impartial image of the man and to supply hitherto unpublished information about his origins, supported by his baptismal certificate.

By an amazing coincidence, a baptismal certificate has also been found for his son, Jean-Baptiste. One might have thought that the father, after a life of adventure far from the Catholic Church and its sacraments, would have lost all sense of religion. Not at all: when the opportunity presented itself, he had his son baptized.

Fortune would smile on Jean-Baptiste. Prince Paul of Würtemberg, another genuine prince who visited North America a decade before his fellow German, Prince Maximilian, took a great shine to young Charbonneau and made him his protégé. Jean-Baptiste's destiny was as extraordinary as his father's, say what you will.

Prince Maximilian's journal, translated from German into English by Hannibal Evans Lloyd, was reprinted in volumes 22, 23, and 24 of *Early Western Travels* (1906) edited by Reuben Gold Thwaites. This chapter also refers to excerpts from Maximilian's writings and field notes quoted in *People of the First Man*, edited by Davis Thomas and Karin Ronnefeldt, which includes many of Karl Bodmer's magnificent watercolours of the Upper Missouri and its inhabitants.

"We recognized old Charbonneau and landed at once," wrote Prince Maximilian of Wied-Neuwied on November 7, 1833. Returning to Fort Clark after a tour of the Upper Missouri, the distinguished naturalist and ethnologist was glad to renew ties with his interpreter and informant. This was the man who went with Lewis and Clark to the mouth of the Columbia, noted the prince in his journal (Thwaites, 1906, 23:222-223). What more need one say?

It was largely due to the two explorers that the prince was visiting North America. Their travel journals, published in 1814 by Nicholas Biddle after numerous difficulties, had piqued the interest of scientific circles.

Biddle's colossal work had lifted Lewis and Clark to the rank of heroes, but it was far from satisfying all the expectations stimulated by the mention of one hundred and twenty-two hitherto unknown animals and one hundred and seventy-eight new plants.

In Europe, natural history buffs were enthusiastic. Prince Maximilian among them. They wanted to know more. He had been initiated at an early age into the natural sciences and archaeology. As an officer in the Prussian army he had seen action in the Napoleonic wars, but his military service hadn't prevented him from registering at the University of Göttingen to learn more about the natural sciences, to which he would devote much of his life.

Prince Maximilian of Wied-Neuwied (artist unknown).

On the prince's first major expedition—to Brazil in 1815-1817—he had added the study of native peoples to his scientific preoccupations. In 1832 he set off for North America with the Swiss painter, Karl Bodmer. He intended to follow in the footsteps of Lewis and Clark, in other words, to travel up the Missouri.

On July 4, 1832, Boston welcomed Prince Maximilian to the sound of "Yankee Doodle" as the city celebrated Independence Day with great pomp and circumstance (Thwaites, 1906, 22: 45). The prince felt he wasn't really in America, but rather in "one of the old English towns" (41). He was more attracted to Philadelphia, however, where he noted that German seemed to be the predominant language, but remarked that he couldn't find a work of any substance on the Indians there. "It is incredible how much the original American race is hated by its foreign usurpers," he wrote ✳ (Goetzmann, 1984: 7).

Prince Maximilian fully intended to prepare a work on the Indians, but for the moment he had a burning desire to see them with his own eyes. He planned to reach St. Louis at the mouth of the Missouri by going through the Great Lakes, first travelling up the Hudson and the Erie Canal to Lake Erie, and visiting the already famous Niagara Falls. People discouraged him from following this plan, however, as epidemics were rampant in the region at the time. He took the Pittsburgh route. This led him to the heart of several German settlements, including New Harmony founded by the German, George Rapp. Here he met French naturalist Charles Alexandre Lesueur. The little town was a so-called utopian settlement where harmonists, philanthropists, and socialists rubbed shoulders. Among its attractions was the fine book collection

✳ Despite this comment, Maximilian met a number of scholars worthy of his respect, including Samuel F.B. Morse, Pierre DuPonceau, Henry R. Schoolcraft, and in particular Thomas L. McKenney, recently dismissed from his post as superintendent of Indian affairs by President Andrew Jackson. McKenney had a major project in mind that fascinated Maximilian: a monumental work on the Indians of North America, with drawings and signed portraits by, among others, C.B.J.F. de Saint-Mémin and Charles Bird King (Goetzmann, 1984: 7). It was published as *History of the Indian Tribes of North America* (1844).

Charles Alexandre Lesueur
(detail, Karl Bodmer).

The Steamboat Yellowstone (Karl Bodmer).

of William Maclure, president of the Academy of Natural Science of Philadelphia. Maximilian spent five months in New Harmony gathering information and documentation, and putting the final touches to the preparations for his scientific mission. On March 24, 1833, he finally reached St. Louis, gateway to the West.

William Clark, as superintendent of Indian affairs, gave Maximilian the necessary authorization and, in his personal capacity, provided him with a map that recalled the American's famous expedition to the mouth of the Columbia.

✳ The American Fur Company was a creation of the amazing German immigrant, John Jacob Astor (1763-1848), who arrived in America at the age of twenty-one in 1784 and became one of the richest men of his time. After dominating the fur trade, he sensed its coming decline and turned to real estate.

As always in such cases, the American Fur Company ✳ graciously provided the illustrious traveller with means of transport and accommodation. The prince was lucky, as the company's spanking new steamboat, the *Yellowstone*, was ready to get under way and would be visiting the various trading posts along the Missouri. He was welcomed aboard with Karl Bodmer and a second companion, David Dreidoppel, a hunter, taxidermist, and domestic servant all rolled into one, who had been with the prince on his Brazilian trip.

Snags on the Missouri (Karl Bodmer)

On April 21, 1833, Prince Maximilian trained his telescope on the surrounding countryside and "saw the first Indian, sitting on a sandbank; but our attention was soon called to the obstacles on the river" (Thomas: 20). Driftwood snags and tree trunks kept the steamboat from advancing. The ship's boilers must humbly give place to the ship's engagés, who would pole or "drag the steamer upstream by huge hawsers called cordelles" (19, 24).

The *Yellowstone* finally reached the River Platte early in May, but it took four more weeks to reach Fort Pierre. It was near here that Maximilian first found himself truly immersed in an Indian environment (Goetzmann: 182). "We visited the Indian tents uninvited; in that which we first entered there were several tall, good-looking men; the owner of the tent was a man of middle size; his complexion very light, and his features agreeable. His wives were dressed very neatly, and were remarkably clean, especially the one who appeared to be the principal; she wore a

✳ In 1804, Lewis and Clark met a trapper named Pierre Dorion who said he had made his home among the Sioux for about two decades (Thwaites, 1: 46). He lived with a Sioux woman. His son Pierre married an Indian woman who later became famous. Marie Aioe Laguivoise, alone with her two sons, survived a bitter winter ordeal in the Rockies after part of the Hunt Expedition of 1811, sent out by Astor, was attacked by Indians. Her husband, the younger Pierre Dorion, was among those killed. Gabriel Franchère wrote of her heroic escape in his journal, and the story was widely published. The Dorion whom Maximilian met was certainly of the same line. Throughout the prince's journal we find French names—Belhumeur, Chardon, Descoteaux, Dechamp, Doucette, Beauchamp, Berger, Bissonnette, Morrin, Martin, Lesueur, Fecteau, Picotte, and Papin.

---

❻ James Kipp and Toussaint Charbonneau were both originally from the Montreal region. The former, who married a daughter of Chief Four Bears (Mato-Topé), was a tireless builder of forts and enjoyed an enviable reputation. Charbonneau's case was very different. In his defense it must be said that Sacagawea, his companion during the Lewis and Clark Expedition, has totally eclipsed him. History and historians have ignored him, and unfortunately he didn't always serve his own cause.

very elegant leather dress" (Thomas: 30). Maximilian was among the Teton and Yankton Sioux, where Dorion and Ortubize served as successive interpreters ✳ (Thomas: 31 and 32).

At last, on June 18, the steamboat *Assiniboin*—they had changed boats on June 2 at Fort Pierre—pulled in to shore at Fort Clark. By a gently sloping bank, over six hundred Indians awaited the prince. "Close to the beach, the chiefs and most distinguished warriors of the Mandan nation stood in front of the assembly of red men. ... They were all dressed in their finest clothes, to do us honour. As soon as the vessel was moored, they came on board, and, after having given us their hands, sat down in the stern cabin. The pipe went round, and the conversation began with the Mandans, by the assistance of Mr. Kipp, clerk to the American Fur Company, and director of the trading post at Fort Clark, and with the Minnetarees, by the help of the old interpreter, Charbonneau, who had lived thirty-seven years in the villages of the latter people, near this place"❻ (Thomas: 34).

Toussaint Charbonneau was born in Boucherville near Montreal on March 2, 1767, "of the legitimate marriage of Jean-Baptiste Charbonau and Marguerite Deniau," as his baptismal certificate shows (shown on page 195). He began working for the North West Company at a very young age, and this led him, around 1797, to the Missouri's Grand Bend. Whites who lived with an Indian woman were called "squaw men," of which Charbonneau was indeed one! He had a special penchant for Indian girls. Was it chance that led him among the Minnetaris, also called Hidatsas? Prince Maximilian, who was very sensitive to physical good looks, wrote, "The Minitarees are, in fact, the tallest and best formed Indians on the Missouri, and, in this respect, as well as in the elegance of their costume, the

Until now it was believed that Toussaint Charbonneau was born circa 1757, which would have made him over seventy-five when Prince Maximilian met him in 1833-1834, as described on pages 198-199. On the far right of this scene, portrayed by Karl Bodmer (next page), we can see Prince Maximilian standing between the artist and an interpreter thought to be Charbonneau.

Toussaint Charbonneau's baptismal certificate and a typewitten transcript. (*see below*)
B 1767, 22 March – Charboneau, Touss
In the year seventeen hundred and sixty-seven the twenty-second March, by us, the curé and Grand Vicar, was baptized Toussaint born yesterday of the legitimate marriage of J Baptiste Charbonau and Marguerite Deniau, the godfather was Toussaint Decardonet and the godmother Angelique Dussault who stated that they did not know how to sign.

B 1757, 22 mars - Charboneau, Touss

L'an mil sept **cent soixante sept** le vingt deux Mars par nous curé et Grand Vicaire a été baptisé Toussaint né d'hier du legitime mariage de J Baptiste Charbonau et de Marguerite Deniau, le parain a été **Toussaint Decardonet** et la marainne Angelique Dussault qui ont declarés ne scavoir signer. Marchand V G

Prince Maximilian meets the Minitari (Hidatsa) Indians. (Karl Bodmer).

✳ "Mr Chabonah Sent a frenchman of our party to say that he was Sorry for the foolish part he had acted and if we pleased he would accompany us agreeabley to the terms we had proposed and doe every thing we wished him to doe &c.&c.," wrote Clark on March 17, 1804. "He agreed to our tirms and we agreed that he might go on with us &c." (Thwaites 1: 275).

Crows alone approach them, whom they, perhaps, even surpass in the latter particular." The prince was clearly captivated, and added, "Several tall, athletic men were on horseback, and managed their horses, which were frightened by the noise of the steam-boat, with an ease which afforded us pleasure." And the women? "Among the young women we observed some who were very pretty, the white of whose sparkling hazel eyes formed a striking contrast with the vermilion faces. I regret that it is impossible, by any description, to give the reader a distinct idea of such a scene, and there was not sufficient time for Mr. Bodmer to make a drawing of it" (Thomas: 37).

A Good Cook

Toussaint Charbonneau was a bon vivant, one who preferred to indulge in pleasure rather than hard work. When he offered his services as an interpreter to Lewis and Clark in the fall of 1804, he warned them of his demands. He would accept no task but that of interpreter, although he changed his mind later on. *(See note on previous page.)* ✳

Lewis and Clark differed in their opinion of Charbonneau. Malicious tongues will say that the only thing Lewis appreciated about Charbonneau was the white pudding that the French Canadian prepared so well.☉ Charbonneau did indeed like to cook. In later years, Francis Chardon, in command of Fort Clark, mentioned in his journal several feasts prepared by the interpreter, including "a feast of Mince pie and Coffee which was excellent" on Thursday, September 15, 1836 (Chardon: 80).

Charbonneau missed no occasion to offer his hosts gourmet treats. On Friday, January 6, 1837 (the feast of Epiphany), "This being a Holliday with the French Old Charbonneau gave us an excellent dinner of Pudding, Pies, fryed & Roasted Meat &&" (Chardon: 93). If he was religious, he was also patriotic! He would celebrate July 4.

☉ "This white pudding we all esteem one of the greatest delicacies of the forest." Lewis was so enthusiastic on this day, May 9, 1805, that he undertook to describe in detail how to prepare, cook, and serve the *boudin blanc* (Thwaites 2: 15-16). Lewis's description is a true piece of anthology, and on that day he loved his "wrighthand cook Charbono."

Charbonneau and Women

Many people were illiterate in those days, but those who knew how to write noted down everything. An unbelievable number of travel accounts and personal journals is available today. Unfortunately for his reputation, Charbonneau's foibles come under scrutiny in some of them.

In the *Journal of John Mac Donell 1793-1795* written at Fort Qu'Appelle (also called Fort Espérance), we find Charbonneau occupied in hunting both fur-bearing animals and pretty Indians. On March 4, 1795, he left the fort with two companions named Saint-Denis and Saint-Pierre to court "Foutreau's daughter," a great beauty. On March 9 we learn that Charbonneau and one Bédard had decided to stay at "the low mountain" and had been replaced by two men, Bellair and Coquotte. Then on May 30, calamity! Charbonneau had gone too far. The journal reveals that "Tousst. Charbonneau was stabbed at the Manitou-a-banc end of the P. l. P. [Portage la Prairie] in the act of committing a Rape upon her Daughter by an old Saultier woman with a Canoe Awl—a fate he highly deserved for his brutality. It was with difficulty he could walk back over the portage" (*Journal of Mac Donell* cited in Chardon: 271).

Indian Girls Swinging. (Alfred Jacob Miller, Ross: No. 47). The artist's eye was attracted by this Indian girl swinging on the branch of a tree, "in the genial season of youth," sighed Alfred J. Miller, adding "The common earth, the air, the skies / to her were opening Paradise"—a quote inspired by the final lines of Thomas Gray's (1716-1771) "Ode On The Pleasure Arising From Vicissitude." Miller wrote, "Her elfin locks of long black hair are streaming in the wind, like the mane of a wild colt; to crown all, her picturesque, but scanty robe 'floats as wild as mountain breezes.'"

✳ Charbonneau may not have had to run very fast among the Minitaris. One evening in November 1833, Maximilian, the hardened bachelor, noted, "The female sex was everywhere being called upon by the young men and put into action. This type of pastime is the main entertainment of the Indians, as almost all are lewd" (Thomas: 184).

Many years had passed by the time Maximilian knew Charbonneau. For the naturalist, the interpreter was an inexhaustible source of information about the Indians of the Missouri. The two men discussed Indians—their mores, habits, and unpredictable nature, agreeing that the Mandans were the most trustworthy—that is, of all the Indians in the region. Maximilian's curiosity was insatiable. He was particularly interested in the Minitaris, with whom Charbonneau "was well acquainted" (Thomas: 187). His informant wasn't always available, however. On February 4, 1834, Maximilian noted dryly that Charbonneau "was absent again. This seventy-five-year-old man is always running after women" (Thomas: 194). ✳

In 1834, Charbonneau was actually about ten years younger than the prince thought. This mistake persisted. Four years later, on October 27, 1838, Francis

Chardon thought he was eighty. On this autumn Saturday, Chardon wrote that "Old Charboneau, an old Man of 80, took to himself and others a young Wife, a young Assinneboine of 14, a Prisoner that was taken in the fight of this summer, and bought by me of the Rees [Minitaris], the young Men of the Fort, and two rees, gave to the Old Man a splendid Chàrivèree, the Drums, pans, Kittles &c Beating; guns fireing &c. The Old gentleman gave a feast to the Men, and a glass of grog—and went to bed with his young wife, with the intention of doing his best" (Chardon: 173). ℗

℗ Chardon wrote "Chàrivèree." Annie Heloise Abel, in her exceptionally full notes, explains: "Charivari was a custom brought from France and improved upon, being a sort of mockery and used when a marriage was unseemly or ill-assorted" (Chardon: note 514). It is defined in the *Dictionnaire des canadianismes* (Septentrion, 1999) by Gaston Dulong as a noisy demonstration on the occasion of an unconventional marriage (recent widows, elderly people, a couple with a great age difference), or to mark the end of bachelorhood. The custom existed as the "shivaree" in many English-speaking communities in North America.

Charbonneau was a survivor. He had come through numerous perils unscathed. Like a grass snake, he was always able to take shelter, to wriggle out of a tight situation and slip away. He was neither bellicose nor boastful, and he didn't tempt fate. He got the Indians to accept him and knew how to talk to them, as recounted in innumerable anecdotes. Not only could he speak their language, he knew what to say.

The Assiniboin girl Charbonneau gathered to his bosom, like Charbonneau himself, had come through the terrible epidemic of 1837 that had wiped out the Mandans and cut down more that a quarter of the Minitaris, Arikaras, Sioux, Blackfeet, and Assiniboins.

Charbonneau was more than a "squaw man," however. He was a ladies' man with undeniable charm, but he also had courage. He stood up to angry Indians on several occasions. Sometimes he acted in their interests. During the War of 1812, when the British and Americans were fighting one another, he urged the Indians to remain neutral (Speck: 120). American authorities appreciated Charbonneau and sought his services. Archival records of payments spread out over many years have left traces of this fact (Chardon: 277-282). Charbonneau was also mentioned in countless travel journals. In general, he was valued.

A Violent Man and a Coward?

Among the many charges levelled at Charbonneau, two are particularly severe: that of unacceptable brutality, and an inability to keep a cool head.

He had already demonstrated his limitations as a boatman during the Lewis and Clark Expedition. On April 13, 1805 a sudden squall rocked the white pirogue dangerously while Charbonneau was at the helm. He panicked, and George Drouillard had to come to his aid. Lewis emphasized this incident. Although nothing was lost, it had given him a bad scare. A precious cargo of instruments, papers, medicine, and merchandise were stored in this pirogue, believed to be "the most steady and safe" (Moulton, 4: 29-30).

Strange to say, Charbonneau was again at the helm of the white pirogue with its vital cargo on the evening of May 14. A strong wind had been blowing for days. Emotions were already running high because earlier in the evening a huge brown bear had cornered six experienced hunters. They had escaped the animal's fury by the skin of their teeth. It took eight bullets to kill the animal. Then when a violent squall struck the pirogue, which was under sail at the time, Charbonneau panicked and lost control of the rudder, howling and calling on heaven in desperation. Cruzatte—an excellent boatman—had to bring Charbonneau back to earth, so to speak, by threatening to "shoot him instantly if he did not take hold of the rudder and do his duty." The boat was nearly swamped and had to be unloaded and bailed out. Such, *grosso modo*, was Lewis's version (Moulton, 4: 151-152).

Clark's version was slightly different. He wrote that Cruzatte had to threaten Charbonneau, although he doesn't say in precisely what terms, to bring him back to his senses. Yes, the accident could have been disastrous, but thanks to Cruzatte's decisive action the worst was avoided. Clark also calls attention to Sacagawea's presence of mind. Realizing her husband's blunder, she set about limiting the damage. Where was Pomp—her baby Jean-Baptiste—at that moment? Clark doesn't say, merely commenting that "the articles which floated out was nearly all caught by the Squar who was in the rear" (Moulton, 4: 154).

According to various details recorded in the Lewis and Clark journals, Charbonneau and Sacagawea were usually together and helped each other. Once Sacagawea was reunited with her family in August 1805, however, she could have made it clear that her journey had ended, especially as there was a potential husband among her own people. After all, wasn't her brother Cameahwait chief of his tribe? But no: she liked being with the Corps of Discovery, and—why not?—with Toussaint Charbonneau.

Alas, a spat between the couple might indicate otherwise. On August 14, 1805, Lewis noted that "this evening Charbono struck his indian woman for which Capt. C. gave him a severe repremand" (Thwaites, 2: 348-349). Clark merely recorded, "I checked our interpreter for Stricking his woman at their dinner" (Moulton, 5: 93), not mentioning Charbonneau by name but by his function, sign of a certain reserve. However this may be, it involved an isolated incident that was certainly not unexpected, coming from a *coureur des bois* or a mountain man.

William Clark's Opinion

Clark had long forgotten this incident when he said goodbye to the little family. On the way home the Corps stopped at the Mandan village. The two captains were anxious to convince the Indian chiefs to accompany them to Washington so they could visit their "Great Father," the president of the United States. Only Big White (Sheheke), the Mandan chief, agreed to go. The others refused, mainly fearing that the Sioux might stop them. René Jussaume, who helped convince Big White, went with the chief and insisted on bringing along his wife and two children. Big White took his own wife and son.

Lewis didn't witness this scene. He spent August 14, 1805, at the Shoshone camp negotiating for horses while Clark went ahead with the pirogues. Lewis's lengthy journal entry for this day ends with what is clearly a rewrite of Clark's brief entry for the same day.

The time had come to say goodbye to Charbonneau. In the circumstances, Clark felt the need for his services as an interpreter was over. "As none of those Chiefs of whoes language he was conversant would accompany us, his services were no longer of use to the U. States and he was therefore discharged and paid up," he noted on August 17, 1806. But the separation weighed heavily on the captain. "We offered to convey him down to the Illinois if he chose to go, he declined proceeding on at present, observing that he had no acquaintance or prospects of making a living below, and must continue to live in the way that he had done." Clark was especially attached to little Jean-Baptiste, "a butifull, promising child who is 19 months old." He settled it with the parents that, in a year, "provided the child had been weened," he would be old enough to be entrusted to Clark, "if I would be so freindly as to raise the child for him [Charbonneau] in such a manner as I thought proper, to which I agreed" (Thwaites, 5: 344-345).

The voyage down the Missouri continued at top speed. On the evening of August 20, 1806, the journals recorded that the expedition had covered 70 miles (115 kilometres) during the day. It had now reached the Arikara village. Clark was filled with nostalgia. Jussaume's children and Big White's son reminded him of Pomp and Pomp's parents. He mused about all that he would have wanted to say to them.

On the same day Clark prepared a letter for Charbonneau, written from "on Board the Perogue near the Ricara Village," and addressed to "Mr. Teousant

Charbono, Menetarras Village" (Thwaites, 7: 329-330). This letter had been running through his head for three days. They had parted too quickly. He had not had time to speak to Charbonneau as he would have wished. All the time spent together had created ties. He regretted not having been able to list all the merits of Sacagawea, reiterating his affection for Pomp and his strong desire to bring him up as his own son.

William Clark, that robust, six-foot-tall, veteran soldier, a respected and decisive leader, was suddenly undecided, visibly troubled! He tried to find the right words, a way of convincing Charbonneau to come downriver to St. Louis as soon as possible. He evoked everything he could think of. If Charbonneau wanted to live among whites, Clark would buy him land, horses, cows, and pigs. If he wanted to visit his people in Montreal, Clark would lend him a horse and take care of his little family during his absence. If he wanted to return to the Minitaris as an interpreter for American troops, Clark would do what was needed to get him the job. If Charbonneau wanted to continue in trade, and if he entrusted Pomp to Clark, the latter would supply his share of trade goods.

Whatever the choice, Clark recommended that Charbonneau bring with him "Your famn Janey to take care of the boy until I get him" (Thwaites, 7: 330). Clark was no doubt imitating the words usually used by Charbonneau to describe Sacagawea. The American's feelings were manifest.

The success of the Lewis and Clark Expedition had depended on the coinciding of several factors: the captains' capacity for leadership and intelligent planning, their sense of discipline, and the abilities of Drouillard, Cruzatte, Labiche, and others, but also such elements as York's good humour, Cruzatte's violin, Seaman's loyalty, Sacagawea's gentleness, and last but not least the gurgles, smiles, and first steps of young Jean-Baptiste.

On August 20 Clark certainly entertained strong feelings for the child and its mother, whose "attention and services" he had so appreciated, as well as for Charbonneau himself. This was the man whom Lewis described as being "of no particular merit" and "useful as an interpreter only," although he added "in which capacity he discharged his duties with good faith" (Thwaites 7: 359). Lewis, the Virginian, had strong reservations about Frenchmen. He considered them often undisciplined, rowdy, careless, and generally employed by rival (that is, British) fur-trading companies to the north. Moreover, they mingled with the Indians in an easy, informal way, married their women, and shared their life. It was too much for Lewis.

Clark was more human. He knew how to appreciate Charbonneau's good nature, simplicity, and *joie de vivre*. The man was affable and easy-going. He didn't play the hero, didn't go looking for trouble. He was aware of his limitations. He had learned much from nature and the Indians, felt comfortable where he was, and knew what he wanted. Clark himself admitted that throughout this perilous expedition Charbonneau behaved in a manner to win his friendship.

In his letter of August 20, 1806, Clark made endless recommendations to Charbonneau. A letter would be waiting for him at St. Louis; he, Clark, would be in St. Louis or Clarksville on the Ohio; and a final bit of advice—to wait until they met before deciding about Clark's offer. The letter closed "with anxious expectations of seeing my little dancing boy Baptiest, I shall remain your friend, William Clark" (Thwaites, 7: 330).

Jean-Baptiste and His Prince

Jean-Baptiste was eighteen when he met Prince Paul of Württemberg. As agreed, the boy's parents had entrusted him to William Clark who wished to watch over his education. When? And for how long? It's difficult to know exactly. Obviously Jean-Baptiste Charbonneau's school reports haven't been found, but a few clues have survived.

Clark was named superintendent of Indian affairs for the Louisiana Territory in March 1807, and married Julia Hancock on January 5, 1808. She was sixteen, he thirty-seven. Together they would have five children, three of whom died very young. In 1809 Clark was travelling with his wife and son, Meriwether Lewis Clark, when he read in the newspapers of the dramatic death of his friend Lewis. Unlucky in love, short of money, and at a loss as to how to succeed in getting the expedition journals published, Lewis had committed suicide. Clark inherited the task of getting the journals published. He and Jefferson worked together to find various solutions. There was even question of the former president taking on the task himself.

Clark only returned to St. Louis in early July 1810, probably when the Charbonneau family came downriver to the city. In the spring of 1811, Toussaint Charbonneau and Sacagawea set out for their Minitari village, leaving Pomp, now seven years old, in Clark's care. The boy stayed with Clark for five years. When he was around twelve, Jean-Baptiste turned resolutely toward the school of nature.

As for Sacagawea, she died "of a putrid fever" in December 1812, four months after giving birth to a daughter called Lizette ✳ (Chardon, n. 314). At the time, Toussaint Charbonneau was working as interpreter for an expedition to the Gros Ventres led by Manuel Lisa (Chardon: n. 280).

✳ According to a note by John C. Luttig, an agent of the Missouri Fur Company, Clark apparently acted as this baby girl's guardian. He also helped with the upbringing of a third child, named Toussaint after his father. Jean-Baptiste, the eldest, was named after his paternal grandfather, as can be seen on Charbonneau's baptismal certificate (Appleman, 2000: 252, 378, n. 180).

Jean-Baptiste was therefore left to himself at a very young age—which is not to say that his two fathers had forgotten him. William Clark watched over his protégé from a distance and received news about him regularly. In 1823 he was in St. Louis to give an official welcome to an illustrious visitor, Prince Paul (officially Duke) of Württemberg (Lottinville: 180 and 190). Clark helped to organize the prince's expedition to the Missouri region and no doubt spoke to him about Jean-Baptiste. The prince met young Charbonneau on June 21, 1823, near "a very small creek, the Eau Bleue," flowing into the Missouri not far from the mouth of the Kansas River (Lottinville: 270).

Paul Wilhelm, originally called Prince Friedrich Paul, was connected by blood and marriage to the highest European aristocracy, from George III of England to Catherine the Great of Russia. He became Duke of Württemberg when his brother ascended to the throne of this small German kingdom. But he had neither political nor military ambitions, dreaming instead of freedom and the great outdoors. His taste for the natural sciences drew him toward the forests and wide open spaces. At twenty-five he embarked for America, equipped with scientific instruments and

Pierre (Alfred Jacob Miller, Ross: No. 53).
This young Métis of seventeen was a skilled hunter. One day, according to Miller, he almost drowned. "What was your last thought?" asked his rescuer. "Je le pense à Montréal," Miller recorded in French.

sophisticated weapons. He began with a lengthy visit to Cuba, then started up the Mississippi. Everything interested him: history, geography, toponymy, the European inhabitants, the Indians, the animals, and especially the plants. ☞

What was it about Jean-Baptiste Charbonneau that struck the prince? He was surprisingly discreet in this respect. After summarily describing the trading post at the mouth of the Kansas River in his journal, the prince added, "Here I also found a youth of sixteen [actually eighteen, as he was born at Fort Mandan on February 11, 1805], whose mother, a member of the tribe of Shoshones, or Snake Indians, had accompanied the Messrs. Lewis and Clark, as an interpreter, to the Pacific Ocean in 1804 to 1806. This Indian woman married the French interpreter of the expedition, Toussaint Charbonneau, who later served me in the capacity of interpreter. ❦ Baptiste, his son, whom I mentioned above, joined me on my return, followed me to Europe, and has since then been with me" (Lottinville: 271). This statement shows that the journal was revised and completed after the prince's return to Europe. But it covers the travels in America, and not the stay in Europe, making no comment on the activities of Jean-Baptiste and his patron during these European years.

Jean-Baptiste Goes to Europe

We do know that Jean-Baptiste and Prince Paul left New Orleans on December 24, 1823, and reached Newfoundland a month later. They were in Honfleur on February 14 and in Stuttgart on March 4. Three years later, in April 1827, the prince married just long enough to have a child. Divorce followed in April 1829. In need of a change of air, Prince Maximilian decided to take Jean-Baptiste to visit France for a few weeks before returning to America. By early August, 1829, they were in Haiti, and in St. Louis on December 1. Prince Paul left America without Jean-Baptiste at the end of 1830. He would return in 1851.

Jean-Baptiste wasted no time going back to his own people. In the fall he

☞ Prince Paul also found the way of life fascinating but was extremely distressed by the practice of slavery. He referred to it continually. He remarked that in the state of Louisiana a great wrong was done to people of colour of African descent. He felt that the black slavery tolerated in this state was responsible for the separation of whites and blacks, noting that the law forbad interracial marriage, and that the situation was a troubling one which could only lead to dire consequences (Lottinville: 118).

The prince admitted that slavery couldn't be eliminated without a heavy cost to planters, but that it would be wiser for the states to deal with black people and their descendents more compassionately (Lottinville: 119). Later he noted important differences between southern and northern states, in particular that Kentucky had become a popular refuge for fugitive slaves without abolishing slavery.

❦ Toussaint Charbonneau acted as interpreter for Prince Paul from Council Bluffs to Fort Kiowa (Von Sachsen-Alterburg: 79).

Paul Wilhelm of Württemberg

Mergentheim Castle

Prince Paul Wilhelm, Duke of Württemberg, set out on October 17, 1822, for New Orleans. He meant to go to Mexico first, but because of the political situation decided to stop in Cuba beforehand. He then decided to go up the Mississippi as far as St. Louis. Possibly he had already thought of travelling up the Missouri and crossing the Rockies to the Pacific. In any case, this was finally his aim.

Prince Paul of Württemberg remains an enigmatic figure. He wrote much, but spoke little of himself and even less of his money troubles or his love life. Ann W. Hafen (211) quotes him as saying that, in a palace, he would feel like a wild animal in a golden cage. The royal ermine, sceptre, and crown would be the emblems of slavery, and he would long for the silence of great open spaces and a modest life among the free and simple children of nature — of whom, in his eyes, Jean-Baptiste was no doubt a fine example.

joined a supply team headed by one Robidoux. We know this because he got lost and wisely decided to retrace his steps. One of his companions, W.A. Ferris *(see note on next page),* ✳ who would write an account of his own life in the Rockies, noted this incident while recalling that this was the child who had travelled with Lewis and Clark. Jean-Baptiste couldn't escape the fact that he was known and even famous.

Evidently he didn't take advantage of his fame. He worked as an interpreter, guide, and hunter. Sometimes he led a convoy carrying furs, sometimes he took charge of a trading post. In 1842 he had the opportunity of offering hospitality to John C. Frémont, then still a neophyte explorer. Jean-Baptiste took after his father in his penchant for good food. "Mr. C. [Charbonneau]," wrote Frémont, "received us hospitably. One of the people was sent to gather mint, with the aid of which he concocted very good julep; and some boiled buffalo tongue, and coffee with the luxury of sugar, were soon set before us" (Hafen: 215).❧

A few weeks later it was the turn of Rufus B. Sage, who later wrote the best-selling *Rocky Mountain Life*, to partake of Jean-Baptiste's hospitality. This time the commentary was particularly interesting: "The Camp [St. Helenas island, South Platte, Colorado] was under the direction of a half-breed, named Chabonard, who proved to be a gentleman of superior information. He had acquired a classic education and could converse fluently in German, Spanish, French, and English, as well as several Indian languages. His mind, also, was well stored with choice reading, and enriched by extensive travel and observation. Having visited most of the important places, both in England, France, and Germany, he knew how to turn his experience to good advantage" (Hafen: 216). Sage couldn't praise Jean-Baptiste often enough. All contemporary accounts give the same impression.

✳ W.A. Ferris, *Life in the Rocky Mountains*, (Denver, 1940).

❧ T.L. Loftin gives a characteristic account of Jean-Baptiste's welcome in *Westward Go!*—a work published at the author's expense in 2000. It is pleasantly illustrated by a team of artists directed by Beth Berryman. See "Sacajawea's son serves mint juleps."

Jean-Baptiste: a Conscientious and Widely Appreciated Man

In November 1847 Jean-Baptiste was named alcade [mayor] of San Luis Rey, a small mission north of San Diego. His job was not an easy one. The Indians were staging an uprising. The alcade was accused of complicity. He defended himself in writing and submitted his resignation to the district commander, Colonel S.D. Stevenson, who forwarded it with the following note: ♛"Encloses the resignation of J.B. Charboneau as Alcade for San Luis Rey, and says that he has done his duty to the best of his ability, but being a half-breed Indian

♛ Jean-Baptiste's depositions are probably the only documents written in his hand that have been preserved (Hafen: 219). He began by defending his position vis-à-vis the authorities and announced that he intended to demonstrate his innocence during the forthcoming trial. Finally, however, he decided to submit his resignation to the district commander, Colonel J.D. Stevenson.

Jean-Baptiste Charbonneau's Baptismal Certificate

"In the year eighteen hundred and nine on the twenty-eighth of December, I, Brother Urbain Guillet R of the mon[astery] of N[otre] Dame de Bon Secours de la Trappe near Cahokias, in the territory of Illinois, have baptized a child born the eleventh of February in the year eighteen hundred and four of Toussaint Charboneau domiciled in this parish and of ... an Indian woman of the Snake nation. The godfather was Auguste Chouteau and the godmother Eulalie Chouteau both of this parish."

The curé, godfather, and godmother signed the certificate, whereas Toussaint Charbonneau placed his mark (a cross) beside "father of the child" on the document. Sacagawea was not invited to do the same, probably because the priest didn't know how to write her name.

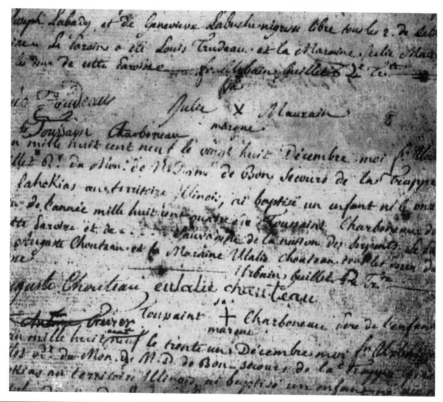

of the U.S. is regarded by the people as favoring the Indians more than he should do, and hence there is much complaint against him" (Hafen: 220).

Despite this misadventure, Jean-Baptiste decided to remain in California where a boom had begun with the discovery of gold. He worked at various trades, then decided to try his luck in Montana. He was travelling toward the area where he was born when he was struck down by pneumonia. A number of newspapers

Marie-Thérèse Chouteau   *Auguste Chouteau, Jean-Baptiste's godfather.*

Portraits of Madame Chouteau and Her Son Auguste Chouteau

Madame Chouteau (Marie-Thérèse Bourgeois), born in New Orleans of a French father and a Spanish mother, had only one son, Auguste, from her marriage with René-Auguste Chouteau, who decided one fine day to go back to France for an unspecified period. When he returned, his wife had settled in St. Louis with Pierre Laclède. Marie-Thérèse and her new companion eventually had four children who bore the Chouteau name. This Pierre Laclède was the same who is said to have founded St. Louis with Auguste Chouteau in 1763-1764. The members of the Chouteau family made St. Louis an important city. They were Louisiana French who were perfectly at home with French Canadians, Americans, and especially Indians.

Pierre Laclède died in 1778. Madame Chouteau, born in 1733, survived her companion until 1814. Referred to as "La Veuve Chouteau" (the Widow Chouteau), she was known equally for her good business sense and loyalty to her extended family. The fact that Auguste and his daughter Eulalie, aged twelve, acted as godfather and godmother to Jean-Baptiste suggests that Toussaint and Sacagawea enjoyed some measure of public renown.

Readers may be surprised to learn that Toussaint wanted to have his son baptized. He was not married and certainly far from being a practising Catholic. However, a deep-rooted religious background was sufficient in itself to account for the baptism. Toussaint was a Roman Catholic, and therefore his son would be, too.

"The home of Madame Chouteau, mother of St. Louis"

reported his death in the summer of 1866, all of which called attention to his merits.

Like his father, Jean-Baptiste was to be eclipsed in the American imagination by the memory of Sacagawea. Today, for many Americans, the child who appears on the current U.S. gold dollar, clinging to his mother's back, is called Pomp. Quebecers are surprised to learn that his real name is Jean-Baptiste, a classic first name for *Canadiens*—Jean-Baptiste Charbonneau, the son of Toussaint born in Boucherville near Montreal, and the grandson of Jean-Baptiste Charbonneau and Marguerite Deniau. ℗

℗ After Toussaint Charbonneau's death, his son Jean-Baptiste inherited a small sum of money from the sale of some land (Hafen: 217). Jean-Baptiste died unmarried and, as far as is known, led a bachelor's life.

The story of Jean-Baptiste Charbonneau illustrates yet again the astonishing mobility of the French Canadians and their descendants. Their march across America was not halted by the British Conquest of 1760; they simply continued on their way in the service of new masters.

Chapter 12

The Indians

The journals kept by Lewis and Clark and their officers are an absolutely unique source for studying the Indians of North America. It is amazing that there is so little reference to these journals in the numberless Amerindian studies that have appeared. However, since the publication of James P. Ronda's *Lewis and Clark among the Indians* in 2000, several books on the subject have come out.

The fact is that few documents exist in which first contact with Native Americans is recounted, as when the Lewis and Clark Expedition met the Shoshones, Nez Percés, and many other Indian groups. This material is all the richer for Jefferson having insisted beforehand that Lewis and Clark bring back answers to a host of questions about Native Americans.

In this chapter my aim is to render a brief homage to the Indians. Not only did they refrain from trying to block the expedition, they also made its success possible in countless ways. This was especially true of the expedition's dangerous passage through the Rockies, going and returning.

The Indians possessed a natural sense of hospitality. They shared what they had. They liked festivities and were more responsive to Cruzatte's violin than Lewis's cannon. Jefferson had asked Lewis to take smallpox vaccines with him to give to the Indians. The subject of the incredible ravages caused by smallpox among the Indians has yet to be adequately studied.

The Indians survived with great difficulty, mainly through mixed breeding, a phenomenon that underlies this book as a whole. The development of a Métis population was a first stage toward survival. The irony here was that native societies exercised such a powerful attraction on their members that they were unable to integrate themselves into white society, although they knew how to integrate others into their own. And so they remained marginal, locked in their traditions and laid low by epidemics.

❧

The winter spent at Fort Clatsop had been a gloomy one, despite the presence of Chinook women, whose favours were for sale.✻ It seemed to go on forever. The two captains were impatient, and on March 23, 1806, they gave the long-awaited signal to start the return journey. It was premature.

As the expedition moved along the homeward route, they met the Indians whom they had encountered on the way west. The meetings were mostly cordial, and the Indians showed their willingness to help. By this time the Americans had almost run out of trade goods to repay their hosts, and compensated by caring for their sick people. Nevertheless the Corps of Discovery pushed on. The Walla Walla chief Yellept proved particularly attentive and benevolent. He realized how pressed for time his visitors felt and told them about a shortcut that would provide water and all-important grazing for the horses, as well as an abundant supply of "Deer and Antilopes" (pronghorn). The terrain was level and the trail clear. The crucial benefit was that it shortened their journey by 80 miles (130 km) (Thwaites, 4: 330). The trail led them to Nez Percé country by early May. On Saturday, May 4, they met their former river pilot as well as the young

✻Among the Mandans there was great sexual freedom. The women gave themselves willingly to strangers. At Fort Clatsop, however, actual prostitution flourished. There can be no argument. By the time the Americans arrived there, Chinook women had learned to deal with strangers and bargain for favours given. On the evening of November 21, 1805, the wife of Chief Delashelwilt brought along six other women for this purpose. "Many are handsom," Clark admitted (Moulton, 6: 73). We learn from Sergeant Gass's journal that such visits were a regular thing. The two captains, noting the generosity of their men, undertook to hand out ribbons to serve as money. In return for such payment, the men acquired venereal diseases that Lewis continually had to treat. He wondered how the Indians managed, as they didn't appear to suffer unduly from the disease.

Clatsop hat

chief Tetoharsky, who had accompanied them the previous autumn as far as the great falls on the Columbia. As before, the two Indians were well disposed toward the expedition and led it to the village of Twisted Hair, to whom the expedition's horses had been entrusted.

Full of good will, one of Twisted Hair's relations "gave us a sketch of the principal · watercourses West of the Rocky Mountains" (Thwaites, 5:5). The information was much appreciated, and Lewis carefully preserved it, but for the moment the Corps wanted more than anything to get their horses back. To the captains' surprise and dismay, "Twisted Hair received us very coolly," wrote Lewis. It quickly became clear that a quarrel of some sort had occurred between Twisted Hair and the Cutnose chief, Neeshneparkkeoök, who was then present. The captains, worried by an earlier rumour that their cache of saddles had been dug up and their horses scattered, asked for explanations, but the interpreter, a Shoshone boy, refused to act on the ground that he would be interfering in a controversy between chiefs, even if only to translate. In the end it was Drouillard, back from a hunting excursion, who

Nez Percé Indian (Alfred Jacob Miller, Ross: No. 33).

The Nez Percés were all peaceful and particularly honest people. However, the origin of their name is less than straightforward (Josephy: 645). On August 14, 1805, Lewis first wrote of the "persed nosed Indians." The French had spread the name Nez Percés, which had been reserved for the Chopunnish, although the practice of nose piercing was not unique to them. The descendants of the Nez Percés have occasionally denied the existence of this ancient custom, but archaeological research would seem to confirm it.

acted as intermediary. It appeared that the Cutnose chief had kept an eye on the horses over the winter. Matters were soon mended; saddles and horses were retrieved and assembled (Thwaites, 5: 5-7).

The expedition stayed with the Nez Percés for some time, as the captains were busy making diplomatic overtures to the many visiting chiefs, urging them to visit Washington. They also continued their medical attentions to the sick people who flocked to the village, not to mention little Jean-Baptiste who was afflicted with a painful sore throat accompanied by a high fever. Lewis wrote, "Charbono's child is very ill this evening; he is cuting teeth, and for several days past has had a violent lax, which having suddonly stoped he was attacked with a high fever and his neck and throat are much swolen this evening. we gave him a doze of creem of tartar and flour of sulpher and applyed a poltice of boiled onions to his neck as warm as he could well bear it" (Thwaites, 5: 56).

The Spectre of the Rockies

The Corps got ready to depart "in the most ample manner in our power to meet that wretched portion of our journey, the Rocky Mountains, where hunger and Cold in their most rigorous form assail the w[e]aried traveller," wrote Clark on June 2, 1806, facing the prospect squarely.✳ The memory of their first crossing still sent chills down his spine. "[N]ot any of us have yet forgotten our sufferings in those mountains in September last, I think it probable we never shall" (Thwaites, 5: 101).

Preparations dragged on. On June 10, despite the Indians' advice against leaving so early and the fact that the expected guides had failed to appear thus far, the two captains decided to resume their journey. Their supplies were meagre and they had been warned that grass for the horses would be hard to find. Nevertheless they headed undaunted into the Bitterroot Mountains, moving gingerly on starving, stumbling mounts. Soon the men were exhausted. The spectre of September 1805 haunted them.

On June 17 they resigned themselves to retracing their footsteps while the horses could still move. They realized it would be "maddnes[s] . . . to proceed without a guide." Lewis noted tersely that, "This is the first time since we have been on this long tour that we have ever

✳ Soulard's maps were fairly reassuring and indirectly confirmed the likelihood of a watershed or a height of land from which all rivers ran either toward the Gulf of Mexico, or toward the Gulf of California and the Pacific Ocean. The Mandans and Hidatsas had talked of an easy passage across the mountains. Despite the help of Old Toby, the Shoshone guide, the crossing was extremely difficult and exhausting, especially along the Lolo Trail. It was winter, game was rare, and the men had to kill their own horses in order to eat (Moulton, 5: 3).

been compelled to retreat or make a retrograde march" (Thwaites, 5: 141, 142). Clark, as was often the case, echoed Lewis's comment word for word. They cached all unnecessary baggage on scaffolds and set off at 1 p.m.

Drouillard—he was always called upon in a crisis—and Shannon were sent in advance to the Nez Percés village in the hope of finding the Indian guides they had been expecting, or possibly someone who would agree to lead them to Travelers' Rest Creek.

Days went by. As they waited, the captains imagined various solutions. In despair, they considered moving forward behind scouts who would try to indicate a possible route. But time was of the essence. They had to reach the Missouri before the next winter—before the river froze. In fact, they relied completely on the mission entrusted to Drouillard and Shannon. On June 23, the two were back, bringing with them "three indians who had consented to accompany us to the falls of the Missouri for the Compensation of 2 guns," wrote Clark, immensely relieved. "Those are all young men of good Charrector and much respected by their nation." One of them was "the brother of the *cutnose*," he noted (Thwaites 5: 157).

Wonderful Guides

The Corps set off without delay. Not only were the guides familiar with the mountain passes, they knew the distances between one patch of grass and the next. ☙ On June 27, Lewis' confidence returned. The expedition halted "on an elivated point" at the request of their guides "and smoked the pipe," Lewis wrote. "From this place we had an extensive view of these stupendous mountains principally covered with snow like that on which we stood; we were entirely surrounded by those mountains from which to one unacquainted with them it would have seemed impossible ever to have escaped; in short without the assistance of our guides I doubt much whether we who had once passed them could find our way to Travellers rest" (Thwaites, 5: 165).

On June 30, 1806, they were back at their camp of the previous autumn on the shore of Travelers' Rest Creek. The nearby hot springs gave them new energy. Lewis observed that "the indians after remaining in the hot bath as long as they could bear it ran and plunged themselves into the creek the water of which is now as

☙ Game had become rare. On June 25, 1806, Sacagawea remarked on the presence of western spring beauty—one of the first flowering species to appear—which she gathered. The Shoshones customarily ate the roots of this small plant, which has a pleasant taste (Moulton, 8: 51-52). The Corps was travelling between a branch of the Clearwater and the magnificent Lochsa River at the time. (Cutright, 1989: 406).

cold as ice can make it," repeating the process several times but ending with the warm bath (Thwaites 5: 171). The Indian guides kept cool heads, however. They felt that they had accomplished their mission and would run the danger of meeting their various enemies if they went any further.

✽ Clark also paid homage to the Nez Percés, especially "the late Great Chief … who had been remarkably kind to us in every instance" (Thwaites, 5: 180).

☙ On August 11, 1806, Lewis was out hunting with Cruzatte. Suddenly a bullet hit him in the left buttock. At first he thought Cruzatte was responsible, then was inclined to suspect that an Indian might have been lurking close by. He walked back painfully to the others in his party and asked them to go in search of Cruzatte, who always protested his innocence. In any case, Lewis felt the important thing was to get his wound treated immediately.

Lewis and Clark breathed a sigh of relief at having finally conquered the mountains. Their exploring instinct reasserted itself, and they decided to separate for a few weeks. Lewis would go north to explore the Marias River, while Clark went south toward the Yellowstone. They would meet at the junction of the Missouri and Yellowstone. The Indians agreed to guide Lewis on his way for a short time.

On July 3, Lewis "took leave of my worthy friend and companion Capt. Clark" and set off "with my party of nine men and five indians." The next day it was the Indians' turn to say goodbye, after giving Lewis detailed instructions about the route to follow (Thwaites, 5: 183-184). "Our guides betrayed every emmotion of unfeigned regret at seperating from us; they said that they were confidint that the Pahkees, (the appellation they give the Minnetares) would cut us off" (188).

Sergeant Patrick Gass had his own commentary in his journal: "It is but justice to say that the whole nation to which they belong [Nez Percés], are the most friendly, honest, and ingenuous people that we have seen in the course of our voyage and travels" (Thwaites, 5: 188, n. 1).

Indians and Americans amused themselves on the evening of July 2, before Lewis and Clark's parties separated. "[T]he Indians run their horses, and we had several foot races betwen the natives and our party with various success," wrote Lewis, who made a point of mentioning that the Nez Percés "are a race of hardy strong athletic active men" (Thwaites, 5: 180). ✽ From every point of view, they were his favourites.

Clark Confronts Black Buffalo

Six weeks later, Lewis and Clark met up as planned. Lewis's party had had a dangerous run-in with a Piegan Blackfoot group on July 26-27, resulting in the killing of one and perhaps two Indians. On August 11, Lewis himself had been

mysteriously shot in the left buttock and couldn't walk. *(See note on previous page.)* ℗
Fortunately, the expedition was now travelling by water and he was able to lie on
his stomach in the pirogue.

The Americans had good reason to be relieved, however. They were homeward
bound. There were no more obstacles before them, except perhaps the Teton
Sioux—who, as it happened, were actually in the area. On August 30, 1806, Clark
saw several men on horseback to the northeast of the river. These, he wrote later,
"with the help of a Spie glass I found to be Indians." He had his pirogue land on
the southwest side of the Missouri. Some twenty Indians immediately appeared
on a hill "a little above us on the opposite Side. one of those men I took to be a
freinch man from his . . . blanket Capoe [hooded woollen tunic] & a handkerchief
around his head" (Moulton, 8: 329). Then, before Clark had time to think, a band
of eighty or ninety Indians armed with guns as well as bows and arrows emerged

Two Sioux on the Lookout
(Ross: No. 18).
According to the artist, Alfred
Jacob Miller, they were watching
over horses and mules grazing in
the area. He also mentioned they
liked to stand on these natural
promontories from where they
could readily see all approaching
danger. In his journal, Jean-
Baptiste Trudeau portrays the
Sioux as being fairly warlike.

from a wood on the opposite bank, about a quarter of a mile downriver.

As a precaution, Clark took "three french men" who could speak "the Mahar Pania and some Seioux" and canoed out to a sandbank, "close enough to converse." Three young Indians swam out to the sandbank to parley (Moulton, 8: 330).

The Indians were Teton Sioux. Black Buffalo was their leader. Clark's heart swelled with indignation. The events of the autumn of 1804, when the expedition had nearly come to blows with this same band, were ever present in his mind. He showered angry reproaches on the Indians and warned them to return to their camp at once, adding that, "if any of them come near our camp we Should kill them certainly" (Moulton, 8: 330).

For once Clark—usually a man of few words—had plenty to say, proclaiming his woes and recalling his grievances. He told the Indians "that we had not forgot their treatment to us as we passed up this river," that they would not be able to block river traffic, and that when other whites "wished to visit the nations above they would Come Sufficiently Strong to whip any vilenous party who dare to oppose them." Furthermore, he said, he knew that some of their people were at war with "the Mandans &c, and that they would be well whiped as the Mandans & Menetarres had a plenty of Guns Powder and balls, and we had given them a Cannon." In sum, "keep away from the river or we Should kill every one" (Moulton, 8: 330-331).

The Teton Sioux then tried to appease the Americans. "Those fellows," wrote Clark, "requested to be allowed to come across and make cumerads." The answer was "No". The Indians moved off, but the Americans held their ground, for Clark was worried about Shannon and the Field brothers, who were off hunting. When they finally returned, "[W]e proceeded on," Clark wrote for the nth time, "down about 6 miles and encamped on a large Sand bar in the middle of the river" (Moulton, 8: 331). He was taking no chances.

Was Clark afraid? Lewis, still recovering from his gunshot wound, was in no condition to back him up. Clark was clearly nervous. His threats to the Indians were serious, but in taking stock of the event a few days after his return to St. Louis, he was well aware that it was infinitely preferable to avoid squabbles or, even worse, actual conflict. Lewis's skirmish with the Piegans was already one incident too many. They had better steer clear of further trouble.

A Generally Warm Welcome

The warlike attitude of the Teton Sioux made Clark aware of just how welcoming most Indians had been. One nation after another, they had listened politely while Lewis told them about the sovereignty of the United States over native territory! They watched, sometimes warily, as medals, flags, and certificates were handed out. They shrugged at the idea of being or becoming the children of a Grandfather far away in the direction of the rising sun.

What the Indians dreamed of was trade. The white men's products had already reached them through a vast trading network. Perhaps they would have a chance of improving their position in the chain. Some, such as the Teton Sioux, had no intention of losing the few advantages they held, based on their position on the Missouri trade route.

All in all, the Indians had behaved very naturally as human beings. The Americans may have had heavy equipment, but they seemed to lack resources and to be worried, at the very least, if not actually at a loss about what to do. It took but a single glance to see that these strangers were out of their element. Still, the Indians welcomed them cordially, and most often with good humour.

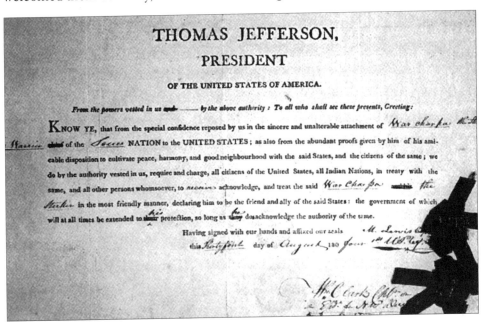

Type of document given to the Indians by the white "Grandfather" in Washington.

Lewis tried to impress his hosts with his air gun and his instruments, parading the white man's skills. It was the interpreters who really made contact, however: Drouillard (with his sign language), Dorion, Gravelines, Jussaume, Charbonneau, and Sacagawea. Whenever possible the Americans organized hunting trips, sporting competitions, feasts, and dances. Cruzatte and his violin never failed to break down any lingering resistance.

With few exceptions, the Indians were hospitable. ✳ They were also generous. They liked commerce and often traded for the sheer pleasure of bargaining. It was the white man's weapons that interested them; the rest merely amused them. They willingly shared their food, even when they themselves were on short rations. Above all, they shared their knowledge. They didn't stint on information; they drew maps, supplied descriptions, warned of difficulties, indicated resources, and furnished guides. They taught the Americans how to make canoes and looked after their horses.

✳ Relations with the Indians were generally so good that Lewis felt it necessary to warn his soldiers to be on their guard. On February 20, 1806, after a pleasant meeting with Tâh-cum, a Chinook chief, Lewis insisted on the need for taking precautions. All the Indians were told to leave the fort. Lewis stated that despite their apparent good nature, the Indians "might be treacherous" and the men should never place themselves at their mercy, that their duplicity was well known. Clark, as was often the case, repeated his colleague's aggressive and unjustified comments word for word (Moulton, 6: 330-332). Ronda (212) noted that "the Corps of Discovery had to be taught to hate."

Consequences for the Indians

The expedition led by Meriwether Lewis and William Clark was a success. The Indians could have prevented it; instead, they made it possible. In doing so, had they opened the way for the American conquest of the West? Strange to say, the return of Lewis and Clark didn't create much of a stir. Of course there were festivities and celebrations, but even Jefferson took his time about plunging into the mass of information gathered.

Then the War of 1812 against the British, fought mainly in Upper Canada (Ontario), shifted attention somewhat from the West. The Americans provisionally renounced their claim to the mouth of the Columbia River. Publication of the expedition's travel journals became bogged down. Patrick Gass's journal was the only one to appear promptly. The rest, when they did appear, were poorly distributed and went almost unnoticed. They would not surface again until sixty-five years later.

The fact remained, however, that in 1803 the immense Louisiana Purchase had come under Washington's authority. The Spanish disputed the boundaries, the French Canadians crossed and recrossed it in all directions, and the British tried to limit its expansion to the north and west.

Meanwhile the Indians acquired ever increasing supplies of firearms and horses, yet at the same time their numbers were dwindling as terrible epidemics decimated the indigenous nations. The survivors were moved from their homelands and would be progressively shunted onto reserves. They kept the memory of Lewis and Clark, who may indeed have been ambassadors of peace, but in the service of a new power that emanated from Washington. These Indians would be the first, but not the last, to bend the knee.

Native peoples, either from a sense of nostalgia or a vengeful spirit, can always say that their ancestors had at least a hundred chances to wipe out the Corps of Discovery as it passed through their territory between 1804 and 1806—but there is no turning back the clock.

Oct. 1, 1806.

By the last Mails.

MARYLAND.   BALTIMORE, OCT. 29, 1806.

A LETTER from *St. Louis* (*Upper Louisiana*), dated *Sept.* 23, 1806, announces the arrival of Captains LEWIS and CLARK, from their expedition into the interior.—They went to the *Pacific Ocean* ; have brought some of the natives and curiosities of the countries through which they passed, and only lost one man. They left the *Pacific Ocean* 23d March, 1806, where they arrived in November, 1805 ;—and where some American vessels had been just before.—They state the Indians to be as numerous on the *Columbia* river, which empties into the *Pacific*, as the whites in any part of the U. S. They brought a family of the Mandan indians with them. The winter was very mild on the *Pacific*.— They have kept an ample journal of their tour ; which will be published, and must afford much intelligence.

Mr. ERSKINE, the new British Minister to the United States, is warmly attached to the U. States. He married, about seven years since, an American lady, daughter of Gen. CADWALLADER, of *Pennsylvania*. He has a daughter now in the U. States.

On October 1, 1806, a Baltimore newspaper announced "the arrival of Captains Lewis and Clark from their expedition into the interior" in St. Louis, noting that they had brought with them a Mandan family and that their "ample journal" would soon be published; also that the Indian population along the Columbia was as numerous "as the whites in any part of the U.S." This brief report was based on a letter of September 23, 1806, from St. Louis in Upper Louisiana.

The tragedy lies not in the contact and meeting, but in the subsequent difficulty for Indians and whites to build a new society together. The development of a half-breed population was a first stage, but—by a curious turn of fate—the force of attraction of Amerindian societies was too strong. They knew how to integrate others into their society, but not how to integrate themselves into white society, and so they stayed marginal, locked in their traditions.

Like individuals, nations are born, live, and die.

Chapter 13

York and Sacagawea

In Lewis and Clark's day, twenty percent of the United States' population was made up of black slaves. York was one of them; Clark was his master.

York was a "good" slave, Clark a "good" master. And yet nothing was easy, at least after the expedition had returned. For York, the great journey had been a moment of grace.

A slave could dream of freedom, but he was not prepared for it. There are many forms of slavery and dependence.

York had no family name, neither did Sacagawea. York had been willed to Clark, Sacagawea was bought or won in a gambling game. Today she has become the most celebrated woman in the United States. Apparently, there are now more statues of her than any other American woman. As a supreme consecration, she appears on the face of the U.S. Mint's new golden dollar coin.

How did the Sacagawea legend develop? What is true, what is false? The answer to these questions takes us back to John McLoughlin, born in Rivière-du-Loup on the Lower St. Lawrence, who married an extraordinary French-speaking Métis woman and became the "father of Oregon."

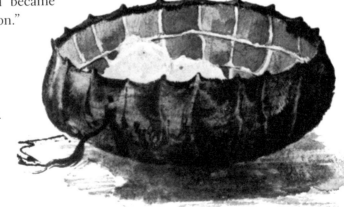

Mandan "bull boat" constructed of a single bull buffalo hide over a willow frame. Note the handy tail as a towrope. Karl Bodmer (Thompson: 176).

It was in the wake of a best-selling book on McLoughlin that an American novelist, Eva Emery Dye, sought and found a new subject for her pen, the so-called "humble Shoshone princess."

At the very bottom of the ladder of the humble and disenfranchised in the Lewis and Clark Expedition were York, Clark's black slave, and Sacagawea, the young Shoshone woman who accompanied the interpreter Toussaint Charbonneau.

"My black Servent & the segassity of Capt. Lewis's Dog" astonished the Shoshones, wrote Clark on August 17, 1805 (Thwaites, 2: 363). In fact, everything amazed them: the general appearance of the Americans, their clothes, their watercraft, their highly sophisticated weapons. The Shoshones had never seen whites—or blacks. In fact, Plains Indians in general had never seen blacks. York quickly became one of the Corps of Discovery's main attractions, as he had first discovered in October 1804 among the Arikaras.

* Jean-Baptiste Trudeau and David Thompson had already written of the sexual freedom common among the nations of the Upper Missouri. The Arikara and Mandan villages were veritable paradises.

The Americans watched curiously as the Indians manoeuvred their round canoes "made of a Single Buffalow Skin" across the river carrying three squaws, "in waves as high as I ever Saw." The Arikaras, meanwhile, stared unbelievingly at the strangers and especially at York. "Many came to view us all day, much astonished at my black Servent," wrote Clark, adding, "this nation never Saw a black man before" (Thwaites, 1: 185). The Indians considered York "big medicine."

The village children circled round him, examining him with curiosity. York played with them, pretending to be a wild beast. It has been suggested that the Indian women, naturally welcoming to strangers, fantasized about York, some of them even offering themselves to him with the complicity of their husbands.* At least so it is told! What is the truth, exactly? It seems possible that York's attraction and his reputed sexual prowess are pure invention, born of the imagination of highly prejudiced historians. This is the view of Gary Moulton, who points out that nothing in the journals of the two captains justifies such a portrait of York. It is Clark himself, however, who seems to be at the origin of the reputation acquired by his "black servent." Did he not tell Nicholas Biddle, while the latter was preparing the expedition's journals for publication, that an Arikara husband had offered his wife to York and retired from the house—even preventing someone from entering until the thing was done (Jackson, 1978, 2: 503)?

Clearly York was a true male, hardy, strong, and athletic, as well as being jovial and good-natured. Indian women and men were astonished at his love of music and his agility. He willingly danced for them, demonstrating these qualities to the full.

When a Hidatsa chief known as "Le Borgne" (French for "the one-eyed man") decided to unmask him, convinced that he was covered in black paint, York submitted readily to the inspection, amused by this skepticism and by the chief's subsequent annoyance (Jackson, 1978, 2: 539; Moulton, 3: 331).

York's Story

William Clark had inherited York. Clark's father, John, had left York to his son in his will (1799). York's father had also been John Clark's slave.

York (we know of no other name for him) and William Clark were the same age. They had been brought up together, but in a master-slave relationship. They were greatly attached to one another, but in very different ways. As master, Clark considered that York belonged to him and was in his service. York knew that he must anticipate his master's wishes, carry his baggage, and keep an eye out for his welfare. ☙

Throughout the expedition—two years and four months—York's conduct was without reproach. He took part in all the work parties and joined the other members of the expedition in doing all sorts of tasks. Some of these held immense significance for the slave. He was allowed to bear firearms, to hunt, and to fight when necessary. For him this was an entirely new situation. He became accustomed to what was in those days a strange kind of fraternization—spontaneously watching over the dying Sergeant Floyd in August 1804, and generally enjoying a form of equality. The two captains asked his opinion, along with that of the others in the expedition, before choosing the site for their second winter camp. "It was the first time in American history that a black slave had voted," as Stephen Ambrose remarked (1996: 316).

Upon returning from this long and wonderful adventure, York naturally saw life differently. He was audacious enough to ask his master to free him.

☙ Every night, from Fort Mandan to Fort Clatsop, York set up the buffalo-hide tent in which the two captains and the Charbonneau family slept (Thwaites, 1: 285). The tent belonged to Toussaint Charbonneau. An agreement had been made that Lewis and Clark would sleep there.

Le Borgne tries to unmask York.
Detail from a painting by Charles M. Russell.

⊚ York and Sacagawea were the only members of the expedition who were not paid. If nothing else, York's wages should have been paid to Clark.

Clark reacted badly. There was absolutely no question of being separated from his "servent."

At the most, he allowed York to take several weeks' leave to visit his wife, whose master lived in Kentucky. York had the temerity to suggest finding work in Kentucky and sending his wages to Clark. ⊚ If Clark refused this request, he would then ask to be sold. Clark fulminated, uttered dire predictions as to York's future, and even thought of finding him a cruel master somewhere in New Orleans. In a letter of November 1808, addressed to his brother Jonathan, Clark explained his dilemma and enlarged on his sinister plans while wishing that York might never learn about them if he would only return to the fold "and conduct himself well" (Ambrose, 1996: 457-458). In his letters to his brother (Holmberg, 1992: 7-9), Clark tells of his many problems with his slaves, and how he thought he might "turn negrows into goods & cash."

Sadly, York's story ends in accordance with a fate written in his origins. Clark freed him some time after 1811. The former slave found temporary work carrying merchandise between Tennessee and Kentucky, but the enterprise foundered. The most probable version of York's fate is that he died of cholera around 1832 while travelling to St. Louis, apparently ready to return to Clark's service.

There are other versions. The Indians had not forgotten York, nor had he forgotten them. There were those who naturally made up a story about how York had travelled to the Rocky Mountain region and ended his days among the Crow people (Moulton, 2: 525).

York may be long forgotten, but with Sacagawea it is a quite different story.

Sacagawea: the Basis of a Legend

Anniversaries have their advantages, often providing an occasion for bringing important people and facts out of oblivion.

In the years 1890-1900, Oregon was in a state of continual excitement. Each year brought a chance to mark a centenary of some sort. Sea-going explorers George Vancouver and Robert Gray had their turn. Other centenaries followed, celebrating the expeditions of Lewis and Clark, the Astorians, David Thompson, and, shortly after, of John McLoughlin. The novelist Eva Emery Dye latched on to McLoughlin as a subject and in 1900 published a book called *McLoughlin and Old Oregon* in 1900. It was an overnight success, and the public wanted more.

Dye faced a daunting challenge. As a subject, John McLoughlin was a giant who bowed to no man. Combative, colourful, and determined, McLoughlin was everything a writer could desire. Dye had set herself a high standard: she had to find another extraordinary character. She began combing the archives, scanning all the historical accounts she could find. She finally opted for an Indian girl who had accompanied Lewis and Clark to the Pacific. The girl's story was simple and touching. Dye had found her heroine, and decided to lift her story into the realm of

John McLoughlin (1784-1857) was born near Rivière-du-Loup on the lower St. Lawrence. His father was of Scottish origin, and his mother, Angélique Fraser, was half Scottish. He studied medicine, but signed on with the North West Company in 1803 to work as a physician and apprentice clerk. This brought him as far as the mouth of the Columbia River, where he finally settled with his Métis wife, Marguerite Waddens (*DCB*, 8: 575-581). He was then working for the Hudson's Bay Company. Historian F.V.V. Holman published *Dr. John McLoughlin:, the Father of Oregon* in 1907.

the legendary. Her style and writer's flair gave birth to the character whom she initially described as "a humble Shoshone princess"—which wasn't entirely false. Sacagawea's father had been the chief of his tribe, succeeded by her brother, Cameahwait. Now it was up to the novelist to construct a Sacagawea worthy of her origins.

Sacagawea was born around 1790 into a small tribe referred to as the Shoshone in the western section of the Great Plains. They lived near the sources of the Missouri, in the foothills the Rockies. Sacagawea belonged to the Snake nation. For a good hundred years the Shoshones had been acquiring horses from the south and southeast. Raising them had become something of a speciality. The Shoshones sold horses to their neighbours to the north, such as the Crow people, and to the northwest, such as the Nez-Percés whom they joined each year for the buffalo hunt in territories where their Hidatsa enemies were on the prowl. Like the Nez Percés or the Salish Indians, the Shoshones had not had direct contact with whites and were unable

✷ Toussaint Charbonneau had several "wives," sometimes more than one at a time. When he met Lewis and Clark he had two and perhaps three, according to Patrick Gass. The journals of the two captains contain only one ambiguous reference by Clark, dated November 11, 1804: "two Squars of the Rock Mountains, purchased from the Indians by (2) a frenchmen (Chaboneau) Came down" (Moulton, 3: 232-233).

A painting of Indians herding horses by Alfred Jacob Miller. When horses were first reintroduced into the Americas by the Spanish in the early sixteenth century, the Indians lost no time in taming them for their use. They quickly became superb horsemen and could train their mounts for either war or hunting. Sometimes the hunted animal had to be killed—buffalo, for example—and sometimes the object was to take it alive. In this case, there was a method for momentarily paralyzing a horse by putting a bullet in the base of the neck. The most spectacular method was the use of the lasso, a thin strip of leather about 25 feet (8 metres) long, usually attached to the hunter's mount and ending in a running noose.

to get firearms. Trading partners like the Blackfeet and Assiniboins acquired guns now and then, but were loath to sell them.

Sacagawea was kidnapped during a Hidatsa raid and eventually became the wife of Toussaint Charbonneau, a French-Canadian trader who lived among the Hidatsas. *(See note on previous page.)*✳ Charbonneau, hired as an interpreter by Lewis and Clark, took Sacagawea with him. It was the story of this adventure that Dye decided to recount in *The Conquest: the True Story of Lewis and Clark*. The novelist was bewitched by Sacagawea and made her the madonna of the expedition.

Dye's enthusiastic pen produced a Sacagawea of epic proportions. "Madonna of her race, she had led the way to a new time. To the hands of this girl, not yet eighteen, had been entrusted the key that unlocked the road of Asia" (Clark and Edmonds: 92).

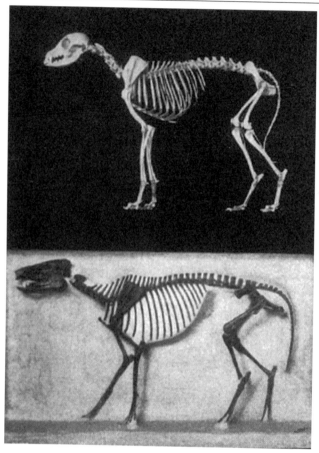

Illustrated here: the skeleton of a modern horse, above. Below is the skeleton of the horse present in North America during the Pleistocene (early Quaternary) era, that is, the last Ice Age, from about 1.6 million years ago to about 10,000 years ago.

The Return of the Horse

The Americas gave much to the rest of the world, but they also received much (apart from devastating micro-organisms)—many vegetables, fruits, and animals, including the horse. There is fossil evidence of prehistoric horses existing millions of years ago in North America, which might explain why it adapted so quickly when first reintroduced. A recent find in southern Alberta by a team from the University of Calgary (2001) offers conclusive evidence of early (Clovis) people hunting pony-sized horses. Modern horses reached Quebec in 1665, and within a hundred years there were fourteen thousand horses in the St. Lawrence Valley. They multiplied at an even greater rate in the more southerly areas of the continent as European settlers arrived. Although the Spanish refused to give horses (or guns) to the Indians, they soon lost control of the situation. The Pueblo Indians were among the first Native Americans to get hold of modern horses, followed by the Apaches, Kiowas, and Utes. It was the Utes who became the main suppliers of horses to the Comanches and Shoshones. The arrival of horses revolutionized the lives of Plains Indians, and a number of tribes went back to a nomad life. The Mandan and Hidatsa villages became centres of vast trading networks, bringing firearms from the north and horses from the south. A new type of Indian, often with a strong Métis component, was in the process of being born.

The Trapper's Bride
(Alfred Jacob Miller, Ross: No. 12).
The artist painted several pictures
of the same subject, but his
comments were always the same:
the price was very high and, in
particular, the young bride was
very demanding. "She wants a
dress, horse, gorgeous saddle,
trappings, and the deuce knows
what beside," wrote Miller. In
less time than it takes to tell, the
trapper was crippled with debt,
and had no choice but to "sell
himself, body and soul, to the Fur
Company for a number of years."

President Jefferson had given Lewis and Clark instructions to find the most direct navigable waterway to the Pacific. Dye didn't hesitate to state that Sacagawea had shown it to the explorers. In less time than it takes to say (or rather to write), her heroine sprang from the pages, soaring beyond Dye's conception. Suffragette organizations took over Sacagawea, and many writers set out in search of her. What had been "an obscure Indian girl" became, for George Creel, writing for *Collier's American Weekly* in 1926, the guiding spirit of the Corps of Discovery (Clark and Edmonds: 93-102).

The Real Story

Sacagawea was about ten years old when she was kidnapped along with a number of others from her tribe. On the day the Corps of Discovery reached the spot where she had been taken captive, Lewis, who had already expressed surprise at her unemotional nature, couldn't help noting in his journal how placid and almost resigned or fatalistic she was.

It was July 28, 1805. The Americans had set up camp "precisely on the spot that the Snake Indians were encamped at the time the Minnetares of the Knife R. came in sight of them five years since . . . pursued, attacked them, killed 4 men 4 women a number of boys, and mad[e] prisoners of all the females and four boys" (Thwaites, 2: 282-283). ⊘ This is probably what the Hidatsas had told Lewis. He now watched Sacagawea, looking for some reaction. Had she not been captured on the very spot where they stood? She had clearly recognized it because of the Three Forks, where the Missouri divides into its three sources.

⊘ The micro-organisms brought by Europeans to the Americas unleashed devastating epidemics. Smallpox took an unimaginable toll. The Indians already practised the custom of bringing men and women captives back from their wars. The epidemics that decimated their populations gave them yet a further reason to bring back captives in order to help reconstitute their communities. The Indian custom of adopting outsiders was well-established. There are hundreds of recorded tales of white men and women being completely integrated into Indian communities, to the point of not wanting to return to their families. In Quebec, the importance of captives in the communities of Kahnawake, Wôlinak, Odonak, and Wendake, for example, is well known. Many inhabitants of these modern-day communities have several captives among their ancestors.

✳ Clark applied bark or decoctions of bark with curative powers, such as quinine (*quina quina*), the best known.

Lewis was an emotional man. He empathized with the trauma she had experienced, and yet, as he admitted, "I cannot discover that she shews any immotion of sorrow in recollecting this event, or of joy in being again restored to her native country; if she has enough to eat and a few trinkets to wear I beleive she would be perfectly content anywhere" (Moulton 5: 9).

Lewis had absolutely no idea of Sacagawea's stoic nature. For three months he had watched her walk with her baby, never complaining, never showing the least impatience or mentioning fatigue. On the contrary, she was always looking for ways to be useful. Sacagawea was in fact an example of steadfastness, determination, and willingness. Her mere presence was a source of inspiration to the men of the Corps of Discovery.

In his unobtrusive way, Clark took Sacagawea and her son under his wing. They established a fine rapport. We can sense Clark's genuine anxiety when she fell ill in the middle of June, 1805. On June 10 he bled her, noting "Sa cah gah we â our Indian woman verry sick." The verdict was the same for the next two days. At this point Clark decided to put her in the back of the pirogue, which was covered, to protect her from the sun. The night of June 13 to 14 was a painful one. Sacagawea moaned constantly. Clark felt helpless and considered her case grave (Moulton, 4: 294). On June 15 he decided to "give her the bark & apply it exteranely [externally] to her region." ✳ She recovered after bathing in sulfur hot springs in the area at Lewis's suggestion.

By August 17 Sacagawea was finally back to her old self. It was on this day that she saw her people. Strangely enough, she, the Shoshone interpreter, was with Clark that day. Lewis had ridden ahead with a party, desperately searching for Shoshones. When he finally chanced upon some on August 13, he experienced great difficulty establishing communication.

Contact did take place, however, despite problems in communication. Meanwhile, Clark and his party on the river were catching up, and on August 17 saw "Several Indians on horsback" approaching. "The Interpreter & Squar who were before me at some distance danced for the joyful sight, and She made signs to me that they were her nation," wrote Clark (Thwaites, 2: 365). Lewis, already ensconced in the Shoshone camp, wrote more fully of the final encounter. "The meeting of these people was really affecting, particularly between Sah-cah-gar-we-ah and an Indian woman, who had been taken prisoner at the same time with her and who, had afterwards escaped from the Minnetares and rejoined her nation" (Thwaites, 2: 361). The passive young Indian of yesterday had disappeared. Lewis had discovered her in a new light.

When, on November 5, 1805, Lewis and Clark were very anxious to buy a magnificent robe of sea-otter skins from a coast Indian, it was Sacagawea who came to the rescue. The Indian had refused all offers. The two captains had never seen such fine furs, and they were determined to have them. Sacagawea's belt of blue beads, which she wore with such pride, finally convinced the Indian to make the trade (Moulton 6: 72-73).

How a Myth Was Built

The titles used in the magazines of the day were each more enticing than the last. Sacagawea's name was almost whispered in the ear of the reader. Finally, it was suggested, the name of this astonishing woman could be established. Among all the possible contributors to the myth, Grace Raymond Hebard deserved the medal of honour! Her 1907 article in the *Journal of American History* was entitled, "Pilot of First White Men to Cross the American Continent." And to be sure of reaching her target audience, she explained, in two interminable subtitles: "Identification of the Indian Girl who led the Lewis and Clark Expedition over the Rocky Mountains in their Unparallelled Journey into the Mysteries of the Western World—Recognition of Sacagawea as the Woman who Guided the Explorers to the New Golden Empire." Dr. Hebard—she had a Ph.D. from the University of Wyoming—did not stop there. She based herself on texts, she asserted, citing Coues and Thwaites and referring to the actual journals of the explorers. Then (without mentioning it, of course) she proceeded to fabricate excerpts, for example: "Sacagawea had a good memory, remembering locations not seen since her childhood. . . . With her helpless infant she rode with the men, guiding us." Who is speaking. Who is writing? For whom is the "us" intended? Dr. Hebard's pen was out of control: "Sacagawea inspired us all," she had the captains say. Of course, neither Lewis nor Clark wrote such words, although they may well have thought them.

Lewis proudly wore the clothes brought back from his expedition for this watercolour portrait by C.B.J.F. de Saint-Mémin (1807). The jacket and trousers were made of leather. The cape-like overgarment with the wide collar may be made of otter. It is decorated with what appear to be twelve white weasel tails. On Christmas Day, 1805, Sacagawea gave Clark two dozen of these tails, ornaments apparently much valued by the Shoshone people.

Sacagawea was a proud and generous woman. Lewis gradually discovered her nature. Was he surprised when she insisted on going with the men as they were leaving to see a beached whale? She got her way, for once. "The Indian woman," wrote Lewis, "was very impo[r]tunate to be permited to go . . . she observed that she had traveled a long way with us to see the great waters, and that now that monstrous fish was also to be seen, she thought it very hard she could not be permitted to see either" (Thwaites, 3: 314-315).

After all, Sacagawea could very well have stayed with her people. She had accomplished what was expected of her. But she probably had a number of reasons for wanting to continue the journey. She knew very well that she was in the midst of a unique experience. She felt secure, and probably not very enthusiastic about the Shoshone husband proposed by her father. Lewis, who was always curious about the customs of the Indians he met, had in fact known that Sacagawea had been promised to a man who already had two wives. When the proposed husband learned that she had borne Charbonneau a child, he decided he no longer wanted her (Moulton, 5: 120). Sacagawea loved her child and accepted her lot with Charbonneau. Possibly she enjoyed his company. If not, the adventure that he made possible for her was compensation enough. Clark's kindness did the rest. She was well aware of it and appreciated his care and consideration. She knew how to show her gratitude, as Clark understood. At the end of November 1805, when hunger stalked the Corps, she gave him a piece of bread "made of some flower she had cearfully kept for her child." She had waited too long: the bread was slightly mouldy. Nevertheless, Clark claimed to have eaten it with "great satisfaction," no doubt appreciating it as much for the gesture as for "it being the only mouthful [of bread] I had tasted for Several months past" (Moulton, 6: 97). When Christmas 1805 came round, gifts were exchanged. Sacagawea gave Clark "two Dozen white weazils tails" (ermine), ornaments that her people prized (Moulton, 6: 137).

Guide and Interpreter

Contrary to the legend that probably originated with Dye's novel, Sacagawea did not hold the key to open the door of Asia. It was a rather artful phrase, in any case, as Dye well knew that her heroine was completely ignorant of the Pacific Ocean and therefore of any route leading to it. On the outward journey, at least as far as the Rockies, Sacagawea had been a useful and even reassuring addition to the party, since she was able to confirm that the Corps was approaching Shoshone country, the land of the "horse people." On August 8, 1805, Lewis noted that she had recognized a huge boulder which her people called Beaver's Head because of its resemblance to this animal. The Shoshone summer camp was actually near by. An anxious Lewis wrote that "it is now all important with us to meet with those people as soon as possible" (Moulton, 5: 59). The Corps needed horses, and Lewis decided to go looking for them the next day with a small detachment.

On the return journey that began in the spring of 1806, once the Rockies had been crossed Lewis and Clark separated on July 3 in order to do as much exploring as possible. On July 4 Clark patriotically called his party to a halt in order to celebrate Independence Day. Two days later, as the party was following a trail used by the Flatheads, Sacagawea told him that she recognized a possible shortcut to the spot where their canoes had been cached (Moulton 8: 167.) A week later, on July 13, Clark could write that, "The Indian woman, who had been of great service to me as a pilot through this country recommends a gap in the mountain more south which I shall cross" (Moulton, 8: 180), referring to what is now the Bozeman Trail.

Although Sacagawea's contribution as a guide was slender, her merits were far from meagre. Clark realized this in a personal letter that he wrote to Charbonneau on August 20, 1806, when he stated, "Your woman who accompanied you [on] that long dangerous and fatigueing rout to the Pacific Ocian and back diserved a greater reward for her attention and services on that rout than we had in our power to give her" (Jackson, 1978, 1: 315).

After their unfortunate episode with the Teton Sioux on the westward journey, Lewis and Clark had been obliged to face up to the fact that the lack of an interpreter had been a determining factor. It was mainly thanks to interpreters that all went well with the Yankton Sioux, Arikaras, Mandans, and Hidatsas. This was why the "Frenchman" Charbonneau and his wife had been

At last, on August 13, 1805, Lewis met the Shoshones, as depicted in this watercolour by Charles M. Russell. Lewis "went forward . . . leaving my gun behind me," and displaying the American flag. Drouillard and Shields watched as the Indians "embraced me very affectionately in their way . . . till I was heartily tired of the national hug" (Thwaites, 2: 340).

hired. Lewis relied heavily on Sacagawea in this respect. When she became gravely ill in June 1805 he was worried for her and her baby—but also, it must be admitted, because she was "our only dependence for a friendly negotiation" with the Shoshones "for horses to assist us in our portage from the Missouri to the columbia river" (Moulton, 4: 299).

Lewis was right. They couldn't be sure the Shoshones would willingly deal with them. What could the Americans offer in exchange? Lewis's promises of future trade relations and supplies of weapons were very vague and distant. Cameahwait, the Shoshone chief, was no fool. He almost broke off negotiations and was ready to take his people, who were starving, on a much-needed hunting expedition. In fact it was actually as an interpreter that Sacagawea proved to be significantly valuable for the expedition's success. But apart from this, the physical presence of the young Indian and her son contributed immensely to the morale of the Corps.

A Symbol of Courage and Peace

According to Clark's very apt expression, Sacagawea was "a token of peace" who "Reconsiles all the Indians, as to our friendly intentions" (Thwaites, 3: 111). Even Jean-Baptiste, little "Pomp" as the men called him, became a source of pleasant distraction. Clark developed a profound attachment for Sacagawea, who was not only maternal with her baby, but somewhat motherly and nurturing toward the men of the expedition. She gathered berries or roots for them, sometimes cooked for them, and no doubt mended their clothes. On the day that Charbonneau lost control of his pirogue, she dove into the water to save precious articles, thus limiting the damage. She immediately sensed Lewis's inevitable anger, especially as he had little love for Charbonneau.

Returning to normal life would be difficult, as much for Sacagawea as for York or even Lewis. But her impassive nature, an innate form of resignation, apparently enabled her to go back to a simpler life. Death came to her very soon. On December 20, 1812, John Luttig, who was in charge of Fort Manuel, wrote: "This evening the Wife of Charbonneau a Snake Squaw, died of a putrid fever, she was a good and the best woman in the fort, aged abt 25 years she left a fine infant girl" (Clark and Edmonds: 106; Chardon 233 and 289).

As with York, legend arose around Sacagawea's death. Thanks to Grace R. Hebard (see inset page 233) a tradition was started, intimating that Sacagawea had lived in Wyoming until 1884 under the name of Porivo.

If Sacagawea did survive "a putrid fever," it was in the collective American memory.

Sacagawea Mania

The humble Shoshone princess long ago conquered the hearts of Americans, although perhaps not Native Americans, some of whom consider her to have been a contemptible collaborator.

Today, near Bismark, North Dakota, less than two-thirds of a mile (about a kilometre) apart, you can find a bust of Sitting Bull and a small obelisk in memory of Sacagawea. The former is in pristine condition, with even a few coins left at its base, whereas the latter was vandalized in the summer of 2002. A random act? Or a form of protest?

This sweet and gentle Indian woman, as she was described by Henry M. Brackenridge, author of *Views of Louisiana: together with a journal of a voyage up the Missouri River, in 1811* (1814), continues to arouse controversy about her role in the expedition, the date of her death, or simply the spelling of her name, which Lewis and Clark usually avoided by calling her "the Indian woman" or "the squaw of Shabono."

Novelists have let their imaginations roam freely, positing a liaison between Sacagawea and Clark, or a quarrel between the two captains who were supposedly in love with her. That Clark felt affection for Sacagawea is clear. His words reveal his feelings. When she was ill, she became "our" Indian woman, not just Charbonneau's wife. When he wanted to recall her merits he was more distant, as in the letter of August 20, 1806, mentioned above where he wrote, "*Your* woman who accompanied *you* [on] that long dangerous and fatigueing rout to the Pacific Ocian and back diserved a greater reward for her attention and services on that rout than *we* had in *our* power to give her" (italics mine). This is rather mysterious: had some payment for her been envisaged? She was an Indian, and no contract had been made regarding her participation in the expedition. In any case, acting in his personal rather than official capacity, Clark wanted to do something for her. He invited the little family to St. Louis, reiterating his offer to take charge of "my boy Pomp" and insisting that "Janey" come too. He offered Charbonneau many inducements. If the interpreter wanted to travel to Montreal to see his friends, "I will let you have a horse, and your family shall be taken care of untill your return" (Jackson, 1978, 1: 315).

Indifferent to all the nonsense that has been written, and clearly above trivial controversy, Americans undertook to shape the memory of Sacagawea in a thousand and one ways. It is said that there are now more statues of her than any other American. Possibly; but what is impressive is the number of objects and commemorative sites taken as a whole. A river was named after her as early as May 20, 1805 (it has become today's Crooked Creek). Lakes, mountains, historical plaques, works of art, musical theatre, parks, events, a club, a school—in fact several schools—evoke facets of her existence and significance.

The supreme consecration came, however, from the United States government and the U.S. Mint. On June 9, 1998, the mint's Dollar Coin Design Advisory Committee, created two months earlier, recommended that the new golden dollar coin bear the image of Sacagawea, "the Native American interpreter and navigator who accompanied Lewis and Clark on their historic expedition to the Pacific Ocean and back" (www.usmint.gov). A month later the proposal was accepted.

Late in 1998 mint officials received twenty-three design proposals. These were submitted forthwith to Amerindian leaders, members of Congress, historians, numismatists, artists, and others. Sculptor Glenna Goodacre's proposal was chosen

(she is best known for her design of the Vietnam Women's Memorial). To prepare her sketches, Goodacre went in search of the ideal model, a young Shoshone. She also visited the Santa Fe Museum of American Indian Arts. An employee showed Goodacre photographs of her three daughters who had been brought up at Fort Hall, an Indian reserve in Idaho. One of them, Randy'L He-Done Teton, twenty-two, was a

This statue, by sculptor Leonard Crunelle, was erected in 1910 in the grounds of the State Capitol building of North Dakota. Sakakawea (variant spelling) meant "bird-woman" in Hidatsa. This was the name given their captive by her Hidatsa kidnappers. Moulton (3: 229) hesitates between a Shoshone and a Hidatsa origin for the name. For many years the spelling was given as Sacajawea, until the Bureau of American Ethnology suggested a hard "g" instead of a "j" in order to better accommodate the spelling used by Lewis and Clark.

student at the University of New Mexico. Goodacre had found her model.

Most of the preliminary sketches submitted showed a young Indian woman seen in profile or three quarter face, but alone. One of Sacagawea's absolutely undeniable merits was that of having carried a newborn child throughout this difficult expedition. Going and returning, she had to cross the many obstacles presented by the Rocky Mountains at that latitude. On the return journey Toussaint Charbonneau was able to get her a horse for short distances, but for most of the journey she valiantly carried her little Jean-Baptiste. This was the image finally chosen.

Jean-Baptiste Charbonneau appears on the golden dollar with his mother. This son of a French Canadian is the first and no doubt last of his breed to appear on a United States coin. Perhaps it's a step toward a common currency!

The reverse side of the dollar shows a magnificent eagle surrounded by

seventeen stars corresponding to the seventeen American states of the time. It reminds us that the Lewis and Clark Expedition coincided with the acquisition of the former French Louisiana, which paved the way for the formation of some thirty new states.

Sacagawea has outstripped Pocahontas and possibly even George Washington in the popular imagination. Her bright eyes look out at William Clark and Toussaint Charbonneau. She may not be guiding them, but she is certainly encouraging them to "proceed on." Pomp is snuggled on Sacagawea's back, sleeping the sleep of the just. He rests at the meeting place of two worlds, America and Europe. He is the future.

Conclusion

What was the key to the success of the Lewis and Clark expedition? They reached the Pacific via the Missouri and the Columbia. They brought home all the members of the Corps of Discovery except one, Sergeant Floyd, who died of an appendicitis attack. They gathered a mass of material about the Indians and the territory through which the expedition passed, and Clark prepared absolutely remarkable maps.

The Indians retained good memories of the Americans, with two or three exceptions. But what followed? What did the future hold for them? Native Americans were soon to learn. Progress was coming!

Lewis and Clark were exceptional men who complemented each other perfectly. It would have been difficult to find better. Lewis was more emotional, more sensitive, but also more intolerant, more intractable. The only people he liked were Americans. Clark was calm and collected by nature, and more open-minded than his colleague. He found that he had a brilliant gift for mapmaking, but wrote his journal more out of a sense of duty than anything else. He was always to the point and interesting. Lewis was too, of course, but differed in style and emphasis.

The quality of the journals kept by the two captains is one of the main reasons why their epic journey has fascinated readers and scholars for over a century. The journals of the expedition's soldiers, Patrick Gass, Joseph Whitehouse, and John Ordway, are of a different order, but not lacking in interest for all that.

Lewis and Clark were hardy, energetic, and disciplined. From the outset they were demanding of their men and behaved like true soldiers, tolerating no breach of orders. They said it and they practised it, sometimes to the amazement of the Indians.

While the main reason for the expedition's success rests on the actual qualities of Lewis and Clark, these alone would not have sufficed.

This Success Had Its Little Secrets

In the first place, the fact that the two captains were delayed and by a stroke of luck spent the winter of 1803-1804 near St. Louis, allowed them to acquire information and complete their recruitment with men accustomed to the Missouri. Without the team of French Canadian engagés, without these men to manoeuvre watercraft over shallows and around snags with poles and cordelles, without the two experienced pilots, Cruzatte and Labiche, they would have had a very hard time getting their keelboat as far as Mandan country.

How would the various encounters with Native Americans have gone without the interpreters recruited as the expedition went up the Missouri? What would the Corps of Discovery have eaten without a clever and resourceful hunter like Georges Drouillard, whose name the captains anglicized as "Drewyer"? Incidentally, they knew nothing of the word *Canadien* and had a habit of carelessly mispronouncing the names of all the French Canadians, the so-called "Frenchmen," whom they met. The British were rivals and the French-Canadians didn't exist. However, it must be said that they also had difficulty with the names of their own soldiers.

In the final analysis, however, the success of the expedition rested on the Indians themselves. It bears repeating: without them, without their friendly welcome and support, the expedition would not only have been doomed to failure, but a good many of its members would have died. The Indians gave so much and received so little.

All along its route the Corps of Discovery often found itself in difficulties, but never really in extreme distress. Why? Because the Indians were never far away. Cameahwait got horses for them. Old Toby took them over the Rockies. A Nez Percé guided them on the Columbia's tumultuous waters. Sometimes the help was very modest, but very vital. This was the case with the dogs that the Indians provided for Lewis and Clark when the expedition was desperate for food. (Indians didn't eat dogs as a rule, and were greatly astonished when the Americans survived well on this diet.)

While Sacagawea and her husband didn't save the Corps from failure, they did help it succeed. Chance played a part, as in Sacagawea's unexpected meeting with her brother, or in the intervention of the Nez Percé woman who had been saved by white men from captivity with hostile Indians, and who defended the Americans when her fellow tribesmen were inclined to give them a frosty reception.

Life hangs by a thread. This was constantly the case with the fate of the Lewis and Clark Expedition. The thread held. It was well deserved.

Thwaites and the History
of the Lewis and Clark Journals

The name "Thwaites" is a familiar and prestigious one for Canadian and Quebec historians. He produced a scholarly, bilingual edition of the Canadian *Jesuit Relations*, but this is about all that most people know about him.

When I closed *Undaunted Courage*, Stephen Ambrose's marvellous study of the expedition, I naturally wanted to know more about Lewis and Clark. I found what I could in bookshops—a reprint of Elliot Coues's three-volume history of the expedition, as well as modern abridged editions of the journals edited by John Bakeless, Frank Bergon, Landon Jones, and especially Bernard DeVoto, to whom we also owe a very personal survey of the colonial history of North America. Further burrowing produced the two-volume compilation of documents with commentary, *Before Lewis and Clark, 1785-1804*, edited by A.P. (for Abraham Phineas) Nasatir, an exceptional researcher, and *Letters of the Lewis and Clark Expedition (1783-1854)*, also in two volumes, edited by Donald Jackson, one of the great Lewis and Clark scholars.

One name continually surfaced throughout all these invaluable works—that of Reuben Gold Thwaites. To him we owe him the complete edition of the Lewis and Clark journals. Roger Auger, an antiquarian bookseller, found me a numbered set that had come on the market. It had hand-coloured illustrations and was printed on imperial Japan paper. The price was $64,000 U.S.—out of my league! Finally he found me a reprint of the 1904 edition by Dodd, Mead & Co. This reprint, published by Arno Press in 1969, had an added introduction by Bernard DeVoto.

It was time to find out more about Thwaites, whose name appears on the title page of *Original Journals of the Lewis & Clark Expedition 1804-1806* as the editor of *The Jesuit Relations and Allied Documents*. The *Relations* is a monumental seventy-three volume work, completed in 1901, and was greeted by scholars with great respect and admiration, as well as appreciation by all who couldn't read the *Relations* in the original language, generally French.

The centenary of the Lewis and Clark Expedition was approaching. The American Philosophical Society, which held the Lewis and Clark manuscripts, was seriously considering an *in extenso* edition of the journals written during the expedition (Cutright, 1976: 105). Officers of the American Philosophical Society got in touch with the New York publishers Dodd, Mead & Co. In the fall of 1901 they agreed to take on the project. Robert Dodd suggested ten percent royalties on the sale price of the work, payable to the American Philosophical Society, which would keep the copyright while agreeing not to authorize any new editions for four years. The society's officers had in mind a format for the edition and wondered to whom they could entrust the project. Some had naturally thought of Thwaites, the dynamic secretary and superintendent of the State Historical Society of Wisconsin, fresh from his laurels for editing *The Jesuit Relations*. Discussions were still under way when they were indirectly interrupted by a Boston publisher. The secretary of the American Philosophical Society, Isaac Minis Hays, was awaiting an imminent decision when he received a surprising letter from Thwaites himself, asking for permission to consult the Lewis and Clark manuscripts with a view to publication, no less! Houghton, Mifflin & Co. had just asked him to edit the Lewis and Clark journals.

What followed isn't too clear, but surviving documents indicate that Thwaites was told about the society's project with Dodd, Mead & Co. With sportsmanlike consideration he told Houghton, Mifflin & Co. how things stood: in his view the important thing was to bring the project to fruition, no matter by whom, and he wished the society well. Things moved quickly, and the ideal solution was soon found. Thwaites was chosen by the society as editor, and early in 1902 he set to work with Dodd, Mead & Co. The first volume appeared in July 1904, the seventh in September 1905. An eighth volume, actually a boxed set of maps, was added in October 1905. The entire project had been completed in four and a half years, in time for the centenary celebrations.

Scholar and Entrepreneur

Thwaites was a phenomenal combination of scholar and entrepreneur. In a relatively short life (1853-1913) he published over one hundred and fifty works. In 1887 he succeeded Lyman Copeland Draper as secretary and superintendent of

Reuben Gold Thwaites was secretary and superintendent of the State Historical Society of Wisconsin for twenty-six years, from 1887 to 1913, the year of his death. The son of immigrants who settled in Massachusetts, he followed his family to a Wisconsin farm. After successful college studies, a little teaching, and some journalism, he took literature and history courses at Yale University. His interest in history soon earned him the top position in the State Historical Society of Wisconsin, where he succeeded Lyman C. Draper.

the State Historical Society of Wisconsin, a position he held until his death. The onetime editor of the *Wisconsin State Journal* wanted to reach the general public. In this respect he changed the society's focus. His works were scholarly, but he also wanted them to be accessible to the ordinary reader.

Wisconsin was Thwaites's adopted state and he became passionately interested in its history. This was also the history of the French in North America, as shown in his study *Wisconsin: the Americanization of a French Settlement.* He published *France in America* (1905) while his edition of the Lewis and Clark journals was appearing, and also while overseeing the publication of thirty-two works in a collection entitled "Early Western Travels." The latter included the travel accounts of Gabriel Franchère, John Bradbury, and the naturalist, Prince Maximilian of Wied-Neuwied.

Thwaites was particularly fascinated by New France and its explorers, missionaries, and pioneers—men like La Hontan, La Salle, Father Hennepin, and Father De Smet. He kept a constant lookout for new subjects, new people, and new documents, and was a peerless organizer, especially of publishing ventures. Each project gave birth to a small factory. Thwaites chose the subjects, but didn't hesitate to call on others to participate. There were many of these—translators, of course, but also researchers whom he groomed as specialists. In this sense he was a precursor of all the universities that today take on major projects.

The Original Journals of the Lewis and Clark Expedition was just such a project. Indeed, it couldn't have succeeded without a high level of organization. Endeavours of this nature can't be the work of only one person. Even so, there is every indication that Thwaites was very involved personally in the case of the Lewis and Clark journals. It was a subject worthy of his gifts, and there was everything to be done.

Biddle and Coues—Thwaites's Predecessors

More than seven years passed between the return of the Lewis and Clark Expedition and the first publication of the journals. All sorts of difficulties had initially arisen, including the death in 1809 of Lewis, who was primarily responsible for taking steps to get the journals published. He certainly had talent, and when one reads his wonderful pages written in the heat of action there is no doubting his ability. Fate decided otherwise, however.

War with Britain in 1812 caused fresh delays and held up the work of Nicholas Biddle, who had taken on the challenge of getting the journals published. Not only was he not paid, he himself had to pay an assistant, Paul Allen, to complete the editorial work. Whether out of bitterness or modesty, Biddle didn't even want his name to appear anywhere in the work. He declined Clark's proposal to share "half of every profit." Biddle had married an extremely rich woman and had no need of money. He was also accustomed to using a pseudonym for his own writings, and even fooled his own biographer, Thomas P. Govan, who, as Paul R. Cutright noted (1976: 71), attributed barely one out of four hundred and thirteen pages to Biddle's role as editor of the Lewis and Clark journals.

Clark himself was apparently overwhelmed by the generosity of Biddle, who wrote to him on March 23, 1814, "I have at last the pleasure of informing you that the Travels are published. . . . The gentleman who revised and prepared it for the press, Mr. Allen is a very capable person, & as I did not put the finishing hand to the volumes I did not think it right to take from him the credit of his own exertions and care by announcing personally the part which I had in the compilation. I am content that my trouble in the business should be recompensed only by the pleasure which attended it, and also by the satisfaction of making your acquaintance which I shall always value" (Jackson 1978, 2: 598). Biddle only regretted that Clark had not had time to revise the work and modestly hoped that not too many "errors and inadvertencies" had "crept" into it.

Biddle graciously told Clark, "Henceforward you may sleep upon your fame which must last as long as books can endure."

Was this edition a success? Biddle seemed to think so. In reality, the run of some fifteen hundred copies was distributed slowly and with some mystery. Clark himself waited over two years before being able to get a copy—and then had to borrow one. As the years went by the Biddle edition became extremely rare. Today some twenty copies are known to exist; each is worth between $35,000 and $50,000 U.S.

In 1892 Elliott Coues, a natural history enthusiast, decided to produce a so-called "faithful" reproduction of Biddle's edition of the journals as a contribution to his own field. He performed a great service, although his work was somewhat flawed by his lack of respect for the actual manuscripts. Thwaites, who had insisted in having all the originals handed over to him, discovered to his horror that Coues had scribbled all sorts of marks on them and had even added writing. It was later revealed that he had secretly made a copy for himself. Whatever its drawbacks, the Coues edition of the journals appeared in 1893 and was welcomed by the public. It had a far more successful career than Biddle's edition.

Thwaites's Contribution: the Start of a New Adventure

The manuscripts in their original state remained unpublished until they were confided to Thwaites. As he became familiar with them, he also became convinced that other documents existed. Biddle had used Sergeant John Ordway's journal. Thwaites looked for it in vain, but he did discover the journal of Sergeant Joseph Whitehouse as well as Clark's maps and notebooks.

Dodd, Mead & Co. were enthusiastic and paid Thwaites $2,500 instead of the $1,500 agreed upon, promising another $500 when "we sell enough to cover expenses," although "the initial sale has been disappointing" (Cutright, 1976: 122). Nevertheless, the publisher expressed immense satisfaction with the work. Indeed, everyone was aware of the exceptional nature of the project. Two limited editions were prepared for collectors, one being the numbered edition on imperial Japan paper mentioned earlier (Cutright, 1976: 121, n. 20).

How was the Thwaites edition received by the public? It's difficult to say today, but it was certainly a critical success, if not a commercial one, and isn't this the most meaningful and lasting kind of success? In one sense, Thwaites brought Lewis and Clark to the world by allowing them to speak directly to their readers.

Nowadays, with the hindsight provided by numerous studies, it's easy to criticize the Thwaites edition. It has undeniably aged, but nevertheless it was the springboard for the numberless research projects that gradually dated it. Thanks to Thwaites, the voices of Lewis, Clark, Whitehouse, and Sergeant Charles Floyd were heard. Interest in their remarkable expedition took on new life, and the hunt for documents intensified. Thwaites had set the example. His flair for unearthing documents had led him to examine even the papers of Draper, his predecessor and mentor in the State Historical Society of Wisconsin. Among these Thwaites found Floyd's journal. The soldier had made entries until August 20, 1804, the day before he died.

It was through Clark's descendants, however, that Thwaites hit the jackpot. The Voorhis family, mother and daughter, had inherited a large number of documents. When Thwaites was able to examine them in October 1903, he found "five note books by Wm. Clark," one of them "an actual field book," as well as the precious maps drawn by Clark (Cutright, 1976: 119).

Thwaites was a decidedly gifted and tenacious researcher. It was these qualities that finally enabled him to get hold of Whitehouse's journal when its then owner tried to sell it to the Library of Congress. Word got around, and Dodd, Mead & Co. acquired this journal. Thwaites was less lucky with Ordway's journal. It had been in Biddle's possession, and there was every reason to believe he had given it back to Clark who, jointly with Lewis, had bought it from Ordway in 1808 or 1809 (Jackson, 1978, 2: 462). However, the Ordway journal was not among the Voorhis papers brought to light in 1903.

Ten years went by before Nicholas Biddle's grandsons, Charles and Edward Biddle, were approached. In 1913 they came upon Ordway's journal in a mountain of documents collected by their grandfather exactly ninety-five years earlier. They also found a previously unknown journal kept by Lewis during his journey from Pittsburgh to Camp Dubois—a document that later became known as *The Ohio Journal*, edited for publication by Milo Milton Quaife (1916).

Fifty years later, in 1953, another surprise turned up among papers handed down to the heirs of General John Henry Hammond. It was an unknown diary kept by Clark, now known as his "Field Notes." They were published in 1964, edited by Ernest S. Osgood.

To all these discoveries were later added the four hundred documents tracked down and published by Donald Jackson, which were particularly interesting for putting the actual expedition in perspective. Thwaites had already understood the importance of placing the expedition in context. He saw it as far more than a mere round trip between St. Louis and the Pacific Ocean and back. For him, it represented the encounter with native peoples, some of whom—like the Shoshones and Nez Percés—had never seen Europeans. It also represented the discovery of animal and botanical species hitherto unknown to Americans, as well as heralding the onset of inevitable confrontation with the Spanish colonial empire and fierce commercial rivalry with the British. For historians, the expedition offered a chance for a last look at the former New France.

Of all those who have written about Lewis and Clark, Thwaites is one of the rare authors to take an interest in the North America of the French, the Indians, and the British. All three fascinated him, for had they not opened the way for the United States of America?

As for the expedition itself—its trajectory, its various stages, difficulties, and observations—everything had already been said, or almost everything.

Gary Moulton—Editor Extraordinaire

Everything had been said, or almost . . . But what about the innumerable books and articles that had brought new insights to the subject and the text. By 1979 the idea that a new edition of the journals was needed had made considerable headway. Donald Jackson, a top Lewis and Clark scholar, ardently promoted the idea, envisioning a project of considerable scope: nine volumes in nine years.

The Center for Great Plains Studies had been founded in 1976. Its directors felt that a scholarly edition of the Lewis and Clark journals was exactly the sort of major project they were looking for. The pieces fell quickly into place. Spurred on by Steve Cox, the University of Nebraska Press (already highly specialized in the humanities, especially in history) decided to get involved. The University of Nebraska–Lincoln created a position for an editor, and the venerable American Philosophical Society offered its collaboration as well as access to its priceless treasures of national history.

Donald Jackson was asked to establish a project outline and timetable, to prepare a budget, to identify funding sources, and find that rare pearl, an editor for the projected new edition.

Gary Moulton modestly recounted his great adventure in an article written for *We Proceeded On* (November 2000, vol. 26, no. 4: 9-16). "I probably knew less about the expedition than many members of the Lewis and Clark Trail Heritage Foundation," he admitted at the outset. Why did he put his name forward, in that

Gary Moulton

case? His wife had seen a recruiting advertisement for the project in 1978 and he didn't have a project lined up for the coming year!

Moulton had just finished editing the papers of the Cherokee chief John Ross. He was interested in the history of the American West. The jury chose him, rightly perceiving him as someone able to launch, manage, and finalize a vast project within a reasonable period of time. He was a good editor; he would become one of the great Lewis and Clark specialists.

With the help of Professor W. Raymond Wood of the University of Missouri and John Allen of the University of Connecticut, Moulton first tackled the job of preparing an atlas. Thwaites, who only discovered Clark's maps while working on the journals, had made the final volume of his edition an atlas. Moulton's atlas was the first volume of the new edition, in folio format so that maps wouldn't have to be folded.

Jackson, guessing the limits of Moulton's knowledge, had suggested he "get the story straight" and "know the precise location of places like the Lolo Trail." As Moulton tells it, "I nodded knowingly, although I hadn't the faintest idea where or what the Lolo Trail was. I hit the books right away."

The atlas came out in 1983. It contained one hundred and twenty-nine old maps, most of them due to Clark's genius as a cartographer. The journals of the expedition's two leaders appeared in volumes two to eight between 1986 and 1993, followed by volumes nine, ten, and eleven, containing the journals of other expedition members.

Moulton was proud of the wonderful collaboration he received from over a hundred scholars, particularly in the fields of botany and geology, sciences with which he was less familiar. Possibly because he felt that the expedition's botanical aspect hadn't received the attention it deserved, he brought out a twelfth volume, the herbarium, in 1999.

Each volume except the atlas contained a good index, but the wealth of information throughout the edition was such that Moulton felt the importance of preparing a comprehensive index (volume thirteen), not only of proper names, but also of subjects, larger themes, concepts, and even objects, behaviour, difficulties encountered, and more.

In 2003 Moulton produced an abridged, single-volume edition entitled *The Lewis and Clark Journals: An American Epic of Discovery*. Now it's a question of what lies ahead.

Looking to the Future

The Moulton thirteen-volume edition is clearly a formidable synthesis of knowledge gathered over the past two centuries on the subject of the Lewis and Clark Expedition. It marks the end of an impressive journey—a goal achieved.

In the nature of things, the work of Moulton and his many collaborators will be a jumping-off point for new research, as was the work of Thwaites a hundred years ago. The subject is inexhaustible.

Moulton himself admits that the members of the expedition are not generally well known. He has in mind the soldiers and the Charbonneaus, father and son. He would like to see a good biography of William Clark. He is right on all counts. Although he doesn't mention them specifically, he is no doubt thinking of Drouillard, Cruzatte, Labiche, Lepage — and why not the explorers who preceded or succeeded Lewis and Clark, as well as a history of the United States in the light of the expedition?

Lewis was a remarkable narrator, Clark an amazing cartographer. How were they able to keep up their journals so faithfully? Of course there are gaps, particularly on Lewis's part, but each day for two years they were able to write or at least to say to themselves, "We proceeded on."

This must surely have become Moulton's motto as he realized the growing scope of the challenge, looked back at what his team had done, and considered what remained. The project took twenty years rather than the nine planned by Jackson or the seventeen foreseen by Moulton. Inspired by Lewis and Clark, he brought his undertaking to completion. Hats off to Gary Moulton!

Bibliography

The abbreviation *DCB* in the main text refers to: *Dictionary of Canadian Biography*. Edited by George W. Brown. Toronto: University of Toronto Press, 1966.

ALLEN, John Logan. *Lewis and Clark and the Image of the American Northwest: With 47 Maps*. New York: Dover Publications, 1991.

AMBROSE, Stephen E. *Undaunted Courage*. New York: Simon & Schuster, 1996.

_____. *Lewis & Clark: Voyage of Discovery*, with photographs by Sam Abell. Washington, D.C.: National Geographic Society, 1998.

ANDERSON, Irving W. *A Charbonneau Family Portrait: Biographical Sketches of Sacagawea, Jean-Baptiste, and Toussaint Charbonneau*. Rev. ed. Astoria: Fort Clatsop Historical Association, 1992.

APPLEMAN, Roy E., *Lewis and Clark's Transcontinental Exploration, 1804-1806*. Washington, D.C.: United States Department of the Interior, National Park Service, 1975.

AUDUBON, John James, 1785-1851. *Audubon and His Journals*, 2 vols. edited by Maria R. Audubon. With zoological and other notes by Elliott Coues. New York, Dover Publications [1960].

_____. *Journal du Missouri*. Introduction by Michel Le Bris (9-31). Paris: Éditions Payot et Rivages, 1993.

_____. *"Les Oiseaux d'Amérique:" Exposition au Musée de la Province de Québec du 2 mars au 2 avril 1944*. Montreal: Canada Steamship Lines Limited, c1944.

_____. *The Birds of America*. 2d ed. New York: The MacMillan Company, 1941.

BALESI, Charles John. *The Time of the French in the Heart of North America, 1763-1818*. Chicago: Alliance française, c1991.

BELYEA, Barbara. *Columbia Journals: David Thompson*. Montreal and Buffalo: McGill-Queen's University Press, 1994.

BURPEE, Lawrence J. *The Search for the Western Sea: The Story of the Exploration of North-Western America*. Vol. 2. Toronto: The MacMillan Company, 1935.

BOORSTIN, Daniel J. *The Discoverers*. New York: Random House, 1983.

CATLIN, George. *Catlin's Letters and Notes on the North American Indians*, 2 vols. North Dighton: J. G. Press, 1995.

_____. *North American Indians: Being letters and notes on their manners, customs and conditions, written during eight years' travel amongst the wildest tribes of Indians in North America, 1832-1839*, 2 vols. Philadelphia: Leary, Stuart and Company, 1913.

CHARDON, Francis A. *Chardon's Journal at Fort Clark, 1834-1839*. Introduction and notes by Annie Heloise Abel. Bison Book Edition. Lincoln: University of Nebraska Press, 1997.

CLARK, Ella E. and Margot Edmonds. *Sacagawea of the Lewis & Clark Expedition*. Berkeley: University of California Press, 1983.

CLARKE, Charles G. *The Men of the Lewis and Clark Expedition: A Biographical Roster of the Fifty-One Members and a Composite Diary of their Activities from all Known Sources*. Glendale: The Arthur Clark Co., 1970.

CLEARY, Rita. "Charbonneau Reconsidered," *We Proceeded On*, 26, no. 1 (February 2000):17-23.

COLTER-FRICK, L.R. *Courageous Colter and Companions*. Washington, Mo.: Colter-Frick, 1997.

COMBET, Denis, ed. *In Search of the Western Sea: Selected Journals of La Vérendrye/ À la recherche de la Mer de l'Ouest. Mémoires choisis de La Vérendrye*. Winnipeg and Saint-Boniface: Great Plains Publications and Les Éditions du Blé, 2001.

CÔTÉ. Louise, Louis Tardivel and Denis Vaugeois. *L'Indien généreux: Ce que le monde doit aux Amériques*. Montreal and Quebec: Boréal and Septentrion, 1992.

COULTER, Tony. *La Salle and the Explorers of the Mississippi*. New York and Philadelphia: Chelsea House Publishers, 1990.

CUTRIGHT, Paul Russell. *A History of the Lewis and Clark Journals*. Norman: University of Oklahoma Press, 1976.

_____. *Lewis and Clark: Pioneering Naturalists*. Lincoln and London: University of Nebraska Press, 1989.

DECHÊNE, Louise. "Étienne Véniard de Bourgmond." *Dictionary of Canadian Biography*. Edited by George W. Brown. Toronto: University of Toronto Press, 1966. 2:645-647.

DESROSIERS, Léo-Paul. *Les Engagés du Grand Portage*. Montreal: Fides, 1957.

DEVOTO, Bernard. *The Course of Empire*. Boston: Houghton Mifflin Company, 1952.

DILLER, Aubrey. "A New Map of the Missouri River Drawn in 1795." *Imago Mundi*, 12 (1955): 175-180.

DORIGNY, Marcel and Marie-Jeanne Rossignol, ed. *La France et les Amériques au temps de Jefferson et de Miranda*. Paris: Société des études robespierristes, 2001.

DUNCAN, Dayton and Ken Burns. *Lewis & Clark: The Journey of the Corps of Discovery*. New York: Alfred A. Knopf, 1997.

DUVIOLS, Jean-Paul. *L'Amérique espagnole vue et rêvée: Les livres de voyage de Christophe Colomb à Bougainville*. Paris: Éditions Promodis, 1985.

FARNHAM, Charles Haight. *A Life of Francis Parkman*. Boston: Little, Brown and Company, 1922.

FOLEY, William E. *A History of Missouri*. Vol. 1, 1673-1820. Columbia, Mo.: University of Missouri Press, 2000.

FOUCRIER, Annick. *Meriwether Lewis et William Clark: La traversée d'un continent, 1803-1806*. Paris: Michel Houdiard éditeur, 2000.

FRANCHÈRE, Gabriel, *Journal of a Voyage on the North West Coast of North America during the Years 1811, 1812, 1813 and 1814*. Toronto: The Champlain Society, 1969.

GLOVER, Richard, ed. *David Thompson's Narrative, 1784-1812*. Toronto: Champlain Society, 1962.

GOETZMANN, William H. *Karl Bodmer's America*. Lincoln: Joslyn Art Museum and University of Nebraska Press, 1984.

GOETZMANN, William H. and Glyndwr Williams. *The Atlas of North American Exploration: From the Norse Voyages to the Race the Pole*. New York: Prentice Hall, 1992.

GORDON-REED, Annette. *Thomas Jefferson and Sally Hemings: An American Controversy*. Charlottesville: University of Virginia Press, 1997.

GRAYMONT, Barbara. "Mary Brant: Koñwatsi Tsiaiéñni." *Dictionary of Canadian Biography*. Edited by George W. Brown. Toronto: University of Toronto Press, 1966. 4:416-419.

HAFEN, Ann W. "Jean-Baptiste Charbonneau." *The Mountain Men and the Fur Trade of the Far West*. Edited by LeRoy R. Hafen. Spokane, Wa.: The Arthur H. Clark Company, 1965. 1:205-224.

HARRIS, Burton. *John Colter: His years in the Rockies*. Lincoln: University of Nebraska Press, 1993.

HAYNE, David M. "Pierre-François-Xavier de Charlevoix." *Dictionary of Canadian Biography*. Edited by George W. Brown. Toronto: University of Toronto Press, 1966. 3:103-110.

HECKROTTE, Warren. "Aaron Arrowsmith's Map of North America and the Lewis and Clark Expedition." *The Map Collector*, no. 39 (summer 1987):16-20.

HERBERT, Janis. *Lewis and Clark for Kids: Their Journey of Discovery with 21 Activities*. Chicago: Chicago Review Press, 2000.

HINE, Robert V. and John Mack Faragher, *The American West: A New Interpretive History*. New Haven and London: Yale University Press, 2000.

HOLMBERG, James J. "A Man of Much Merit:" George Drouillard, The Corps of Discovery's Hunter and Interpreter, Went Down Fighting in the Country He Loved." *We Proceeded On*, August 2000: 8-12.

HUBERT-ROBERT, Régine. *L'Histoire merveilleuse de la Louisiane française: Chronique des XVIIe et XVIIIe siècles et de la Cession aux États-Unis*. New York: Éditions de la Maison française, 1941.

HUNSAKER, Joyce Badgley. *Sacagawea Speaks: Beyond the Shining Mountains with Lewis & Clark*. Guilford, Conn.: TwoDot Books, 2001.

HUNTER, William A. "Elizabeth Couc." *Dictionary of Canadian Biography*. Edited by George W. Brown. Toronto: University of Toronto Press, 1966. 3:147-148.

JACKSON, Donald, ed. *Letters of Lewis and Clark Expedition with Related Documents 1783-1854*, 2 vols. 2d ed., with additional documents and notes. Urbana and Chicago: University of Illinois Press, 1978.

_____. *Thomas Jefferson and the Stony Mountains: Exploring the West from Monticello*. Norman and London: University of Oklahoma Press, 1993.

JACQUIN, Philippe, Daniel Royot and Stephen Whitfield. *Le Peuple américain: Origines, immigration, ethnicité et identité*. Paris: Seuil, 2000.

JENKINSON, Clay Straus. *Jefferson's Vision of the Visit of Lewis to the American West*. Woksape: The North Dakota Humanities Council, Inc., [1991].

JENNINGS, Francis. *The Invasion of America*. New York: W.W. Norton and Company, 1976.

JOSEPHY, Alvin M., Jr. *The Nez Perce Indians and the Opening of the Northwest*. Boston: Houghton Mifflin Company, 1965.

KUKLA, Jon. *A Wilderness So Immense: The Louisiana Purchase and the Destiny of America*. New York: Alfred A. Knopf, 2003.

LAGARDE, Lucie. "Le Passage du Nord-Ouest dans la cartographie française du 18e siècle: Contribution à l'étude de l'œuvre des Delisle et Buache." *Imago Mundi*, no. 41 (1989):19-43.

LANGE, Robert E. "George Drouillard (Drewyer): One of the Two or Three Most Valuable Men on the Expedition." *We Proceeded On*, May 1979.

LAMALICE, André L. "François-Antoine Larocque." *Dictionary of Canadian Biography*. Edited by George W. Brown. Toronto: University of Toronto Press, 1966. 9:455-456.

LAMAR, Howard R. *The New Encyclopedia of the American West*. New Haven: Yale University Press, 1998.

LAMB, W. Kaye. "Alexander Mackenzie." *Dictionary of Canadian Biography*. Edited by George W. Brown. Toronto: University of Toronto Press, 1966. 5:537-543.

LAROCQUE, François-Antoine. *Journal de Larocque dans la rivière Assiniboine jusqu'à la rivière "aux roches jaunes," 1805*. Edited with notes by L.J. Burpee. Ottawa: King's Printer, 1911. (Originally in English, *The Journal of Larocque from the Assiniboine to the Yellowstone, 1805*. Edited with notes by L.J. Burpee. Ottawa: Publications of the Canadian Archives, 1910.)

LAUVRIÈRE, Émile. *Histoire de la Louisiane française, 1673-1939 avec 52 illustrations, dont cartes et plans pour la plupart inédits*. Paris: G.-P. Maisonneuve Éditeur, 1940.

LAVENDER, David. *The Way of the Western Sea: Lewis and Clark across the Continent*. Lincoln and London: University of Nebraska Press, 1998.

LE BRIS, Michel, éd. *M. Lewis. W. Clark, Far West: Journal de la première traversée du continent nord-américain, 1804-1806*, 2 vols. Paris: Phébus Libretto, 1993.

LEWIS, Jan Ellen and Peter S. Onuf. *Sally Hemings & Thomas Jefferson: History, Memory and Civic Culture.* Charlottesville: University Press of Virginia, 1999.

LEWIS, G. Malcolm, ed., *Cartographic Encounters: Perspectives on Native American Mapmaking and Map Use.* Chicago: The University of Chicago Press, 1998.

LIBRARY AND ARCHIVES CANADA, l'équipe des. *Trésors des Archives nationales du Canada.* Quebec: Septentrion, 1992.

LOFTIN, T.L. *Westward Go! Fremont, Randy, and Kit Carson Open Wide the Oregon Trail.* Illustrations by Beth Berryman. Santa Fe: Tee Loftin Publishers, 2000.

LOGAN, Allan John. *Lewis and Clark and the Image of the American West.* With 47 Maps. New York, Dover Publications, 1991.

LOTTINVILLE, Savoie, ed. *Travels in North America 1822-1824*, by Paul Wilhelm, Duke of Württemberg. Norman: University of Oklahoma Press, 1973.

MACKENZIE, Alexander. *Voyages from Montreal on the river St. Laurence through the continent of North America to the Frozen and Pacific Oceans in the years 1789 and 1793 with a Preliminary Account of the Rise, Progress, and Present State of the Fur Trade of that Country.* London, 1801. Reprint. Master Works of Canadian Authors Series. Toronto: [Radisson Society of Canada, 1927].

MARGRY, Pierre, ed. *Découvertes et Établissements des Français dans l'Ouest et dans le Sud de l'Amérique septentrionale, 1614-1754.* Cinquième partie, *Première formation d'une chaîne de postes entre le fleuve Saint-Laurent et le golfe du Mexique (1683-1724).* Paris: Maisonneuve Frères et Ch. Leclerc Éditeurs, 1887.

_____. *Découvertes et Établissements. . . .* Sixième partie, *Exploration des affluents du Mississippi et découverte des montagnes rocheuses (1679-1754).* Paris: Maisonneuve Frères et Ch. Leclerc Éditeurs, 1888.

MASSON, Louis-Rodrigue. *Les Bourgeois de la Compagnie du Nord-Ouest.* Quebec: A. Côté, 1889.

McDERMOTT, John Francis. *A Glossary of Mississippi Valley French. 1673-1850.* St. Louis: Washington University Studies, 1941.

_____. *The French in the Mississippi Valley.* Urbana: University of Illinois Press, 1965.

MILLER, Alfred J. *Braves and Buffalo: Plains Indian Life in 1837.* Toronto: University of Toronto Press, 1973.

MILNER II, Clyde A., Carol A. O'Connor and Martha A. Sandweiss. *The Oxford History of the American West.* New York: Oxford University Press, 1994.

MOORE, Bob. "Pompey's Baptism." *We Proceeded On*, 26, no. 1 (February 2000):10-17.

MORRIS, Richard B. and Jeffrey B. Morris. *Encyclopedia of American History.* 7th ed. New York: Harper Collins, 1996.

MORSE, Eric W. *Les Routes des Voyageurs: hier et aujourd'hui.* Ottawa: Queen's Printer, 1969.

MOULTON, Gary E., ed. *The Journals of the Lewis and Clark Expedition*, 13 vols. Lincoln and London: Center for Great Plains Studies in association with the University of Nebraska Press, 1983-2001.

NASATIR, A. P. *Before Lewis and Clark: Documents Illustrating the History of the Missouri, 1785-1804*, 2 vols. St. Louis: St. Louis Historical Documents Foundation, 1952.

NICKS, John. "David Thompson." *Dictionary of Canadian Biography.* Edited by George W. Brown. Toronto: University of Toronto Press, 1966. 8:878-884.

NISBET, Jack. *Sources of the River: Tracking David Thompson across Western North America.* 2d ed.

Seattle: Sasquatch Books, 1995.

NORALL, Frank. *Bourgmont, Explorer of the Missouri, 1698-1725*. Lincoln and London: University of Nebraska Press, 1988.

NUTE, Grace Lee. *The Voyageur*. 1931. Reprint. St. Paul: The Minnesota Historical Society, 1955.

OSGOOD, Ernest S., ed. *The Field Notes of Captain William Clark, 1803-1805*. New Haven and London: Yale University Press, 1964.

OSGOOD, Ernest S. and JACKSON, Donald. "The Lewis and Clark Expedition's Newfoundland Dog." *We Proceeded On*, Supplementary Publication no. 12.

PARKMAN, Francis. *La Piste de l'Oregon: À travers la Prairie et les Rocheuses*. La Bibliothèque des voyageurs. Paris: Fayard, 1980.

_____. *The Oregon Trail: Sketches of Prairie and Rocky Mountain Life*. Toronto: George N. Morang and Company, 1899.

PARKS, Douglas R. *A Fur Trader among the Indians at the Upper Missouri River: The Journal and Description of Jean-Baptiste Truteau, 1794, 1796*. Forthcoming.

PERRIN DU LAC, François-Marie. *Voyage dans les deux Louisianes, et chez les nations sauvages du Missouri, par les États-Unis, l'Ohio et les provinces qui les bordent en 1801, 1802 et 1803, avec un aperçu des mœurs, des usages, du caractère et des coutumes religieuses et civiles des peuples de ces diverses contrées*. Paris: Capell et Renaud, 1805.

PETERSON, Donald A. *Early Pictures of the Falls: A Lewis and Clark Portrait in Time*. Great Falls: Lewis and Clark Heritage Foundation, 1998.

QUAIFE, Milo M., ed. *The Journals of Captain Meriwether Lewis and Sergeant John Ordway*. Madison: Publications of State Historical Society of Wisconsin, 1916.

RICH, E.E. "Philip Turnor." *Dictionary of Canadian Biography*. Edited by George W. Brown. Toronto: University of Toronto Press, 1966. 4:740-742.

RONDA, James P. *Lewis and Clark Among the Indians*. Lincoln: University of Nebraska Press, 1984.

_____. *Voyages of Discovery: Essays on the Lewis and Clark Expedition*. Helena: Montana Historical Society Press, 1998.

_____. *Jefferson's West: A Journey with Lewis and Clark*. Monticello Monograph Series. Charlottesville, Va.: Thomas Jefferson Foundation, 2000.

RONSIN, Albert. *Découverte et baptême de l'Amérique*. 2d ed. Janville–La Malgrange: Éditions de l'Est, 1992.

ROSS, Marvin C. *The West of Alfred Jacob Miller (1837) from the Notes and Water Colors in the Walters Art Gallery*. Norman: University of Oklahoma Press, 1951.

RUXTON, George Frederick. *Mountain Men. Illustrated by Glen Rounds*. 1906. Reprint. New York: Holiday House, 1966.

SANDOZ, Mari. *The Beaver Men: Spearheads of Empire*. New York: Hastings House, 1964.

SCHAMA, Simon. *Dead Certainties: Unwarranted Speculations*. Toronto: Vintage Canada, 1992.

SHORTT, Adam and Arthur G. Doughty, eds. *Documents relatifs à l'histoire constitutionnelle du Canada, 1759-1791*. Ottawa: Public Archives of Canada, 1921.

SKARSTEN, M. O. *George Drouillard: Hunter and Interpreter for Lewis and Clark and Fur Trader, 1807-1810*. Glendale: The Arthur H. Clark Company, 1964.

SOBEL, Dava. *Longitude: The True Story of a Lone Genius Who Solved the Greatest Scientific Problem of His Time*. New York: Penguin Books, 1995.

SPECK, Gordon. *Breeds and Half-Breeds*. New York: Clarkson N. Potter, 1969.

STEVENS, Walter B. *Missouri: The Center State*. Vol. 1. Chicago: The S.J. Clarke Publishing Company, 1915.

THOM, James Alexander. *Sign-Talker: The Adventure of George Drouillard in the Lewis and Clark*

Expedition. New York: Ballantine Books, 2000.

THOMAS, Davis and Karin Ronnefeldt, eds. *People of the First Man: Life Among the Plains Indians in Their Final Days of Glory. The Firsthand Account of Prince Maximilian's Expedition up the Missouri River, 1833-34.* Watercolours by Charles Bodmer. New York: E.P. Dutton & Co. Inc., 1976.

_____. *Le Peuple du Premier Homme: Les Indiens des Plaines au temps de leur dernière splendeur. Carnets de route de l'expédition du prince Maximilien sur le Missouri, 1833-1834.* Aquarelles de Charles Bodmer. Translated by Guy Casaril. Paris: Flammarion, 1976.

THORP, Daniel B. *An American Journey: Lewis & Clark.* New York: Metro Books, 1998.

THWAITES, Reuben Gold, ed. *Original Journals of the Lewis and Clark Expedition, 1804-1806.* 8 vols. 1909. Reprint. New York: Antiquarian Press Ltd., 1959.

TYKAL, Jack B. *Etienne Provost, Man of the Mountains.* Liberty, Utah: Eagle's View Publishing Company, 1989.

VAUGEOIS, Denis. *Québec 1792: Les acteurs, les institutions et les frontières.* Montreal: Fides, 1992.

VAUGEOIS, Denis. "Élisabeth Couc." *Le Devoir*, July 5, 1993.

VINCENS, Simone. *Madame Montour et son temps.* Montreal: Québec/Amérique, 1979.

VILLIERS DU TERRAGE, Marc de. *La Découverte du Missouri et l'histoire du fort d'Orléans.* Paris: Librairie ancienne Honoré-Champion, 1925.

_____. *Les Dernières Années de la Louisiane française: Le Chevalier de Kerlérec d'Abbadie-Aubry Laussat.* Paris: E. Guilmoto, éditeur, 1903.

VON SACHSEN-ALTENBURG, Hans and Robert L. Dyer. *Duke Paul of Württemberg on the Missouri frontier, 1823, 1830 and 1851.* Boonville, Mo.: Pekitanoui Publications, 1998.

WALDMAN, Carl, ed. *Atlas of the North American Indian.* Illustrated by Molly Braun. New York: NY Facts On File, 1985.

WALLACE, F. C. Anthony. *Jefferson and the Indians: The Tragic Fate of the First Americans.* Cambridge, Mass. and London: The Belknap Press of Harvard University, 1999.

WARHUS, Mark. *Another America: Native American Maps and the History of our Land.* New York: St. Martin's Press, 1997.

WEBER, David J. *The Spanish Frontier in North America.* New Haven and London: Yale University Press, 1992.

WIED-NEUWIED, Maximilian, Prince of. *Maximilian Prince of Wied's Travels in the Interior of North America, 1832-1834,* translated from the German by Hannibal Evans Lloyd (1771-1847). Reprinted in *Early Western Travels 1748-1846.* Vols. 22, 23, and 24. Edited by Reuben G. Thwaites. Cleveland: The Arthur H. Clark Company, 1904-1907.

_____. *Voyages dans l'intérieur de l'Amérique du Nord pendant les années 1832-1834.* Illustrations de Karl Bodmer. Cologne: Taschen, 2001.

WOLFERMAN, Kristie C. *The Osage in Missouri.* Columbia, Mo.: University of Missouri Press, 1997.

WOOD, Raymond and Thomas D. Thiessen, eds. *Early Fur Trade on the Northern Plains: Canadian Traders among the Mandan and Hidatsa Indians, 1738-1818. The Narratives of John Macdonell, François-Antoine Larocque, David Thompson, Charles McKenzie.* Norman: University of Oklahoma Press, 1985.

ZOLTVANY, Yves F. "Pierre Gaultier de Varennes et de La Vérendrye." *Dictionary of Canadian Biography.* Edited by George W. Brown. Toronto: University of Toronto Press, 1966. 3:246-254.

Illustration Sources

10, Charles Russell, Amon Carter Museum

14, Waldman (1985)

17, *Encyclopedia of American History* (1996):74

36, painting by L. Edward Fisher, *Lewis and Clark 1804*, Missouri Bankers Association

46, montage based on Côté et al. (1992):116; 47, Côté et al., 147, 169

48, top, *A Book of Old Maps, Delineating American History*, edited by Emerson D. Fite & Archibald Freeman (Cambridge, Mass.: Harvard University Press, 1926), no. 8

48, bottom, David Buisseret, *From Sea Charts to Satellite Image*, (Chicago: The University of Chicago Press, 1991):51

51, Lauvrière

52, author's collection

54, author's collection

55, Norall, 19

57, State Historical Society of Missouri

58, author's collection

62, bottom left, Pierre Cultural Centre, South Dakota

65, Loftin, 106

66, Thomas Jefferson, portrait by Raphaelle Peale, White House Historical Association

69, Barbara Chase-Riboud, photo: Marc Riboud, from the cover of *La Virginienne* (Paris: Albin Michel, 1981)

70, detail, Clay Straus Jenkinson, 16-17

72, Henry Art Gallery, University of Washington, in *We Proceeded On*, 24, no. 3 (August 1998):16

77, author's collection

78, portrait of Meriwether Lewis by Charles Willson Peale, Independence National Historical Park

82, map, Clay Straus Jenkinson, 16-17

85, Jackson (1993):107

88, Jackson (1993):209

91, Jacques Cauna, *Au temps des isles à sucres*, (Paris: Éd. Karthala-ACCT, 1987), ill. 21

92 & 94, de Villiers (1903)

95, Thomas Jefferson, by Parisian artist Edmé Quenedey, 1789

96, map from G. Hanotaux and A. Martineau, *Histoire des colonies françaises, et de l'expansion de la France dans le monde* (Paris: Plon, 1929), 1:271

96, bottom left, Robert R. Livingston by Vanderlyn, bottom centre, James Monroe by Vanderlyn, in de Villiers (1903)

97, Map of Lower Mississippi from LePage du Pratz, *Histoire de la Louisiane* (1758), 1:139. in Lauvrière, *Histoire de la Louisiane française*, 262)

97, lower right, François de Barbé-Marbois by Maurin, de Villiers

98, Fox Indian, by Karl Boomer, in Lauvrière; 98, medal for the Indians of Louisiana, in de Villiers (1903)

99, de Villiers (1903)

101, portrait of William Clark by Charles Willson Peale, Independence National Historical Park

102, "St. Louis: The Way Opened to the Pacific," mural by Ezra Winter, George Rogers Clark Memorial, Vincennes, Indiana.

103, Stevens, vol. 2

104, drawing by Michael Haynes in *We Proceeded On* 27, no. 2, (May 2001):23

107, Stevens, vol. 1

108, de Villiers (1925)

109, Clark's sketch of the keelboat, Duncan and Burns, 29

110, Stevens, vol. 1

115, Mandan lodges, by Karl Bodmer, in Thomas, 185

118-119, Moulton, vol. 1 (atlas); 120, 121, 122 in *Early Pictures of the Falls*, Peterson, (1998)

124, top, Catlin, 1913, pl.10; 125, by Beth Berryman, in Loftin, 73

126, montage of drawings by Glen Rounds in Ruxton (1906, reprint 1966)

128, *Harper's Weekly*, (May 23, 1873) in *We Proceeded On* 24, no. 3 (August 1998):7

129, Catlin, (1913), pl. 40

130, Herbert, 51

131, American Numismatic Society

132, bottom, Amon Carter Museum

134, Ross, no. 37

135, drawings by Beth Berryman in Loftin, 166

138, Duncan and Burns, 26

139, montage of two drawings by Uebing Cavender, in *The Newfoundland Annual* (1998):66-67

141, *The Newfoundland Annual*, (1996)

145, Amon Carter Museum

146, Ross, no. 11

147, Allen, 22

148 & 149, Allen, 185 & 195

152, Duncan and Burns, 7

154-155, Moulton, vol. 1 (atlas)

152, Stevens, 1:109

159, 162, author's collection

163, Carl W. Bertsch in Nute, 23

164, author's collection

169, Carl W. Bertsch in Nute, 2

173, Mississippi kite, J.J. Audubon, author's collection

174, Ross, no. 197

176, Ross no. 76

177, top, Ross, no. 170, bottom, Ross, no. 55

178, Catlin (1995), left side, title page

180, detail from Ross, no. 197

181, Farnham (1922)

182, Karl Bodmer, Joslyn Art Museum, Omaha, Nebraska

183, Catlin (1995), vol. 2

185, Parkman, *The Oregon Trail*, opp. p. 448

190, artist unknown, Joslyn Art Museum, gift of Enron Art Foundation

191, Charles Alexandre Lesueur, detail of a watercolour by Karl Bodmer, Joslyn Art Museum, gift of Enron Art Foundation

192, *Steamboat Yellow Stone*, watercolour by Karl Bodmer, Joslyn Art Museum, gift of Enron Art Foundation

193, *Snags on the Missouri*, watercolour by Karl Bodmer, Joslyn Art Museum, gift of Enron Art Foundation

195, detail of coloured engraving (see opposite page for full view) of a painting by Karl Bodmer, in Wied-Neuwied (2001)

195, bottom, baptismal certificate of Toussaint Charbonneau, Sainte-Famille parish, Boucherville, Quebec

198, Ross, no. 47

204, Ross, no. 53

206, von Sachsen-Altenburg, 36 and 37

208, *We Proceeded On* 26, no. 1 (February 2000):10

209, top (Marie-Thérèse Chouteau), Lamar, 211; bottom left (house), Stevens, 2:23; bottom right (Auguste Chouteau), Stevens, 2:162

212, photo by Hillel Burger, Peabody Museum, Harvard University, in Ambrose (1998):181

213, Ross, no. 33

217, Ross, no. 18

219, The Huntington Library, San Marino

221, Ambrose, (1998):230

223, Karl Bodmer, Thomas, 176

226, detail from a painting by Charles M. Russell, Montana Historical Society

228, Fort Vancouver National Historic Site;

229, Ross, no. 80

230, American Museum of Natural History;

231, Ross, no. 12

234, portrait of Lewis in otter shawl, Missouri Historical Society

236, Charles M. Russell Museum

239, State Historical Society of North Dakota

236-237, www.usmint.gov

249, State Historical Society of Wisconsin

254, *We Proceeded On* 26, no. 4 (November 2000):16

List of Maps

Index

Page numbers in *italics* refer to subjects shown in illustrations or on maps.

OTHER TITLES OF INTEREST

~

Yellow-Wolf & Other Tales of the St. Lawrence
Philippe-Joseph Aubert de Gaspé
Translated from the French by Jane Brierley

Canadians of Old: A Romance
Philippe-Joseph Aubert de Gaspé
Translated from the French by Jane Brierley

A Man of Sentiment
The Memoirs of Philppe-Joseph Aubert de Gaspé
1786-1871
Translated from the French by Jane Brierley

On His Way in the World
The Voyages and Travels of John H.R. Molson, 1841
Edited by Karen Molson and Hilbert Buist

They Were So Young
Montrealers Remember World War II
Patricia Burns

The Shamrock & the Shield
An Oral History of the Irish in Montreal
Patricia Burns

Memoirs of a Less Travelled Road
A Historian's Life
Marcel Trudel
Translated from the French by Jane Brierley